Bircham Newton

A Norfolk Airfield
In War and Peace

JOHN STEVENS

Then out spake brave Horatius,
The Captain of the Gate:
'To every man upon this earth
Death cometh soon or late.
And how can man die better
Than facing fearful odds,
For the ashes of his fathers,
And the temples of his Gods...?'

From Macaulay's *Lays of Ancient Rome: Horatius.*

This book is dedicated to all those who served at Bircham Newton and to all who sacrificed their lives in the defence of freedom.

By the same author:
RAF Great Massingham: A Norfolk Airfield at War 1940-1945 (1990)
Airfield Focus (5): Bircham Newton (GMS Enterprises 1992)

CONTENTS

ACKNOWLEDGEMENTS

I am grateful to Lanceni Press, Fakenham, and in particular, to Mrs Pat Cooke (Director) and Alastair Robinson, for their help with the production of this book. Wing Commander John Stevens MBE, RAF Ret'd (aviation artist) produced the drawings and Alan Gardener, Flight Lieutenant, RAF Ret'd, drew the airfield plans. My sister Elspeth Mackinlay proofread the text and made many useful suggestions, as did Barry H. Abraham, Editor of *Airfield Review*, journal of the Airfield Research Group.

In researching this book I have been assisted by many organisations and individuals over the past few years. These include the Public Record Office at Kew and the Royal Air Force Museum at Hendon. Peter Elliott, Senior Keeper at the RAF Museum, and Christine Gregory, Curatorial Assistant, were most helpful in my researches. Information on the RCAF squadrons was obtained from the Directorate of History and Heritage, National Defence Headquarters in Ottawa, Canada. No. 206 Squadron Association and especially the late Squadron Leader Alan D. B. Smith, former Secretary, have been a source of continual help and encouragement. Thanks are also due to Betty Beaty, widow of the late Squadron Leader David Beaty MBE, DFC and Bar, Flight Lieutenant Jim Glazebrook DFC, RAF Ret'd, Wing Commander J. C. Graham DFC and Bar, RAF Ret'd. Wing Commander Tom Cross, former Commanding Officer of No. 206 Squadron based at Kinloss, and a succession of squadron historians which include Flight Lieutenants Richard Frick, I. D. Macmillan and Tom Talbot have been generous with their advice and help. The Royal Air Forces Association (RAFA) and the publication *Air Mail* put me in touch with many veterans and squadron associations, including the No. 221 Squadron Association whose squadron history was a useful source. I have also sought advice on several occasions from Wing Commander V. A. Stapley OBE, DFC, President of the King's Lynn and District branch of the RAFA and Alderman of the Borough. Huby Fairhead and Bob Collis of the Norfolk and Suffolk Aviation Museum have supplied much information, as has Donald N. Thurston. Photographs have been generously supplied by Peter H. T. Green, Ray C. Sturtivant and Tony Arter. Chaz Bowyer gave me permission to use some of the photographs for which he holds copyright. The Imperial War Museum and Royal Air Force Museum, Hendon, have also permitted me to publish photographs from their collections.

The Buckingham Palace Press Office put me in touch with Air Commodore the Hon. T. C. Elworthy CVO, CBE, Captain of The Queen's Flight from 1989-1994, who supplied me with extracts from the logbook of Flight Lieutenant (later Air Vice-Marshal Sir) Edward Fielden, Captain of the King's Flight in the1930s and 1940s. It was through the help of David Tuck, Assistant Press Secretary to Her Majesty The Queen, that I was able to contact HRH The Duke of Edinburgh for some comments about his time at Bircham Newton during his flying training in the early 1950s.

The Chief Executive, Peter Lobban, and staff of the National Construction College of the Construction Industry Training Board (CITB) at Bircham Newton have permitted me to tour the buildings and also to publish various photographs in their possession. Peter York has been a useful source of information and help on my many visits.

Permission has been granted to use material from the following, acknowledged in the text: *RAF Coastal Command* by Chris Ashworth, Patrick Stephens Limited, an imprint of Haynes Publishing, Sparkford, Yeovil, Somerset BA22 7JJ; *British Military Airfield Architecture* by Paul Francis, also Patrick Stephens Limited; *The Right of the Line* by John Terraine, Hodder and Stoughton Limited; *All Round the Compass* by Ron H. Brown, Janus Publishing Company; *Sholto Douglas: Years of Command* by Robert Wright, HarperCollins Publishers Ltd; *War in a Stringbag* by Charles Lamb, Cassell Military Paperback; *Ensor's Endeavour* by Vincent Orange, Grub Street Publishing Ltd, and extracts from *Flypast* magazine, with permission of Key Publishing and editor Ken Ellis. I am very grateful to Peter Franzen, editor of the *Eastern Daily Press* for permission to use a selection of cuttings and photographs, and to Malcolm Powell, editor of the *Lynn News and Advertiser* and also to the editor of the *Evening News*. Theo Boiten gave permission for me to use information from his book *Blenheim Strike* (Air Research Publications) and Merv Hambling's *Norfolk Crash Diary* series 1939-50 proved another invaluable source. The privately published autobiography of the late Air Vice-Marshal Allan L. A. Perry-Keene entitled *Reflected Glory* has proved a fascinating source of life at Bircham Newton in the early 1920s, and Mrs Marion M. Newman, daughter of A. L. A. Perry-Keene, has kindly lent me many photographs and other material. Airfield plans drawn by Alan Gardener were based on plans held by the RAF Museum. Crown Copyright material is reproduced by permission of the Controller of Her Majesty's Stationery Office. Airfield plans and the location map are reproduced by kind permission of Ordnance Survey. I am grateful to Anthony Maynard who drew the map on page 84.

The following veterans contacted me with information and in many cases photographs, for which I am very grateful: Selwyn Armitage (Flight Lieutenant, RAF Ret'd), Mike J. Applegarth (No. 42 Sqn), Ken Border (No. 279 Sqn), Cyril Bright (No. 279 Sqn), the late Vernon Buckman (*Memories of Life with 206 (GR) Squadron 1938-42*), Terry Bulloch (No. 206 Sqn), R. G. Cardew (No. 279 Sqn), Bob A. Clayton, A. Cockle (No. 59 Sqn), S. H. Daly, Gordon C. Dick, I. R. Dick (Squadron Leader, RAF Ret'd), Graeme V. Donald (No. 206 Sqn), Ernest E. Fitchew (Squadron Leader, RAF Ret'd), John D. A. Floyd (Nos 415/119 Sqns), Neil Grant (Wing Commander, RAF Ret'd), Winifred Gunter, the late Charles Hall (the cartoonist 'Holly'), Mrs Victoria Hall (widow of Charles Hall), E. B. Hammersley (No. 220 Sqn), E. F. 'Ted' Hare BEM (No. 7 Sqn), Jack Holywell (No. 206 Sqn), Thelma Holdaway, Aubrey O. Lancaster (No. 235 Sqn), W. H. H. Lewis, Donald S. MacNeil (No. 519 Sqn), R. G. 'Bob' MacNeil (No. 519 Sqn), J. M. C. 'Jock' Manson (No. 53 Squadron historian), Allan Monaghan (No. 206 Sqn), Don Nelson, T. C. Overend DFC (Squadron Leader, RAF Ret'd), William Parkes (No. 220 Sqn), Mrs Prue Riddiford, daughter of the late Squadron Leader C. H. Hayward (CO No. 7 Sqn), Syd Roberts (No. 279 Sqn), S. J. 'Robby' Robilliard (cartoons of life with No. 206 Sqn), Don Rogers (Squadron Leader, RAF Ret'd), Ron Ross (National Serviceman 1951-2), R. D. Rushen BEM (Squadron Leader, RAF Ret'd), Donald R. Samson, H. Schofield, Edwin A.

Shackleton, Les A. Smith (No. 206 Sqn), Tony Spooner DSO, DFC, Captain Eric Starling (No. 221 Sqn), Mike D. Stimson (No. 1510 BABS Flt), John Stitt (No. 500 Sqn), D. L. Turner (No. 519 Sqn), J. D. Upton, Hugh C. Wilkins (No. 279 Sqn), Squadron Leader R. G. Woodman DSO, DFC, and Peter Wright.

Steve Snelling of the *Eastern Daily Press* and Derek Edwards have provided much encouragement and help, and local people who assisted with information include Roger Sheldrake and members of the Narborough Airfield Research Group, Dudley Crisp of Gressenhall, Janet Hammond of Sedgeford, and Andrew England. The late William H. C. Peacock allowed me access to the former airfield site at Docking (Sunderland Farm), and gave me much useful information as have the present owners, Robert W. and Mrs Perowne. William Barber, present owner of the former airfield site at Sedgeford has permitted me to visit on several occasions. Mike Seymour has been generous in sharing information from his database on aircraft losses. Others who have given freely of their advice and help include Sue and Roger Wood, Winston G. Ramsey, Editor-in-Chief of *After the Battle*, Maurice V. Gardner and Kevin Bidewell. Brian S. Hillman was kind enough to supply me with a copy of his database on the war graves at Great Bircham, which enabled me to fill many gaps in my account. Every effort has been made to trace and acknowledge the copyright of photographs and other material used in the book but I would welcome any additional information if it comes to light. Inevitably, given the passage of time, there are gaps in the historical record and contradictory accounts of various incidents, but I have done my best to present an accurate narrative on the basis of the facts available to me. Nevertheless I apologise in advance for any errors or omissions.

Finally, the starting point for my research in the early 1990s was without doubt the West Norfolk Aviation Society, based at Methwold, when we were granted permission to tour the CITB at Bircham Newton in the company of the then Promotions Service Manager Colin Hawksworth. Going even further back than that was the friendship and encouragement of the notable local historian the late Raymond Wilson, formerly Librarian in King's Lynn and author of *Red Alert - Lynn*. But throughout all of this my wife Janet has cheerfully put up with disrupted holidays, visits to the most inhospitable places, and endless tramps around deserted airfields in rain and shine.

Peter B. Gunn, Docking, Norfolk
May, 2002.

GLOSSARY

Note: some terms are explained in the text and therefore are not included here.

AA	Anti-Aircraft
AACU	Anti-Aircraft Co-operation Unit
AC1	Aircraftman First Class
AC2	Aircraftman Second Class
ACM	Air Chief Marshal
AFC	Air Force Cross
Aldis Lamp	A lamp used to transmit messages and signals in Morse Code.
AOC	Air Officer Commanding
Asdic	Ship-borne sonar detection equipment
ASR	Air-Sea Rescue
ASRTU	Air-Sea Rescue Training Unit
ASV	Air-to-Surface Vessel (radar)
AVM	Air Vice-Marshal
B	Bomber (Sqn)
BABS	Blind Approach Beacon System
BAT	Blind Approach Training
BEF	British Expeditionary Force
C-in-C	Commander-in-Chief
CITB	Construction Industry Training Board
CO	Commanding Officer
DFC	Distinguished Flying Cross
DFM	Distinguished Flying Medal
DSO	Distinguished Service Order
DWI	Directional Wireless Installation
E-Boat	Small, fast craft capable of speeds up to 40 knots, armed with torpedoes and light guns and frequently used in mine-laying operations.
ENSA	Entertainments National Service Association
EVT School	Educational and Vocational Training School
F	Fighter (Sqn)
F/Lt	Flight Lieutenant
F/O	Flying Officer
F/Sgt	Flight Sergeant
FAA	Fleet Air Arm
Flak	Corruption of German term for anti-aircraft fire
FTS	Flying Training School
G/Capt.	Group Captain

GR	General Reconnaissance (Sqn)
GRU	General Reconnaissance Unit
IFF	Identification Friend or Foe: automatic transmitter in aircraft for its identification but could also be used to home in on other aircraft.
'K'-site	Decoy airfield for day use
LAC	Leading Aircraftman
Lorenz system	Blind beam approach radio beacon system
Met.	Meteorological
MF/DF	Medium Frequency/Direction Finding
MT	Mechanical Transport
NAAFI	Navy, Army, and Air Force Institutes
NCO	Non-commissioned officer
Nomad	Operations which involved sea searches for targets of opportunity.
OTU	Operational Training Unit
P/O	Pilot Officer
PoW	Prisoner-of-war
'Q'-site	Decoy airfield for night use
R-Boat	*Räumboot* - slower than E-Boat and used for mine-laying.
R/T	Radio-telephony
RAT	Radio Aids Training
RCAF	Royal Canadian Air Force
Recipe	Pre-planned Met. sortie over Atlantic
Rhombus	Pre-planned Met. sortie over North Sea
Rovers	Armed low-level shipping searches with no specific target
S/Ldr	Squadron Leader
SHQ	Station Headquarters
Sqn	Squadron
U-Boat	*Unterseeboot* - German submarine
u/c	undercarriage
USAAF	United States Army Air Force
VC	Victoria Cross
VHF	Very High Frequency
W/Cdr	Wing Commander
W/T	Wireless telegraphy
WAAF	Women's Auxiliary Air Force
WO	Warrant Officer
WOp/AG	Wireless-Operator/Air Gunner

RAF Bircham Newton Display Board. (CITB)
One accidental omission was that of No. 221 (GR) Squadron, formed at the station in November
1940, departing for Limavady in May 1941. This oversight was partly remedied by a visit of
the No. 221 Squadron Association to Bircham Newton in May 1993, when a signed squadron
crest was presented to CITB.

AUTHOR'S NOTES:
1. The symbol † after a name indicates that the individual is buried in the Churchyard of St Mary, Great Bircham.
2. Full details of aircraft losses are to be found in Appendix IV.

INTRODUCTION

On a late December day in 1962 a nostalgic ceremony took place to mark the official closure of Royal Air Force Bircham Newton, ending 44 years of a service life which had spanned two world wars and seen the comings and goings of well over 80 operational flying units and thousands of personnel. Of the 300 people attending the ceremony, many had their own personal memories of a station which had seen one of the longest periods of continuous service in the country. Among those present that day were two Marshals of the Royal Air Force, Lord Tedder and Lord Portal, both former squadron commanders at the station. Lord Tedder had served with No. 207 Squadron between 1920 and 1922, and was later to become General Eisenhower's Deputy during the Allied invasion of Europe in 1944. Lord Portal had commanded No. 7 (Bomber) Squadron in 1927. The official brochure for the ceremony added the brief comment: 'The unending process of development and change leaves no place for Bircham Newton in the Royal Air Force, and the life of the station comes to an end.'

Fortunately, that was not to be the end of Bircham Newton's story, as it was shortly to become a centre for the Construction Industry Training Board (CITB) and is now the National Construction College. Much of the airfield layout and many of its buildings continue in use today, retaining the unmistakable appearance of its life in sterner days. Bircham Newton remains one of the best preserved airfields in the country today.

The aerodrome began life in 1918 in the fledgling days of the Royal Air Force as a training station for the early fighter and reconnaissance squadrons before they proceeded to the Western Front. The first long-range strategic bombers were stationed there at the end of the war and it continued in peacetime service as a bomber station until its transference to Coastal Command in 1936. In this role it was the only Coastal Command station between North Coates in Lincolnshire and Detling in Kent having responsibility, with its satellites at Docking and Langham, for a huge stretch of the East Anglian coastline throughout the war years. Station strength at its peak numbered nearly 3,000 by the end of World War II, comprising over 2,400 RAF and more than 550 WAAF personnel. During its lifetime many hundreds of aircraft types have operated from Bircham Newton, everything from the de Havilland biplanes and large Handley Page bombers of the Great War era, to the naval Fairey Swordfish biplanes (affectionately known as 'Stringbags'), Avro Ansons, Lockheed Hudsons, Bristol Blenheims, and Vickers Wellingtons of the Second World War - to name but a few. However as the jet age dawned the airfield was not selected for expansion with concrete runways, so its days were numbered as an operational station. But there was a brief appearance in 1965 of the Hawker Siddeley Kestrel VTOL (Vertical take-off) aircraft, forerunner of the famous Harrier, as the airfield was used for trials by the West Raynham-based Tripartite Evaluation Squadron. Thus in a sense Bircham Newton's history has mirrored much of the aviation history of the twentieth century.

For many thousands of airmen and their families a posting to Bircham Newton usually involved a train journey from London to King's Lynn, and then the local train to Docking, to await motor transport to the camp. The first experience of rural Norfolk was not always particularly favourable, as recalled by Mrs Violet Shepherd on her way to No. 27 Airmen's Married Quarters (AMQ) on a soaking wet night in November 1945:

'......We arrived at Docking on a dark day in November 1945 at nightfall due to various delays on the railway, only to find one aged porter who took our tickets and vanished into his lamplit office out of the streaming rain. The train departed and so did everyone else leaving us rather forlorn on the station platform. No transport visible, we wakened the porter again and asked if we could use the phone. Contact was made with the transport section and half an hour later we loaded ourselves, cases, bags, children etc. and set off for a ten minute ride to the camp.'

The effort was well worth it as the married quarter at Bircham Newton was the first home the family had been able to call their own![1]

The last passenger train ran through Docking Station on 31 May 1952 but the line remained open for goods until its closure in 1963 due to the 'Beeching axe'. By that date, the life of the airfield at Bircham Newton was over and a new era was about to begin.

Docking Railway Station during the 1940s. The railway came to Docking in 1866. During the life of the airfield at Bircham Newton many thousands of airmen alighted here on their way to the camp. The line finally closed in 1963. (Tony Arter)

[1] *Flypast* April 1988, article by Paddy Porter.

CHAPTER 1

ORIGINS IN THE GREAT WAR

'The aerodrome has a good surface, a good sub-soil and is very suitable for the purpose in hand.'
(Official Report July 1918 on the potentiality of Bircham Newton as a base for operating large Handley Page bombers)

Little seemed to threaten the somnolent lifestyle of rural Norfolk until the onset of World War One in August, 1914, which brought with it a new dimension to warfare, air power. The immediate threat was of Zeppelin attacks against population centres and responsibility for defence was placed in the hands of the senior service and its newly-formed Royal Naval Air Service (RNAS). An aerodrome was opened at South Denes, Great Yarmouth, but the limited range of aircraft then available made it essential to provide emergency landing grounds at various locations around the coastline of Norfolk and Suffolk. By 1915 RNAS landing grounds were established at Bacton, Aldeburgh, Burgh Castle, Covehithe, Holt, Narborough and Sedgeford.

In April 1916 home air defence became the responsibility of the War Office, and aerodromes like Sedgeford and Narborough were transferred to the Royal Flying Corps. The expansion of that service brought the need to train squadrons for the Western Front, and many Norfolk aerodromes were earmarked for that role. At the same time new areas were being surveyed including a site four miles to the south-east of Sedgeford in the parish of Bircham Newton. This location, just under two miles to the north-east of the village of Great Bircham, is situated on a ridge which commands the higher ground in the immediate vicinity. As the crow flies, the north Norfolk coast was just over seven miles distant and Docking, the nearest railway station and village of any size, lay three miles away.

It is clear that Bircham Newton was from the first planned as a bomber training aerodrome, and with an area of 297 acres would be able to accommodate the heavier aircraft coming into service. Sedgeford's area of 170 acres would restrict its future development and it would soon be eclipsed by its more substantial neighbour.

Building work continued throughout 1917 and for much of 1918. On 1 April 1918 the Royal Air Force came into being from the amalgamation of the Royal Flying Corps and the Royal Naval Air Service, and all existing aerodromes were handed over to the new Service, a total of 250 of which Norfolk's share numbered around 33. Of these, Bircham Newton was one of 13 with what amounted to full station status[1].

The first recorded unit arrived at Bircham Newton on 28 May 1918, No. 3 Fighting School from Driffield (formerly No. 3 School of Aerial Fighting and Gunnery). This was

---

[1] The others being Burgh Castle, Feltwell, Harling Road, Holt, Marham, Mattishall, Narborough, Pulham (airship station), Sedgeford, Thetford, Tydd St Mary and Yarmouth.

DH4 Fighter-bomber. No. 3 Fighting School Bircham Newton 1918. (CITB)

an advanced training unit which brought pupil pilots up to operational standard in gunnery, advanced flying techniques, and aerial fighting, the 1918 equivalent of a 'Top Gun' establishment. A variety of aircraft were employed: the light de Havilland bombers DH4, and DH9; the Camel, Dolphin and Snipe fighters, all of the Sopwith family; the outstanding SE5A fighter, and that workhorse of RFC/RAF training, the Avro 504.

An insight into the daily routine of No. 3 Fighting School is provided by the logbook extract of Second Lieutenant J. Gordon Webster RAF[2], during July and August 1918. The entries from 29 July show that he was making three or four local flights daily, usually of 20 or 30 minutes' duration, and mostly in a DH9. There was reconnaissance, formation flying, firing and aerial fighting practice. On 31 July he was in the air in DH9 Serial No. D1042 for a round trip of 65 minutes on a special 'Air Day' to Cromer and North Walsham, accompanied by Sergeant Van Hoon. On 1 August Lieutenant Webster was on a fighting training sortie in DH9 Serial No. D7311 for 40 minutes, taking in King's Lynn, Narborough, and East Dereham. In October, the unit moved to Sedgeford, by which time Bircham Newton was being developed as a heavy bomber station.

THE PLAN TO BOMB BERLIN!

This new strategy was the outcome of planning at the highest level of government to create an independent air force capable of striking at the heart of targets within Germany itself. German bombing raids on cities and towns by Zeppelins and heavy bombers, culminating in German raids on London during the summer of 1917, were producing

---

[2] Webster, 2/Lt J. Gordon: logbook. (RAF Museum)

near-panic among the population, and a demand for an effective response. One result was the creation of the Independent Air Force in the summer of 1918, commanded by Major-General Hugh 'Boom' Trenchard. Eight bomber squadrons were planned which would be formed as No. 27 Group, consisting of the 86th and 87th Wings.

No. 27 Group's commander, Lieutenant-Colonel R. H. Mulock DSO, was given the task of establishing the new force at Bircham Newton and carefully selected the personnel from battle-hardened bomber pilots and observers. They were to be found among the crews of night bombing FE2b squadrons in France and the most recent heavy bomber, the Handley Page O/400. The chosen crews were promptly sent on a special course of navigation at the School in Andover.

The outcome was that a new squadron, No. 166, was formed at Bircham Newton on 13 June, commanded by Major C. H. Darley DSC, DFC, a seasoned veteran of night bombing on the Western Front, and reputed to have carried out more night bombing raids than any other pilot. Another officer selected was Major F. T. Digby DSO, DFC, also an experienced pilot on bombers. On 13 September the squadron was transferred from No. 3 Group to 86th Wing of No. 27 Group.

The aim was straightforward, to bomb Berlin, and the aircraft selected for this strategic bombing task was the new Super-Handley Page, or the V/1500, the largest British bomber of the First World War, and the first with four engines and a tail gun position. This was in fact one of the first home-based heavy strategic bombers in aviation history. Powered by four 375 hp Rolls-Royce Eagle VIII engines, with a range of 1,300 miles, a crew of six, and capable of delivering thirty 250 lb bombs, the aircraft represented a considerable leap forward in bomber design. However, if one considers its maximum speed of 90 mph (cruising at 80 mph) and service ceiling of 11,000 feet, albeit with an endurance of 17 hours, combined with the absence of modern navigational aids, it was highly optimistic to expect a crew to be able to find Berlin and safely return to base, even in perfect flying conditions.

HP V/1500 of No. 166 Sqn, Bircham Newton 1918. Note the port engine configuration: a tractor and pusher unit mounted on struts between the upper and lower wings. (CITB)

Group photo of No. 166 Sqn in front of a Handley Page V/1500,Bircham Newton 13 June 1918.
(RAF Museum photograph: Ref PO13331)

No. 166 Squadron was very much an élite unit, composed of hardened veterans. Many of these were Canadians, and it was said that affairs of the squadron seemed to be conducted in colonial fashion, with Major Darley holding some sort of 'soviet council' (*sic*) with his men regarding any work to be done on the aircraft[3].

The fact that Norfolk was within easy reach of German industry and the major cities of Hamburg, Cologne and Berlin, led to an assessment of various aerodromes to choose the most suitable operating base for the new large Handley Page bombers. The official report of July 1918 put Bircham Newton at the top of a list which included Sedgeford, Pulham and Narborough. Bircham Newton was commended for its good sub-soil, and the extreme difficulty enemy night-raiding squadrons were expected to have in attempting to locate it! Additionally, the aerodrome was in the process of expanding from its present capacity of 3-400 personnel, with only one General Service hangar completed but a total of four planned in a short time[4]. Although a water supply was not yet available (but being laid on), the station had its own electrical power plant. The nearest railway station was at Docking, only three miles away, making for suitable access to the aerodrome. The conclusion in the report was that up to three squadrons of heavy aircraft could be accommodated there, in spite of the fact that the CO of No. 3 Fighting School was clearly reluctant to relinquish the station!

Judging by the pace of events, it seems clear that the objective of the squadron becoming fully operational and ready to bomb Berlin on more than a token basis, was not going to be realised before the spring of 1919 at the earliest. Major Darley was reported to be collecting aircraft from Glasgow, as subcontractors for Handley Page included Wm Beardmore & Co. Ltd of Dalmuir near Glasgow and Harland and Wolff Ltd of Belfast[5]. However, delays in factory production resulted in only three machines

---

[3] Darley, C. C.: Letter to S/Ldr J.H.C. Wake (1/3/37): quoted in *War in the Air* Vol VI by H. A. Jones (App. B).

[4] RFC General Service Aeroplane Sheds (164/17) - See photos and airfield plans in Ch 4.

[5] Darley: letter (see Note 3).

being delivered by the time of the armistice. In the meantime crews had to train on the FE2b, and by early November the squadron had about 17 officers and 308 other ranks on strength. By 9 November two V/1500s and their crews were ready for operations, and awaiting orders to bomb Berlin, but poor weather led to a postponement and by 11 November the armistice was signed and the crews were stood down.

V/1500 of No. 166 Sqn (serial F7135) c. 5 November 1918 being made ready to bomb Berlin. (CITB)

V/1500 and crew of No. 166 Sqn prior to a long-range endurance flight from Bircham Newton on 9 May 1919, covering 989 miles in 12 hours, 7 minutes. Capt. Sinclair, Capt. Vereker and Lt Bruce Clark were the pilots. Lt Royles was navigating officer and rigger-in-charge was 1st Airman R. Peel. Engine fitters were Cpls Gregory and Peek. (P.H.T. Green Collection)

The rapid run-down of the service did not prevent a sister squadron, No. 167, being formed on 18 November, again with the V/1500. However this unit disbanded on 21 May 1919, with No. 166 disbanding shortly afterwards on 31 May. A third squadron of the V/1500, No. 274, was re-formed at Bircham Newton on 15 June, being allocated eleven of the ex-Nos 166 and 167 Squadron aircraft along with others recently delivered. Its life was short-lived as it disbanded there on 30 January 1920. By then, the V/1500 had vanished from squadron service. History will never be able to relate how far the aircraft and its crews would have measured up to the strategic bombing role intended for them. A generation would pass before a similar challenge presented itself, and few of those who were present at Bircham Newton in the autumn of 1918 could possibly have imagined that within a generation the strategic bomber would become one of the most potent and feared weapons of war in the twentieth and twenty-first centuries.

Sad to relate, Major Darley (now Flight Lieutenant) was killed in a Vickers Vimy crash at Lake Bracciano, north of Rome, on 28 September 1919. His brother, C. C. Darley, navigator on the aircraft, was seriously injured but survived[6]. This episode had arisen from the order to ferry six Vimy bombers from Bircham Newton to Egypt, one of which was commanded by Major Darley. Flight Lieutenant Allan Perry-Keene, whom we will meet later, had been ordered to fly as Darley's co-pilot but at the last moment the major took his brother instead[7].

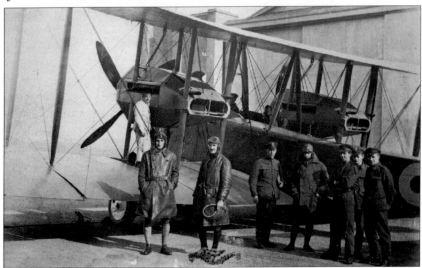

F/Lts C. H. and C. C. Darley photographed at Bircham Newton before starting for Egypt in Vickers Vimy, Sept. 1919. Charles Curtis Darley (extreme left) and his brother C. H. Darley to his right. The aircraft crashed north of Rome, C. H. Darley was killed and his brother seriously injured and hospitalised for 18 months. (A. L. A. Perry-Keene / Marion M. Newman)

---

[6] Ibid.
[7] Perry-Keene, Allan: *Reflected Glory* p22 (privately published).

CHAPTER 2

PEACETIME BOMBER STATION

'A large piece of waste land in north-west Norfolk.'
(Allan Perry-Keene describing the Air Ministry's choice of the airfield site of Bircham Newton as a base for the Super Handley Page bombers in 1918: quoted in *Reflected Glory* by A. Perry-Keene)

'The airmen at Bircham Newton regard themselves as more or less isolated from the rest of the world. This has one advantage in that everyone realises that he must make the most of the facilities afforded by the camp, and a cameraderie develops which may be lacking in less isolated RAF stations.'
(*Lynn News and County Press* May 1935)

The 'peace dividend' following the ending of hostilities and the signing of the Treaty of Versailles led to severe service cut-backs and an exercise in downsizing for all military establishments. A sign of the times was an auction held at Bircham Newton on Wednesday and Thursday 25 and 26 June 1919 by Messrs. Stephen Gregory & Sons. Included in the Sale were 8,000 yards of barbed wire, 4,500 yards of two foot gauge railway track, 59 tip wagons, six turntables and 17 sets of points and crossings. There were also cooking utensils, plates, cups and saucers, 1,700 blankets, 337 single bedsteads, and one 35 hp Crossley Horizontal oil engine along with one Crompton generator[1].

Handley Page O/400 at Bircham Newton, February 1920. This aircraft type had seen service in France as a heavy bomber. (A. L. A. Perry-Keene / Marion M. Newman)

---

[1] Fairhead, Huby: letter to author 14/12/91.

Squadron disbandments continued in early 1920 with the winding up of Nos 56 and 60 Squadrons, previously based at Narborough, flying SE5As. Both squadrons had been associated with the name of Major James B. McCudden VC, DSO, MC, MM, who had served with No. 56 Squadron and briefly commanded No. 60 Squadron, before his death in a flying accident in France during 1918.

By the end of 1919 the Bircham Newton Station Establishment had ceased to exist, but in early 1920 the station re-opened with the formation of No. 207 (Bomber) Squadron (nucleus from 274 Squadron) commanded by Squadron Leader A. W. Tedder (later Deputy Supreme Commander Allied Forces & Marshal of the RAF), and equipped with the de Havilland DH9A light bomber. Flying Officer (later Flight Lieutenant) Allan L.A. Perry-Keene was present during these events, witnessing the odd assortment of aircraft on the station at the time, including V/1500s, the Handley Page O/400, some Vickers Vimys, a DH10, the Bristol Breamore or Pullman triplane (*sic*), the latter having an enclosed cockpit as it was intended for civil aviation. This aircraft was taken away by the manufacturers before it was flown and never developed.

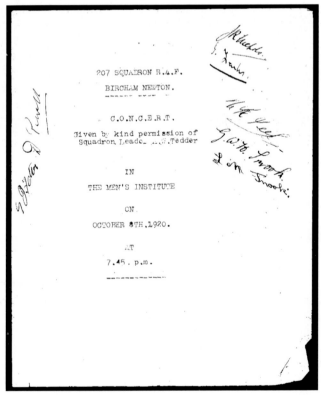

The lighter side of life: Concert at Bircham Newton laid on by No. 207 Squadron, October 1920. Note reference to the CO S/Ldr A. W. Tedder (later Marshal of the RAF).
(A.L.A. Perry-Keene / Marion M. Newman)

Allan Perry-Keene, generally known as 'P-K', was one of the many remarkable characters who saw service in the early days at Bircham Newton. He had served briefly in the Norfolk Regiment before moving on to the Royal Flying Corps as a bomber pilot on the Western Front. Then as one of the founder members of the fledgling RAF he found himself at Bircham Newton in 1920 at the end of the Great War. In later years 'P-K' served in Iraq, Burma and India before becoming the first commander of the Royal Pakistan Air Force shortly after independence in 1947, playing a significant role in preventing a war between India and Pakistan over Kashmir at that time. He retired as an Air Vice-Marshal.[2]

Sports Day, Bircham Newton 1920. F/O Allan Perry-Keene in foreground.
(A.L.A. Perry-Keene / Marion M. Newman)

Allan Perry-Keene was impressed with the V/1500: 'It was certainly a giant bomber, with 125ft wing span and four Rolls-Royce VIII engines, two each in tandem, the rear ones having pusher propellers. It was the first to have a tail gunner's cockpit and one could walk upright from the nose to the tail. Very heavy to fly but I felt like a king of the air behind its enormous control wheel.'[3]

The neglected condition of the airfield over the previous winter gave rise to concerns expressed in the House of Commons in March 1920, when Mr N. P. Jodrell MP pointed to the lack of weather-proofing of the buildings, which might have led to an epidemic of pneumonia had it not been for the mild winter! Major Tryon, for the Air Ministry, replied that there was every hope that something would be done before the next winter for the sake of the station personnel![4]

---

[2] AVM A. Perry-Keene died in November 1987.
[3] Perry-Keene, Allan, *Reflected Glory* p22 (privately published).
[4] *Eastern Daily Press* 24/3/20.

The outlook for the armed services could not have been more bleak during 1921 and 1922 and the very existence of the Royal Air Force as a separate service even came into question. The 250 aerodromes inherited by the RAF in 1918 were reduced to just 27 by 1924. Trenchard was now Chief of the Air Staff, and fought a tough campaign in Whitehall to preserve the air arm and its aerodromes. He undertook a building programme to lay the foundations of a permanent service but was accused by his enemies of extravagance and waste to the extent that the RAF was christened by some 'The Royal Ground Force'[5]. Nevertheless, the service survived the 'Geddes Axe' of February 1922[6], and later in the year it was an emergency beyond Europe in the Near East that seemed to justify Trenchard's arguments about the value of air power.

In September the 'Chanak' crisis erupted in Turkey when the Turkish leader Mustapha Kemal Atatürk went to war with Greece over the post-war Treaty of Sèvres. It was feared that this would threaten the entire post-war settlement and allied interests in the area, not least Britain's imperial concerns. The cheapest and quickest option was

'D' Flight of No. 100 Sqn with Vickers Vimy at Spittlegate in March 1923 which was the basis of the re-formed No. 7 (B) Sqn and transferred to Bircham Newton on 1 June. Left to right: F/O Tallentyre, F/O Thomas, F/O Howard (seated), F/O Savile (standing at rear), F/O A. Perry-Keene, F/O Barraclough, F/O Banting. (A.L.A. Perry-Keene / Marion M. Newman)

---

[5] Longmate, Norman: *The Bombers* (Arrow) p37.
[6] Government committee chaired by Sir Eric Geddes which recommended pay cuts for the armed forces and public servants.

to dispatch an air contingent, so in late September 1922 No. 207 Squadron moved from Bircham Newton to become part of the Expeditionary Force which was sent to Constantinople. Once again, the station was placed on a Care and Maintenance basis until No. 7 (Bomber) Squadron was re-formed in June of the following year. Continuing international tensions were leading to a re-shaping of government defence policies and an expansion of the RAF was planned for 1923-24 involving the provision of new permanent buildings for a number of existing stations, including Bircham Newton.

The situation in Europe was still uncertain, and in spite of the fact that official plans were assuming that there would be no war for ten years (the 'Ten Year Rule')[7], it was decided to form an effective bomber force by creating new squadrons. One outcome was the establishment of No. 7 Squadron (formed from 'D' Flight of 100 Squadron) on 1 June 1923, which confirmed Bircham Newton as a heavy bomber station. The squadron, commanded by Squadron Leader C. H. Hayward, was the first unit to operate the twin-engined Vickers Vimy, and until the spring of 1924 the squadron represented the entire home-based heavy bomber force. The aircraft type has of course been immortalised by the first non-stop transatlantic flight by Alcock and Brown in 1919, although the aircraft flown on that occasion was a private version[8]. This squadron was joined briefly by a day bomber squadron, No. 11, from Andover, equipped with DH9As, which remained until departure for Netheravon the following May.

S/Ldr C. H. Hayward, CO of No. 7 Sqn, at Bircham Newton c.1924.
(Mrs Prue Riddiford / CITB)

---

[7] The 10-year rule was scrapped in 1932.
[8] The Vickers Vimy was designed by Thomas Keppel North, whose grave is in the cemetery at Rougham, Norfolk.

S/Ldr Hayward and his wife outside old married quarters in 1924, plus car.
Note new baby's pram (Prudence Riddiford) on left of car.   (Mrs Prue Riddiford / CITB)

Squadron Leader Cecil Hayward, No. 7 Squadron CO, included golf among his accomplishments and took advantage of the excellent facilities of the Royal West Norfolk Golf Club at Brancaster, Hunstanton, and Sheringham. He was to become RAF golf champion 13 times from 1921-35 and secretary of the RAF Golf Society for several years.[9]

One notable event during this period was a loop performed by Flight Lieutenant Stewart in a Vimy during the summer of 1923! Trials were also carried out with the second prototype of the Vickers Virginia (Mk. II J 6857) in 1923-24, later joined by five Mk. IIIs, an aircraft type with which the squadron was later to re-equip.

Mr E. F. 'Ted' Hare (later awarded the British Empire Medal) recalls joining No. 7 Squadron as an aero engine fitter on 5 September 1923 after apprentice training at Halton. He had joined the RAF in May 1921 and this was his first posting to a regular RAF station. He and another airman Jim Mason, who became his best friend, were collected at Docking Station in a Crossley van, after the train journey from Liverpool Street Station to King's Lynn, and then a change for Docking via Wolferton. One thing he noticed was that Wolferton, being a 'royal' station, had no placards or posters on display. On arrival at Bircham Newton they were sent to 'A' Flight in the charge of a corporal. The billets were very large, with sleeping accommodation for forty men, separated by a central partition. Ted was favourably impressed after the spartan conditions at Halton!

Right from the start Ted enjoyed his time at Bircham Newton and made the most of his surroundings. He enjoyed working with the Rolls-Royce engines of the Vimy and he liked the people on the station. He recalled the presence of No. 11 Squadron and the song 'Seven and Eleven' current at the time. Among the highlights were dances in

---

[9] Mrs Prue Riddiford (daughter of S/Ldr Hayward): letter to author 19/7/93.

'A' Flight No. 7 Sqn at Bircham Newton, 1923, with Vickers Vimy. From right to left: Sgt Denny, F/Lt Perry-Keene, F/O Barraclough, AC1 Brown, Sgt Brett, AC1 Mills, AC1 Holder, AC Langton. (E.F. Hare)

Snettisham, Heacham and in St Nicholas' Hall, King's Lynn. Lord Fermoy was present at one of the events at Snettisham and made the point that the activities at the aerodrome had disturbed his peace and quiet at his family home at Park House, Sandringham! On occasions a dance would be held at the station and a coach would bring girls from King's Lynn for the party.

Ted Hare had many flights in the rear cockpit of a Vimy, on several occasions with Flying Officer (soon Flight Lieutenant) Allan Perry-Keene. The purpose of this was to monitor the performance of the engines as there was little substitute for experiencing the aircraft in flight. In fact, Ted recorded 46 flights in the Vimy mostly of short duration between September 1923 and July 1924. On one of these, the tail skid knocked down a hare on the take-off. After the machine had landed the hare was retrieved and sold to the Sergeant in charge of fitters on 'A' Flight for the sum of two shillings, enough money to buy 24 cups of NAAFI tea! On another occasion a pilot asked him to accompany him in an Avro 504 for reasons which did not seem clear at the time. They landed at a farm where a certain young lady lived, and Ted was asked to keep the engine running while the pilot went inside! Those were the days!

One of Ted's duties was to retrieve the engines of crashed aircraft for examination. There was an occasion when he was required to do this at Wells-next-the-Sea in mid-winter. There were two engines to remove and drag over the sand to be loaded into a lorry. This turned out to be more than a day's work so the airmen stayed overnight, sleeping in one of the lorries. It was bitterly cold and the first night Ted had no sleep at

Above Left: *E. F. 'Ted' Hare (right) and Albert Mears who served as aero engine fitters with No. 7 Sqn 1923-1924. Both trained as RAF apprentices ('Trenchard brats') at Halton before squadron service. Ted was posted to No.19(F) Sqn at Duxford after his time at Bircham Newton. (E.F. Hare)*

Above Right: *The author (left) photographed with Ted Hare at the latter's home in Clacton-on-Sea in 1991.*

all. The next morning he went for his cup of the tea to the local British Legion hall where he received a tip from a Great War veteran to take his boots off. The next night he did this and slept soundly.

Any spare time was used to cycle to Sedgeford where a lady called 'Ma Drewery' would serve free cups of tea to the airmen. All the children around were dressed in various items of RAF clothing which had been handed out by airmen because people were so poor in those days. On Sundays Ted attended church in Docking and Rudham. He remained at Bircham Newton until 30 July 1924 when he was posted to assist in the formation of No. 19(F) Squadron at Duxford. It was a disappointment to leave especially as Ted loved working with Rolls-Royce engines. In fact he did not remain in the Royal Air Force after he had served his six years. Bircham Newton had been the highlight of

Vickers Vimy (No. 7 Sqn) which crashed on 16 October 1923 whilst on night flying. 1 crew member killed. (E. F. Hare)

26

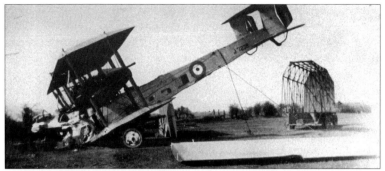

Vimy J7239 (No. 7 Sqn) 13 March 1924. Pilot Sgt Ward. (E.F. Hare)

his service career and working on Sopwith Snipes and Gloster Grebes at Duxford never had the same appeal [10].

Of the many other remarkable personalities who saw squadron service in these pioneering days, Flight Lieutenant Allan Perry-Keene had been present at Bircham Newton from the very early days of the Handley Page bombers and had known Squadron Leader Tedder. In fact, he sometimes flew with Tedder in a Handley Page O/400 'in which we played chess on his portable set'. Perry-Keene was a member of No. 100 Squadron when 'D' Flight was detached to form No. 7 Squadron. He recalls that the Vimy 'was probably the ugliest aeroplane ever built with not a corner rounded off'. He occasionally conveyed the AOC, Air Commodore T. I. 'Webby' Webb-Bowen, on various inspections in a Vimy, as the AOC preferred that aircraft to the more draughty DH9A, and two engines were preferable to one when flying over the Wash! After one flight, the AOC saw the post office telegram which stated: 'Vimy B2607 pilot Fg.Off. Perry-Keene passengers ACs Bowen and Smith left for Bircham Newton 10.25 a.m.' The AOC, none too pleased, commented: 'I seem to have been demoted to Aircraftman, and you've got your hyphen and I haven't.'[11]

During May 1924 the Vimy was gradually being replaced by the larger Vickers Virginia powered by two Napier Lion engines of 450 hp each. This aircraft was to become the backbone of the RAF's bomber force until the late 1930s.

Perry-Keene recalls the night flying training from Bircham Newton which on one occasion nearly led to disaster when an engine fire erupted at 4,000 feet over Hunstanton at 12 o' clock at night, owing to the breaking of a petrol feed tube. He headed for the airfield eight miles away while his observer Flight Sergeant Brett climbed out of the cockpit to extinguish the spreading fire. By the time they reached the airfield the fire was flickering out and they landed without injury. But, the engine was completely burned out and the aircraft was seriously damaged. As a result, Brett was awarded the Air Force Medal.[12]

---

[10] E. F. Hare: letters to author 12/91.
[11] Perry-Keene, p26.
[12] Ibid. pp26-7

On a somewhat lighter note, Perry-Keene and a friend 'Pop' Ritchie had built a monoplane glider at Spittlegate[13], where they had been based with No. 100 Squadron. Perry-Keene's father had been a pioneer in the Birmingham motor industry and with this family background it was not surprising that he was something of an inventor. When the two airmen were posted to Bircham Newton the glider came as well, strapped to the rear fuselage of a Virginia in two separate flights, resulting in little rudder control for the aircraft! A car engine was then purchased for £10 which was fitted to the newly christened 'Bircham Beetle' and the machine flew successfully. Later on, though, Perry-Keene crashed and ended up in hospital: 'I had to pay for my stay there as some hard-hearted official ruled that anyone flying a civil aircraft did so at his own risk'.[14]

In the meantime, September 1923 had seen the arrival of No. 11 Squadron from Andover with its DH9A light bombers, re-equipping with Fairey Fawns during the following spring. This squadron left for Netheravon at the end of May 1924, exchanging places with No. 99(B) Squadron under the command of Squadron Leader G. R. M. Reid DSO, MC. Until the end of the year, No. 99 Squadron flew the Vickers Vimy, but in August the squadron became the first and only RAF unit to be equipped with the

'Bircham Beetle', built by a syndicate including F/Lt Perry-Keene, at Bircham Newton, Sept. 1924. (A.L.A. Perry-Keene / Marion M. Newman)

Air Vice-Marshal A.L.A. Perry-Keene during the 1950s. (A.L.A. Perry-Keene / Marion M. Newman)

---

[13] The RFC referred to Spittlegate but the airfield became known as Grantham between the wars, and then in 1944 the name reverted to 'Spitalgate'. (Info from Peter Elliott, RAF Museum, 24 May 2000).

[14] Perry-Keene, pp28-9.

single-engined Avro Aldershot bomber, which was retained until replaced by the twin-engined Handley Page Hyderabad at the end of 1925. This was the last RAF heavy bomber in squadron service to be of wooden construction. A fighter squadron, No. 32, had also been based at the station during the summer of 1924, flying Sopwith Snipes, returning to its home aerodrome at Kenley in August.

Bircham Newton photographed in 1924. In foreground two Vickers Vimy bombers of No.7 Sqn and to their left two Avro Aldershot bombers of No. 99 Sqn. Note the coupled General Service Sheds which were replaced in the late 1930s by the new Type 'C' hangars. (Tony Arter)

Bircham Newton aerial photo c.1924. (P.H.T. Green Collection)

Bircham Newton aerial photo c.1924/5. Avro Aldershots in foreground. Vimy to left. Avro 504N at rear. (P.H.T. Green Collection)

Avro 504K at the airfield 1920s. These aircraft were often used for training purposes. (Dudley Crisp)

A fatal accident occurred on 27 February 1925 about a quarter of a mile from the aerodrome, involving an Avro 504K (H3083) piloted by Pilot Officer Cecil S. M. Woode of No. 99 Squadron accompanied by his mechanic AC Ernest Forrester. The aircraft, used by the squadron for training purposes, lost control at 2,000 feet and dived into the ground, killing the pilot and seriously injuring Forrester. Cecil Woode was the son of the Rector of Fersfield and was buried at Fersfield on 4 March.[15]

---

[15] Fairhead, Huby: letter to author 14/12/91.

Crash of Avro 504K H3083 in which P/O Cecil Woode and AC E. Forrester were killed.

Grave of P/O Cecil S. M. Woode (No. 99 Sqn), 27 February 1925, St Andrew's Church, Fersfield.

In April 1927 No. 7 Squadron, by now under the command of Wing Commander C. F. A. Portal (later Marshal of the RAF Lord Portal), moved to Worthy Down. In the new year, 1928, No. 99 Squadron left for Upper Heyford, being replaced by the DH9As of No. 39(B) Squadron, arriving from Spittlegate. This unit remained until it moved to India at the end of the year.

De Havilland DH9As on flight line at Bircham Newton during 1920s. These aircraft were built by Mann Egerton. Several of the squadrons at the station during this period were equipped with these aircraft, and some went on to serve in the Middle East. Note the 'Hucks Starter' on right of picture of group of aircraft. (Dudley Crisp)

DH9A in one of the large General Service (GS) Sheds 1920s. (Dudley Crisp)

Bircham Newton had by now developed into a permanent bomber station, in accordance with the plans of 1923-24 referred to earlier. In September 1924 a Station Headquarters (SHQ) had been formed under the command of Wing Commander the Hon. L. J. Twistleton-Wykeham-Fiennes. A number of buildings dating from just after the First World War and the 1920s remain in use to the present day including the Squash

Programme for Bircham Revue December 1926. (Tony Arter)

Local family group by an aircraft, Bircham Newton late 1920s.
Dudley Crisp recalled visiting his grandfather Matthews' farm at Bircham Newton just on the edge of the airfield, when he was a small boy. The family would often visit the airfield and could wander about inspecting the aircraft and attending social functions. Security was not a problem in those pre-war days. (Dudley Crisp)

Courts (1918), the old Guard House (1923), and the four Type 'C' barrack blocks easily visible from the main road (1928)[16].

By comparison with other stations, the accommodation for officers and airmen was of a good standard but in keeping with RAF policy of not encouraging officers to marry early there was little provision for married quarters. Allan Perry-Keene, as a Flight Lieutenant, had married in September 1923 but was able to rent a furnished bungalow for 25 shillings a week at Heacham, some ten miles from the Station. The couple 'engaged a daily maid who for under £1 per week brought us our early morning tea, cooked and cleaned. Known to us as 'Venus', for her not unsurpassing beauty, she stayed with us until we were posted from Bircham Newton.'[17]

An order was then issued by the Air Officer Commanding, that the married officers were to live within five miles of their station. Given the shortage of adequate accommodation in the area, Allan Perry-Keene and his new wife Rene were fortunate to find an unfurnished cottage in the old 'North-West Norfolk Union Workhouse' (now Norfolk Heights). Apparently, this had once been the workhouse master's quarters, and though bitterly cold in winter was well built and probably the best available at the time.[18]

---

[16] See also airfield plans in Ch 4.
[17] Perry-Keene, p33.
[18] Ibid. p34.

Bircham Newton witnessed an unusual event on 15 June 1928 when an Armstrong Whitworth Argosy (G-EBLF) *City of Glasgow* of Imperial Airways landed at the Station to refuel, while taking part in an experimental passenger service from Croydon to Turnhouse near Edinburgh, at the same time as racing the *Flying Scotsman*. After leaving Bircham Newton, another refuelling stop was made at Cramlington near Newcastle, with the aircraft arriving eventually at the destination 15 minutes before the train![19] Little seems to have changed!

A succession of bomber squadrons continued to come and go. No. 101(B) Squadron re-formed at Bircham Newton in March 1928 with DH9A aircraft, some of which had come from No. 39 Squadron. Re-equipment followed with the new Boulton and Paul Sidestrand III in early 1929, before the squadron moved on to Andover in October of that year. A new squadron, No. 35(B), re-formed at the station in March 1929 with DH9A light bombers, under the command of Squadron Leader Gilbert S. M. Insall VC, MC.

Gilbert Insall possessed an outstanding war record, having become only the fifth pilot to be awarded the Victoria Cross in the Great War, as well as earning the Military Cross for a daring escape from prisoner-of-war camp. One of his peacetime passions was archaeology and he was one of the first to realise the potential of aerial reconnaissance in identifying and photographing prehistoric sites. Insall had already surveyed many sites in the Middle East and in 1926 had photographed what was to become the famous Wiltshire Woodhenge site near Durrington Walls. By now a wing commander and squadron CO, Gilbert Insall was in a position to combine his private passion and training requirements. Rank has its privileges! Thus he set out from Bircham Newton on a June day in 1929 to fly along the Tas valley south-east of Norwich, in the

No. 207 Sqn's Fairey IIIF J9172 and others lined up c.1930.
Note the early watch office in the background. (P.H.T. Green Collection)

[19] Fairhead, Huby: letter to author 9/11/91.

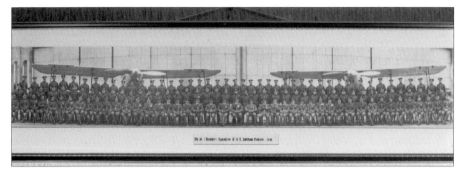

No. 35 (Bomber) Sqn line-up with Fairey IIIF, 1931. (CITB)

course of which he discovered the concentric rings of the Neolithic site of Arminghall 'woodhenge'. The subsequent photographs he took marked Insall out as one of the pioneers of aerial photography.[20]

In November 1929 No. 35 Squadron had converted to Fairey IIIF day bombers and was now joined by No. 207(B) Squadron, returning to Bircham Newton from Eastchurch, also equipped with the Fairey IIIF. By August 1932, both units had re-equipped with the Fairey Gordon, which had originally been developed from the Fairey IIIF.

No. 207 Sqn group photo in front of Fairey Gordon, winning the Armament Officers' Trophy, 1933. (RAF Museum photograph: Ref PO18453)

---

[20] *Eastern Daily Press* Magazine 24/7/99: article by Steve Snelling, with contributions from Derek Edwards.

Until 1933 Bircham Newton came under the control of the Wessex Bombing Area, with its Headquarters at Abingdon.[21] In that year, an organisational change led to that Command being divided, resulting in the day bomber squadrons (including those of Bircham Newton) coming under the command of Central Area, which in turn became part of the newly formed No. 3 Group in May 1936.

The early 1930s was a period of intense activity for Nos 35 and 207 Squadrons, with fighter affiliations and tactical exercises with the Army. One squadron with which there were frequent fighter affiliation exercises was No. 19 (F) Squadron based at Duxford.

Fairey Gordon K2691 of No. 207 Sqn overshot on landing and undercarriage collapsed c.1934. (P.H.T. Green Collection)

A spectacular local incident concerning the crash of a Fairey IIIF from Bircham Newton was reported in the *Eastern Daily Press* on 6 January 1931, when the aircraft's right wing appeared to break up at 4,000 feet above Heacham, and the pilot, Sergeant Hudson (who lived at Heacham) with a mechanic as passenger, both parachuted to safety. They were uninjured and the only casualty was said to be a rat which had run out of a chicken coop in terror and was caught under the falling aeroplane. The machine was wrecked, having 'dug a hole big enough to bury a horse and cart'.[22]

---

[21] In 1925 the RAF had introduced the Air Defence of Great Britain (ADGB) by which bomber and fighter squadrons were grouped geographically.

[22] *Eastern Daily Press* 6/1/31.

AEROPLANE CRASH AT HEACHAM.

TWO MEN ESCAPE BY PARACHUTES

A JUMP AT 4000 FEET.

WATCHERS THRILLED BY DOUBLE DESCENT.

An aeroplane belonging to the R.A.F., on a practice flight from Bircham Newton aerodrome, crashed at Heacham, seven miles from its harbour, yesterday morning. The pilot, Sergeant Hudson, who lives at Heacham, and his companion, finding that the machine was doomed owing to a broken wing, jumped out in their parachutes at a height of 4000 feet and reached the ground without a scratch.

The machine was completely smashed. The only casualty was a rat which ran out from under a chicken coop near which the machine fell and was caught under the wreckage.

The descent of the pilot and his companion was seen by police officers, who were photographing a road in connexion with a police-court case. As soon as the pilot landed one of the officers ran up to him and shook him by the hand.

"You're a very lucky man," he said. "I hope you're not hurt."

"I'm quite all right, thanks," answered the pilot.

The other airman landed only a few yards away, also quite unhurt. The aeroplane wreckage was guarded by the police until R.A.F. men from the aerodrome came to move it.

Mr. W. J. Jones, of Heacham, stated he was at Hill House, Heacham, between ten and eleven yesterday morning when an aeroplane passed flying low. He watched it as it passed over the houses in the direction of Snettisham, and came to the conclusion it was in difficulties. Then he noticed the right wing was doubled up under the machine.

The next thing he saw was a man jump from the machine with a parachute, which did not open. The man passed out of his sight behind intervening houses. He then saw a second man jump from the machine also with a parachute, which opened beautifully. The aeroplane went on a little further before it crashed.

Mr. Jones ran towards the spot and found that the first man's parachute had eventually opened and the man had made a safe landing in the garden of a house belonging to Mr. H. Graver. Going some 40 yards further he found that the second man had also safely landed in a field on Mr. Barrett's farm. The aeroplane, which came down on Mr. W. E. Cross's farm, about half a mile away, had dug a hole big enough to bury a horse and cart. It was smashed to pieces.

'PLANE WING BREAKS IN MID-AIR

4,000FT. PARACHUTE JUMP

Successful parachute descents from a height of 4,000ft. were made by an R.A.F. officer and his companion when the wing of their machine broke, while flying over Heacham, seven miles from Bircham (Norfolk) Aerodrome yesterday.

The pilot is stated to have been Sergt. Hudson. His companion was a mechanic.

The two men landed within a few yards of each other, while the aeroplane crashed in a field some distance away and was completely wrecked.

The only casualty was a rat, which ran out of a chicken coop and was crushed by the falling aeroplane.

Mr. W. J. Jones, of Heacham, who saw the crash, said: "The right wing of the 'plane seemed to double right up."

Press reports 6 January 1931
on Fairey IIIF crash at Heacham.
(Eastern Daily Press via Huby Fairhead)

THE ROYAL CONNECTION AND THE EMPIRE AIR DAYS

By the 1930s flying was becoming increasingly popular in society and it was hardly surprising that the Royal family, and especially its youngest members, would exploit its possibilities. Given the fact that Bircham Newton airfield was just over seven miles from the King's Norfolk home of Sandringham, it became increasingly common for members of the Royal family and their guests to be seen at the aerodrome arriving or departing for various engagements.

One of the first occasions for this was the arrival of the Prince of Wales from Scarborough race-course on 27 May 1928 in a Bristol F2B (a converted Bristol Fighter) serial J8430 en route for a number of Norfolk engagements. This aircraft was the first official Royal aeroplane brought into service but there were several others in regular use at this time including the de Havilland DH80 Puss Moth G-ABBS which made frequent appearances. On 20 August 1930 this aircraft, piloted by Flight Lieutenant Edward Fielden (later Captain of the King's Flight and Air Vice-Marshal), arrived from Northolt at 0940 hrs, leaving at 1125 hrs with Prince George as passenger en route to Hendon. A few days later, on 22 August, Flight Lieutenant Fielden was flying solo in the DH80 from Bircham Newton to Sheringham and Duxford 'over familiar country'.[23] The comings and goings of the Prince of Wales continued, as illustrated by a logbook entry of 24 December 1931, when the Prince arrived at Bircham Newton from Hendon in DH80A G-ABRR piloted by Flight Lieutenant Fielden in 'good weather'.[24]

AIR COOLED
ENGINES FOR
EVERY TYPE OF
AIRCRAFT

ARMSTRONG SIDDELEY MOTORS LTD.
Coventry · · England

SIDDELEY

King and Queen inspecting Gordons of No. 35 Sqn at Empire Air Day 1934. (From Official Programme, Royal Review RAF 1935)

Other aircraft associated with the Royal family at this time and the Prince of Wales in particular were making frequent appearances at Bircham Newton, including a Vickers 259 Viastra Mk X G-ACCC from about 1934, and a DH89 Dragon Rapide G-ACTT from around 1935.

On 24 May 1934 Their Majesties King George V and Queen Mary paid a visit to the station on the occasion of the first Empire Air Day, to inspect the squadrons and personnel, the first such official royal visit to an RAF Station since the end of the war. The King and Queen were accompanied by the station commander Wing Commander (later Air Commodore) Ray Collishaw DSO,

---

[23] Fielden, AVM Sir Edward: logbook extract August 1930.
[24] Ibid. December 1931.

OBE, DSC, DFC. The King had met Wing Commander Collishaw in France during 1918 when the latter was serving as a major, commanding No. 203 Squadron at Le Nieppe. Now, in somewhat different circumstances, the royal party were entertained to an impressive flying display by aircraft of No. 35 Squadron and a bombing demonstration by No. 207 Squadron.

Exactly one year later, on 24 May 1935, the station was opened to the public for the first time to celebrate Empire Air Day. The Royal Air Force was beginning to make serious attempts to throw open its doors in a bid to attract public support, and in the longer-term to boost recruitment. The local newspaper reports were fulsome in their descriptions of 'smiling young aircraftmen with the benevolent air of the vicar at a Sunday School treat' conducting groups around the hangars and workshops, and the parked aircraft. 'The absorbed air with which large numbers of Norfolk's youthful sons of the soil watched or listened to exhibitions or explanations indicated that their interest lay deeper than mere curiosity'. And the report added, significantly: 'Obviously Empire Air Day was an effective method of inaugurating a nation-wide recruitment campaign.' Wing Commander Collishaw, described as a 'wartime air ace who brought down over 60 enemy machines' and a 'Colonial' (he was a Canadian), was seen chatting freely among the crowds.[25]

Apart from the resident Nos 35 and 207 Squadron at the Empire Air Day, there were also Vildebeest bombers of No. 22 Squadron, then based at Donibristle in Scotland. One of the highlights of the day was a mock bombing attack by Fairey Gordons of No. 207 Squadron on 'a realistic desert fort of wood and canvas'. Lest there should be any misunderstanding, the same squadron acted the part of a hostile enemy force attacking a British oil pumping station in the Arabian desert. There was no mistaking the direction from which a future foreign threat was expected to come as far as the defence planners were concerned.

Empire Air Day at Bircham Newton, 1935. Fairey Gordons of No. 35 Sqn on left, a Hawker Hart of No. 24 Sqn from Hendon in centre, and a Handley Page Heyford in foreground. (Ray Wilson)

[25] *Lynn News and County Press* May 1935.

The living quarters were not open to the public although a representative of the *Lynn News and County Press* was invited to inspect some of the airmen's quarters: 'Clean, comfortable quarters are provided and there are facilities for rugby, soccer, cricket and tennis', stated the report. 'It is a fine, healthy and interesting life', said one officer: 'The men have more time off than the average civilian worker and they see more of England and the world than the average young fellow does. The conditions of service are good and we feed them well.'[26] The extent of the facilities provided, it was suggested in the report, reflect the fact that in many respects Bircham Newton was relatively more isolated than many RAF airfields, and therefore a special effort was made to make the most of what was provided. By the end of what must have seemed like a sensational day to those who attended the event, the proceeds amounted to £206, a sum forwarded to the RAF Benevolent Fund.

In what was to be a busy year, Nos 35 and 207 Squadrons took part in the RAF Silver Jubilee Review held at Mildenhall on 6 July 1935 before moving to the Sudan on the onset of the Abyssinian crisis during October, when Mussolini invaded Ethiopia as part of his scheme to create an Italian East African Empire.

The end of the year saw Nos 21(B) and 34(B) Squadrons re-forming at Bircham Newton, equipped with Hawker Hinds, being joined in January 1936 by No. 18(B) Squadron with its Hawker Harts, soon to be replaced by Hinds, from Upper Heyford. In February No. 49(B) Squadron was re-formed from 'C' Flight of No. 18 Squadron. In July 1936, Nos 21 and 34 Squadrons left for Abbotsinch to form the nucleus of No. 2 Group, and No. 49 Squadron moved to Worthy Down in August, with No. 18 Squadron moving to Old Sarum in the same month.

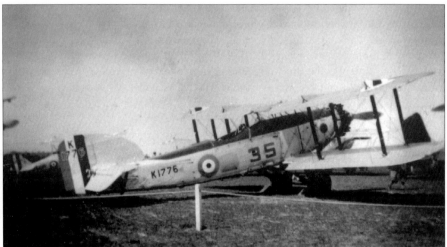

Fairey Gordon of No. 35 Sqn at Open Day 1935, shortly before the squadron left for the Sudan. (Ray Wilson)

---

[26] Ibid. May 1935.

Hawker Hinds at Bircham Newton end 1935 / start 1936 possibly of No. 21 Sqn which re-formed at Bircham Newton in December 1935, the first squadron to be equipped with Hinds. (L.A. Smith)

THE END OF AN ERA

The year 1936 proved to be a momentous one for Bircham Newton, and for the country. King George V died at Sandringham on 20 January. On that day Edward, Prince of Wales, arrived at Bircham Newton from Hendon in DH89 Dragon Rapide G-ADDD, with Flight Lieutenant Fielden at 1220 hrs. At 1455 hrs Lord Hailsham, with Sir John Simon, Home Secretary, and J. Ramsay MacDonald, Lord President, departed for Hendon. Just before midnight on the 20th the King died and Edward, Prince of Wales, was now King.

The next day, 21 January, the new King Edward VIII and the Duke of York were departing for Hendon in the Dragon Rapide (1125 hrs).[27] The cold facts revealed in Flight Lieutenant Fielden's logbook barely provide a hint of the historic significance of this event, for the new King was the first British monarch in history to fly to his capital for the first time. By the time the Dragon Rapide reached Hendon, resplendent in its distinctive blue and red colours associated with the Brigade of Guards in which Edward as Prince of Wales had once served, the world's press were present in force at that aerodrome to report on the occasion[28].

It was during the short reign of King Edward that, on 21 July 1936, the King's Flight was formed at Hendon, with Edward Fielden, now a wing commander, appointed as its first captain. Later that year, on 5 August, the King paid what must have been one of his last visits to Bircham Newton when he arrived from Heathrow in the DH Rapide. It was a brief visit to Sandringham as the King departed at 1845 hrs on the same day, this time for Hendon. King Edward, unlike George V and later George VI, had never particularly liked Sandringham so it is not surprising that his visits were infrequent and brief. The abdication of King Edward in December 1936 ended his association with Sandringham and Bircham Newton.

---

[27] Fielden, January 1936.
[28] Wilson, Ray: article in King's Lynn *Citizen* 11/9/91.

Hawker Tomtit at Bircham Newton. Possibly one of the type used by Edward, Prince of Wales during the 1930s for visits to Sandringham via Bircham Newton. (L.A. Smith)

It was also during 1936 that Bircham Newton's days as a bomber station were coming to a close. The pace of change at home and an increasingly threatening international climate were about to usher in a new era in the station's history.

Logbook extract of Edward Fielden for January 1936, showing historic flight of 21 January. 'Storrier' was Chief Inspector David Storrier, private detective. 'Jenkins' was T. Jenkins, engineer, who often accompanied Fielden. (Crown Copyright)

43

CHAPTER 3

COASTAL COMMAND AND THE APPROACH OF WAR

'A good evening out was a walk to Docking, a few pints in the local pub, and a walk back to camp across the fields and the aerodrome.'
(Les A. Smith on an airman's life at Bircham Newton 1936-9)

'.......The dreaded words "Bircham Newton" reduced me to the depths of despair for it was the most feared posting in the UK in those days.'
(Vernon Buckman's thoughts on being posted to the station in December 1938)

If the crisis in Abyssinia had highlighted weaknesses in Britain's imperial defence, events on the European continent were beginning to concentrate minds on the shortcomings in home defence especially in the air.

Adolf Hitler had become German Chancellor in January 1934 and 'Führer of the German Reich' in August of that year. It was clear that the days of the post-war peace settlement were numbered, especially its disarmament clauses, and the League of Nations seemed powerless to act. Thus, early in 1935 the Luftwaffe was reborn and a massive expansion of the German armed forces was initiated. Hitler's reoccupation of the Rhineland in March 1936 provided yet another nail in the coffin of the Versailles Treaty of 1919 and any hopes for a permanent peace in Europe.

It was against this background that the Air Ministry produced a further series of plans to expand the Royal Air Force by developing new modern aircraft, increasing the number of squadrons to 124 by 1939, and expanding the number of permanent RAF stations from 52 in 1934 to 89 by 1938. On 13 July 1936 the RAF Command structure was reformed by abolishing the geographical groupings of the Air Defence of Great Britain (ADGB) and introducing the Command structure based on functions: Fighter, Bomber, Coastal, and Training Commands.

The need to replace without undue delay existing biplane bombers like the Hawker Hart and Hind by faster monoplane aircraft, led to an enterprising member of the British Purchasing Commission, Sir Arthur Harris (later C-in-C Bomber Command), to look across the Atlantic to the United States. The outcome was an order for 200 of the new maritime Lockheed Hudson reconnaissance aircraft. This act of apparent disloyalty to home industry caused a considerable furore in Britain at the time but during wartime 2,000 of these aircraft were to be delivered to the RAF, becoming an enormous asset to Coastal Command.[1] The Hudson was to play a major and distinguished part in Bircham Newton's wartime history.

The station was transferred to No. 16 (Reconnaissance) Group, Coastal Command on 10 August 1936, the first Coastal unit No. 206 (GR) Squadron having arrived from

---

[1] Terraine, John: *The Right of the Line* (Hodder and Stoughton Limited) pp38-9.

Avro Anson K6206 (No. 220 Sqn) after 'wheels up' landing. (L.A. Smith). Bill Parkes (then AC1, No. 220 Sqn) recalls the problems with the newly-delivered 'beautiful silver bird' - the Anson: 'the pilots were never used to having an aircraft with a retractable undercarriage and a landing speed a little higher than they were used to... and over a period of 14 days <u>five</u> Ansons landed with their u/c fully retracted. Our CO was not pleased. Fortunately both squadrons (Nos 206 & 220) were guilty so the rage was shared.'

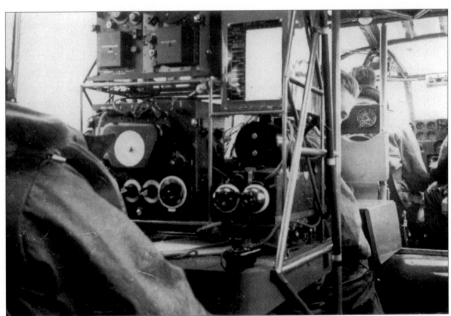

Shot taken inside a 'B' Flight Anson, probably awaiting instructions for take-off c.1937. (L.A. Smith)

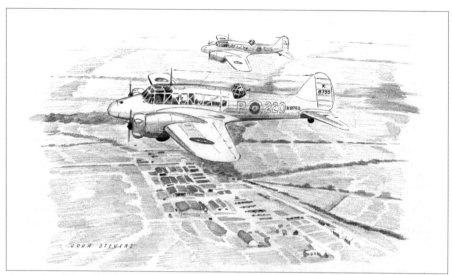

Anson Is of No. 220 Sqn over Bircham Newton c.1937.   (Drawing by Wing Commander John Stevens MBE, RAF Ret'd)

Manston at the end of July under the command of Wing Commander F. J. Vincent DFC, equipped with an aircraft which was to be associated with Bircham Newton for well over a decade, the Avro Anson, known affectionately as 'Faithful Annie'. No. 206 Squadron had first been formed in 1916 but was renumbered in 1919, eventually to be re-formed from 'C' Flight of No. 48 Squadron based at Manston on 15 June 1936. No. 48 Squadron had been the first RAF unit to receive the new Anson, which was the first monoplane to enter RAF service and the first with a retractable undercarriage, although the latter operation was only achieved by hundreds of backward turns on a winding handle. In October, Wing Commander H. O. Long DSO took command of No. 206 Squadron, a unit which was to have a long period of service at Bircham Newton, remaining there until May 1941. Two other Anson squadrons followed, No. 220 in August, and No. 269 for a few days in December before leaving for Abbotsinch. No. 220 Squadron was initially commanded by Squadron Leader W. M. M. Hurley, being replaced in December 1936 by Squadron Leader F. P. Smythies.

On 16 October, the AOC of the Command, Air Marshal P. B. Joubert de la Ferté CB, CMG, DSO, paid his first visit to the station to inspect the new squadrons.

Adjustment to a new station and new aircraft required a lot of hard work and attention to detail. No. 206 Squadron's Standing Orders issued in September 1936 laid down in detail the procedures to be followed, for example in taxying: 'Aircraft are to be taxied slowly, particulary at Bircham Newton, where the ground is hard and rough.' In the event of fog, the nearest alternative airfield to attempt a landing was Mildenhall.[2]

---

[2] No. 206 (GR) Squadron: Standing Orders (1/9/36): courtesy of No. 206 Squadron, RAF Kinloss.

As far as take-off was concerned the Anson only required about one third of the aerodrome area, so in the event of an accident, say, due to a stall (of which there were a small number)[3] ambulance and crash tenders would be on site in a very short time.

On the subject of crashes, an unusual incident occurred in late 1936 when a young pilot officer, J. A. Kent (later Group Captain), who was based at Duxford with No. 19 (F) Squadron, got lost in his Gloster Gauntlet on a cross-country night flight. Somewhere between Hatfield and Duxford he lost his bearings and flew on until he was beginning to run out of fuel. At that point he noticed a beacon on an aerodrome hangar and prepared to make a landing on the south side of that position, assuming that the hangar was on the north side of the field as was the case with most RAF stations. Unfortunately, he had

Anson K6197 (No. 220 Sqn) accident.
(L.A. Smith)

---

[3] See App. IV (Crashes/Losses)

Anson turret. AC L.A. Smith in process of fitting a camera gun in readiness for 'Air to Air' exercise. (L.A. Smith)

miscalculated and nearly hit a row of trees coming to an undignified rest in what appeared to be a field. He had landed at Bircham Newton all right but in the back garden of the station commanding officer! Bircham Newton was unusual in having its hangars on the south side of the airfield. This was an experience the young pilot would not forget especially as he had not only just missed trees in his forced landing but also an old concrete gun emplacement and a 20ft deep stone quarry![4]

Les A. Smith has provided an account of early days with the newly established No. 220 Squadron at Bircham Newton:

'I enjoyed about three years at Bircham from around September 1936 to August 1939. I served as a flight mechanic on 'B' Flight No. 220 (GR) Squadron. There were about 20 mechanics and riggers posted to form the squadron direct from our technical training course at Henlow. When we arrived at Bircham we found that we were the founder members of our squadron. There were no officers, no NCOs and no other ranks. For the first two or three months we were attached to 206 Squadron, also recently formed. However, we eventually detached from 206 and became established as No. 220 Squadron. At this time the airfield could fairly be described as isolated. I believe that the only public transport was the bus to King's Lynn and that it was a poor service. I can still remember getting on the only evening bus at about 6 p.m. with the intention of going to the cinema. The problem was that there was over two and a half hours to wait to see the whole programme and then get the only bus back to camp. Obviously, the

---

[4] Kent, G/Capt. J.A.: *One of the Few* (Corgi 1971) pp 41-44.

most congenial way of spending that time was at the pub almost opposite the cinema. Was it the 'White Hart'? Many were the times I never reached the cinema. I would stagger from the pub directly, more or less, on to the bus back to camp.

'I suppose one of the first things a young airman does when posted to a new area is to explore and get to know the surroundings. We used to go around in groups of three or four, walking or cycling, particularly in the summer. A good evening out was a walk to Docking, a few pints in the local pub, and a walk back to camp across the fields and the aerodrome. Certainly one of my favourite memories is of walking or cycling to Sedgeford and calling on 'Ma Drewery' for tea and cakes[5]. After the tea and cakes we would sit and chat for a couple of hours and she would regale us with stories of all her RFC friends from Great War days who did the same thing all those years ago. This was probably in the summer of 1937 before we had any inkling we would be involved in a war'.[6]

A serious episode of flooding in the Fens during March 1937 led to two corporals and an aircraftman being detached to Mildenhall to assist with the distribution of food and other essentials. A Leyland heavy tender and Morris 6 wheeler covered 724 miles in the course of these duties.

On a somewhat more pleasant note, rehearsals began to take place for another Empire Air Day on Saturday 29 May 1937. This time the station was showing off its recently acquired Avro Ansons along with other types from different parts of the country. A notable newcomer was the new Bristol Blenheim bomber which had entered squadron service with the RAF as recently as the previous March with No. 114 (B) Squadron based at Wyton. Other types on display included the Hawker Hart and Hawker Hind, the latter from Upwood, the Hawker Demon from Hornchurch, the Westland Wallace from Biggin Hill and a Handley Page Heyford bomber from nearby Mildenhall.

Another interesting aspect of life at Bircham Newton during this period was the continuing connection with royal flying. The King's Flight had officially been formed at Hendon by King Edward VIII on 21 July 1936 under the captaincy of Wing Commander (later Air Vice-Marshal Sir) Edward H. Fielden. Edward's successor, King George VI, saw the obvious advantages of the Flight for his royal duties and frequently used Bircham Newton on journeys to and from Sandringham, as well as in the course of other engagements. One of the aircraft used from 1937 was the Airspeed Envoy III G-AEXX acquired for the Air Ministry from the recently re-formed firm, Airspeed (1934) Ltd of Portsmouth (also later of Christchurch, Hants). It so happened that one of Airspeed's joint managing directors was N. S. Norway, better known as the novelist Nevil Shute. One problem highlighted was the aircraft's relative lack of space but after successful trials at Martlesham it was handed over on 3 May 1937. At Bircham Newton the aircraft was a familiar sight during the later 1930s, resplendent in its Brigade of Guards colour scheme. It remained in continual use by the King until it was handed over to No. 24

---

[5] See previous account by Ted Hare.
[6] Smith, L.A.: letter to author 10/8/91.

Airspeed Envoy III G-AEXX of the recently-formed King's Flight, in one of the No. 206 Sqn hangars at Bircham Newton during 1937. The aircraft was a familiar sight at Bircham Newton, conveying the new King George VI to his various engagements while he resided at Sandringham. (L.A. Smith)

Squadron's 'A' Flight at Hendon for the use of the AOC Balloon Command, Air Vice-Marshal O. T. Boyd.

At that time Coastal Command was considered to be less glamorous than Bomber or Fighter Commands as far as the public perception was concerned. This was surprising in a nation that prided itself on its sea power and the Navy assumed that the Command's main role would merely be to act as the eyes of the battle fleet in the event of another engagement like the Battle of Jutland of 1916. Thus maritime reconnaissance took up the bulk of training time along with gunnery practice, bombing practice and formation flying. Little attempt was made to equip the Ansons for anti-submarine work as it was felt that Asdic sonar detection equipment fitted to destroyers would be sufficient in a future war.

The late 1930s were still halcyon days in RAF squadrons, in the opinion of Flying Officer Terence Bulloch (later Squadron Leader, DSO and bar, DFC and bar), who was posted to No. 220 (GR) Squadron in 1937. The most serious crimes for officers were getting into debt and being unable to pay the mess bill, followed by damaging aeroplanes. The most favoured pastimes seemed to be drinking beer and driving fast cars.[7] But the more serious side of life was beginning to make itself felt as international peace was becoming ever more brittle.

January 1938 proved to be a busy month on the station. On the 4th, No. 206 (GR) Squadron, commanded by Wing Commander Long, moved to Leuchars for annual air-firing and bombing exercises which lasted until the 31st. On the 18th, Squadron Leader

---

[7] Spooner, Tony, DSO, DFC: *Coastal Ace* (William Kimber 1986).

Smythies led a striking force of 11 Ansons from No. 220 (GR) Squadron during night exercises with the Home Fleet in the North Sea and Channel. Air Vice-Marshal H. M. Cave-Brown-Cave DSO, DFC, AFC, AOC of No. 16 (GR) Group, arrived on the 25th, remaining to receive King George VI the following day. The King arrived at 11 a.m. on his way to Cranwell in Airspeed Envoy G-AEXX returning to the station after that visit to inspect the Ansons of No. 220 Squadron. The station commander Group Captain J. W. Woodhouse DSO, MC was present along with the AOC in the official welcome of the royal guest. Afterwards, the King departed by road for Sandringham.

Air Vice-Marshal Cave-Brown-Cave returned on 11 March to present to No. 206 (GR) Squadron its motto and crest 'Nihil nos effugit' ('Nought escapes us') with the distinctly maritime 'octopus' motif in the centre of the badge.

Something of the flavour of life at the station during 1938 is provided by AC1 E. B. Hammersley who was posted to No. 220 (GR) Squadron from the armament training school at Eastchurch in May 1938, remaining at Bircham Newton until the squadron left for Thornaby, Yorkshire, in August 1939. He recalls that the CO, Squadron Leader Smythies, was regarded with affection and respect. Another officer he remembers was Flight Lieutenant 'Pincher' Martin, who on one occasion decided to take his wife and family on his aircraft to Armament Training Camp at Leuchars in Scotland. It was only when he was busy loading his cot and baby bath into the aircraft that the CO appeared and demanded to know what he thought he was doing![8]

There was still much of the leisurely atmosphere typical of many RAF stations, which vanished for ever with the onset of war, according to Mr Hammersley. Annual leave was 14 days and had to be taken en bloc. On one of these occasions he hitched a lift on a test flight to his nearest home airfield, Hornchurch, thanks to the offer of Flying Officer Bulloch. Mr Hammersley also recalls an Empire Air Day in which an officer drove an old car up and down the tarmac while it was bombed with bags of flour from various aircraft. Another antic was performed by a character on the station called Pilot Officer Tulloch who was 'a tall, bean-pole of a man. He dressed as a Victorian lady complete with crinoline, bonnet and parasol. He had a specially made dog-lead which was several yards long and which terminated with a little dog. He would walk majestically through the crowd, every now and again stopping to peer backwards over their heads calling "Flossie! Flossie!", and giving a little tug on the lead. All eyes would follow the lead until "Flossie" appeared.'[9]

Another eyewitness account of pre-war life at Bircham Newton is provided by Ron Brown who served as Education Officer and from 1939-1941 as Intelligence Officer.[10] His main task was coaching servicemen for promotion exams and officers applying for permanent commissions. He liaised with local schools to monitor the needs of children of service personnel. Another job was helping to oversee the educational needs of

---

[8]   Hammersley, E.B.: letter to author Nov. 1992.
[9]   Ibid.
[10] Brown, Ron: *All Round the Compass* (Janus 1993).

personnel of the detached de Havilland Queen Bee remote-controlled target aircraft flight at Weybourne, near Sheringham, whose task was to operate drogue-towing for anti-aircraft gunners. He was also in charge of the Station Photographic Section and acted as the Sports Officer. In this latter capacity he organised regular transport to the swimming pool in Hunstanton to enable aircrew to receive swimming instruction. On occasions Ansons might be called upon to transport tennis and rugger teams to various venues. There was no doubting the idyllic lifestyle available to RAF officers in those pre-war days. Shooting parties and dining invitations with the local farmers and aristocracy were commonplace. There was ample time to enjoy leisurely pursuits like sailing and tennis with up to 51 days' leave per year in peacetime plus one long weekend every month. Moreover, given the relative isolation of a station like Bircham Newton, it was not uncommon for an Anson to be available for weekend transport to a suitable RAF station, and training requirements need not be neglected if cross-country flights could be combined with such tasks as collecting turkeys and hams for Christmas from Aldergrove in Antrim, Northern Ireland, or wines and champagnes from the Channel Islands. Whether or not this latter bonus had anything to do with the fact that an officer on the station was Pilot Officer Le Marchand Huchesson from Jersey, whose father was one of the island bailiffs, is not clear. As far as daily life was concerned, most needs were supplied by officers' batmen, the symbols of those pre-war gentlemanly days. On the social scene, there were weekly dining-in nights, not always welcomed by some of the married officers who might be living at some distance from the station in places like Old Hunstanton.

The more serious side of life was of course evident, as in all RAF stations then and now, with the occasional aircraft accident which seemed inevitably to accompany routine training. One such happened when a newly posted or visiting squadron leader attempted low level aerobatics in an Anson, although obviously inexperienced in that type of aircraft. After take-off, he pulled the stick right back, climbing vertically to 200 feet at which point the aircraft turned over and crashed into the ground, killing the wireless operator. The pilot was unhurt but was promptly posted from the station reputedly to be invalided out of the service.[11] When an event of that kind occurred it was customary to hold an auction of the dead man's kit, to assist the bereaved family. The highest price paid was usually for the cap badge.[12]

During the summer of 1938 a number of exercises were held involving the squadrons at Bircham Newton. One of these, planned from 5 to 7 August, was to train air and ground defences against air attack and to test the organisation and efficiency of all the forces taking part. In connection with this a complete blackout was to be organised over large areas of eastern England and the Midlands. The planned exercise included 23 fighter squadrons and 14 bomber squadrons, along with the ground defences and the Observer Corps (including that at King's Lynn), collectively known as the 'Westland'

---

[11] Hammersley, E.B.
[12] Ibid.

Landing of Anson short of the airfield after night flying exercise c.1938. Crew Sgt Bennet (pilot) & AC Jones (WOp) suffered minor injuries. Aircraft dropped into a large crater on edge of airfield. It was stripped in situ and returned by road to A.V. Roe's at Ringway. (L.A. Smith)

defending force and the attacking 'Eastland' force of 36 bomber squadrons. Nos 206 and 220 Squadrons were part of the latter force and more than 20 Ansons were to stand by in readiness. Other stations taking part included Marham, Feltwell, and Mildenhall. In the event, the exercise proved only a partial success as thick fog and low clouds hampered the operation from the start and prevented the Bircham Newton squadrons from taking part at all. Also, tragedy struck when a Handley Page Harrow bomber from Feltwell crashed at Bury St Edmunds with the loss of the entire crew.[13]

A serious loss for No. 206 Squadron on 1 November 1938 was an Anson (K8836) which failed to return from a night navigation exercise over the North Sea with the loss of its crew. No trace of the aircraft was ever found.

An illustration of life at the station during this period has been provided by Vernon Buckman (then Sergeant, later Squadron Leader), who was posted to No. 206 Squadron from Palestine in December 1938 as wireless operator/air gunner, remaining at Bircham Newton for four years, the longest period he served at a single station during his RAF career. The contrast with his time in Palestine could not have been greater, as he relates:

'The journey home was on the troopship *Somersetshire* sailing through the Bay in a northerly blizzard. Hearing that I was to join No. 206 (GR) Squadron caused me no qualms for I knew nothing about it, but the dreaded words "Bircham Newton" reduced me to the depths of despair for it was the most feared posting in the UK in those days.'

---

[13] *Lynn News* 9/8/38.

'Disembarking at Southampton at 4 a.m., still in a blizzard, and waiting about in the transit sheds for four hours I finally travelled by slow train, through London, arriving at Docking at 7 p.m. in snow three feet deep - so fed up that I had forgotten to be overjoyed at being home after four years abroad! On phoning Bircham I was told that no transport could get down that day, so my first day back in Blighty was spent in front of the fire in the station waiting room. On learning next morning that transport could not be sent until the snowplough had got through and, as the snowplough came from Docking, I decided that I would come through with that. They did not tell me that the snowplough was horse-drawn but that is how I eventually arrived, having walked the two miles behind the snowplough with my kitbags balanced on the boards of the plough.

I was warmly welcomed at the station, particularly by Corporal Harry Miller, who ran the squadron orderly room with remarkable efficiency, and who from that moment on

As an important east coast aerodrome, Bircham Newton was visited regularly by aircraft from other stations either in the course of training or for annual Empire Air Day air displays of the later 1930s.

Fairey Hendon at Bircham Newton. Probably from No. 38 Sqn based at Mildenhall, later moving to Marham. The aircraft is parked on the compass base as a result of possible navigational problems or compass checking. (L.A. Smith)

Air Dispatch DH Dragon Rapide at Bircham Newton, for newspaper delivery. A regular visitor between 1937 and 1939. (L.A. Smith)

Boulton and Paul Overstrand at Bircham Newton, from No. 101 Sqn based at Bicester, the only unit to be equipped with this aircraft from 1935 to 1938. No. 101 Sqn had been based at Bircham Newton, equipped with the Sidestrand, during 1929 before moving to Bicester. The Overstrand replaced the Sidestrand until its own replacement by the Blenheim in 1938. The Overstrand was the first RAF bomber to be fitted with a power-operated, enclosed gun turret mounted on the nose. Overstrands left first-line service after 1938 but some went on to serve as gunnery trainers as late as 1940. This particular aircraft (K4552) being the last recorded example at Manby. A further planned version called the Superstrand did not get beyond the drawing board. (L.A. Smith)

looked after me as he did the rest of the squadron.....I was looking forward to a long spell of leave.......However on meeting the CO Wing Commander N. H. D'Aeth that morning, he very apologetically informed me that I could have a long weekend but I had then to accompany the squadron to Leuchars early in the New Year for the annual firing practice.'[14]

Westland Wallace K8678 of No. 1 AACU at Bircham Newton 1937/1938. Various Flights of this unit were based at the airfield during this period, often during summer camps for target towing duties with various AA units. (L.A. Smith)

Mishap at Bircham Newton of Wallace I K4013 of 1 AACU. (L.A. Smith)

Supermarine Walrus refuelling at Bircham Newton c.1938. The Walrus was to play an important part in the rescue of aircrew who ditched in the sea. (L.A. Smith)

Avro Tutor at Bircham Newton, probably from FTS Cranwell during one of the Empire Air Days held annually from 1934. (L.A. Smith)

Hawker Hector K8149 at Bircham Newton c.1938/39. The aircraft's role was mainly Army co-operation duties until its replacement by the Lysander in 1939. (L.A. Smith)

Fairey Swordfish I K8359 at Bircham Newton with Avro Anson in the background, at one of the Empire Air Days. The Swordfish was later to serve in a number of Fleet Air Arm squadrons which flew from Bircham Newton. (L.A. Smith)

[14] Buckman, Vernon: Memories of Life with 206 (GR) Squadron.

On returning to Bircham Newton, Vernon was put in charge of the squadron radio section with the rank of sergeant. Another duty was the maintenance of carrier pigeons which involved a visit to Sandringham's pigeon lofts to fly the King's birds! Such a responsibility was no sinecure as the birds had to be looked after and a cage with two birds had to be provided for a wireless operator proceeding on all maritime flights. The regal source of these birds was something that had always to be borne in mind!

Serious training continued through the early months of 1939, as Vernon recalls, which included navigation exercises at sea, fishery patrolling and night flying. Detailed logs were kept in the complex navigation exercises of position, time, heading and height because although it was not known at the time, the aircraft were under trial RDF (Radio Direction Finding - later radar) surveillance from Bawdsey Research Station.[15] This was the outcome of the work of Robert Watson-Watt and his team who had moved to Bawdsey Manor in 1936 to pioneer this technique. Bawdsey became the first of the 'Chain Home' air defence radar stations of such enormous importance in the Battle of Britain.

Also in early 1939, Vernon attended a course in Standard Beam Approach (SBA) at Wroughton. This system was later installed at Bircham Newton as a bad weather landing aid, a development of the German Lorenz system.[16]

A diversion from routine training occurred on 21 March when fifteen Ansons from No. 220 Squadron were detailed to act as an escort from Calais to Dover for the French President M. Lebrun who was on his way to London for an official visit. Thereafter, exercises in conjunction with the Home Fleet increased in intensity, usually taking the form of 'locate, shadow and report'. There was endless gunnery and bombing practice, the latter activity carried out by eye, there being no bombsight yet available on the Anson. Leuchars was still the location for armament training and night bombing practice took place on ranges such as Acklington aerodrome near Newcastle-upon-Tyne. Other training routines included enemy ship recognition, especially of German battleships, and practice in the skill of aerial photography. An example of this kind of work was the dispatch of some Ansons in June 1939 to locate and photograph the *Queen Mary* on its voyage out of Cherbourg en route to New York.[17] Affiliation with the Spitfires of No. 19 (F) Squadron based at Duxford provided the squadron's gunners with much-needed practice.

Another notable event was a 21st anniversary party to celebrate the founding of the Royal Air Force held at the Duke's Head in King's Lynn on 1 April 1939.[18] Also the final Empire Air Day took place on 22 May 1939 attended by 5,000 people which included displays by Ansons, Wellingtons, a Magister, a Tutor and Hawker Henley target-tugs, the latter most probably from No. 1 Anti-Aircraft Co-operation Unit (1 AACU) which operated with the anti-aircraft range at Weybourne Camp, north Norfolk.

---

[15] Buckman.
[16] Ibid.
[17] Brown, Ron.
[18] Ibid.

Ansons from No. 233 (GR) Squadron arrived from Leuchars in June for a three month detachment and in August No. 220 (GR) Squadron left for Thornaby to be re-equipped with the new Lockheed Hudson, much to the chagrin of members of No. 206 Squadron! In its place came No. 42 (Torpedo Bomber) Squadron from Thorney Island, with the elderly Vildebeest Mark III and Mark IV biplanes.

At the end of August the Duke and Duchess of Kent arrived from Sandringham on their way to Northolt in Airspeed Envoy G-AEXX piloted by Wing Commander Fielden, Captain of the King's Flight. Bircham Newton was an aerodrome in very close proximity to Sandringham House and there was frequent contact with the Royal Family, as we have already seen. A three mile air space forbidden zone was drawn around the main house as Queen Mary disliked noisy aircraft but in January 1939 a mock air raid by RAF aircraft on exercise was carried out, in which Ron Brown took part, when three Ansons made dive-bombing attacks at 200 mph. The only spectators were two small girls (aged 12 and 9 yrs) standing by their white ponies and waving frantically to the 'attacking' aircraft! Ron Brown was also given the task of lecturing to Sandringham household staff on Air Raid Precautions and on German aircraft types. It was also not uncommon for the royal dogs to be transported by air from Windsor to Sandringham via RAF Halton and Bircham Newton. As a special treat the mess dinner table at Bircham was often graced by royal pheasants.[19]

The days of peace were almost over for on 20 August a state of emergency had been declared for the RAF and on 1 September general mobilisation was ordered by the Air Council. On 3 September at 11 a.m. Bircham Newton was once again at war.

Miles Magister L5967 of the Station Flight, 30 August 1939. Note the Hawker Henleys in the background (possibly of No. 1 AACU). (P.H.T. Green Collection)

---

[19] Brown, Ron.

CHAPTER 4

THE AERODROME GROWS

'On arrival at Bircham Newton I was greeted by the Orderly Officer who informed me I was going to 'Ypres', which scared me as my father had fought there in the Great War. However, as it turned out, all the barrack blocks were named after Great War battlefields, Somme, Mons and Passchendaele.'
(Allan Monaghan recalling his posting to No. 206 Squadron in 1941)

As we have already seen Bircham Newton was established as an aerodrome towards the end of the Great War, in 1918. On a point of terminology, the word 'aerodrome' was common parlance for such establishments during the 1920s and 1930s and it was not until around 1943 that the American designation 'airfield' came into common use.[1]

In its basic outward appearance, the station retained its 1918 features throughout the 1920s and well into the 1930s. Most of the buildings straddled the western side of the main Great Bircham to Burnham Market road, with the three large General Service sheds and the smaller Aeroplane Repair Section shed lined along an axis from the north-east to south-west. The Officers' Mess and cabins along with the women's hostel were among the very few buildings on the eastern side of the road, slightly apart from the main airfield.

One of the earliest buildings still in use today is the Squash Court (Bldg 153: 1918 design), on the eastern side of the main road. Something will be said later about the reputed hauntings supposedly associated with this early building. Other early designs include the married quarters (Bldg 150: 1921 design).

The next phase of expansion of 1923-24 has already been referred to, largely undertaken by the short-lived first Labour Government of 1924. Bircham Newton was one of the stations selected and a spate of buildings date from this period, many of which survive to the present day. These include the Guard House (Bldg 101: 1923 design). After the airfield was taken over by the Construction Industry Training Board (CITB), the building became Barclays Bank, and eventually the CITB shop, but it still retains its original outward appearance. Other 1923 designs include the Booster House (Bldg 95), the Power House (old) (Bldg 93), and the Reservoir (Bldg 96).

The year 1928 saw new barrack blocks, Type 'C' (Bldgs 45-48), replacing the original airmen's barracks. Other buildings dating from this period include the latrine (Bldg 91: 1929 design).

The international crises and the period of rearmament from the early 1930s led to the reappraisal of home defences already referred to and the consequence was a gradual redevelopment and expansion in the provision of airfields throughout the country. By

---

[1] Smith, David J.: *Britain's Military Airfields 1939-45* (Patrick Stephens Limited) pp9-10.
Also information from Barry H. Abraham (Editor *Airfield Review*).

1939, these changes had given Bircham Newton the outward appearance it has for the most part retained up to the present day.

The most obvious changes included a new Watch Office with Tower (Bldg 84: 1934 design). The term 'watch office' was standard in the Royal Air Force rather than the American designation 'control tower' which only became current in more recent times.[2] A new Officers' Mess was completed in December 1936 (Bldg 152: also 1934 design). Other developments included a new Station HQ (Bldg 1: 1936 design), Sergeants' Mess and Quarters (Bldgs 16 & 21: 1936 design) and NAAFI (Bldg 49: 1936 design).

By the late 1930s, the old aircraft sheds were being superseded by the substantial Type 'C' aircraft sheds, a common sight today in many airfields across the country. The first Type 'C' Aircraft Shed (Hipped) was taken over by No. 220 Squadron in July 1937 in a location directly to the south-west of the existing sheds. By 1939 two others were in place but a proposed fourth, on the site of one of the demolished sheds, was never built. The foundations of the latter can still be seen today. Additional hangarage was provided by Bellman hangars (Bldgs 132-133). It is worth pointing out that the term 'aircraft shed' was the description used for such buildings in the Royal Air Force at the time. The later word 'hangar' was another foreign import, this time from the French, with the original meaning of a covered space for a carriage.[3]

The other major change in layout by 1939 was the new development directly to the south-east of the main airfield, in a completely new site. Married officers' quarters already existed in that vicinity (Bldgs 108-112: 1937 design), but now they were joined by a new parade ground and a cluster of buildings which included amongst others, new barrack blocks Type 'L' (Bldgs 67, 68 & 70: 1938 design), ambulance garage and mortuary (Bldg 25: 1936 design), gas decontamination block (Bldg 28: 1937 design) and sick quarters and annexe (Bldg 26: 1937 design). On the south side of the airfield, close to the main Great Bircham road, were the bomb stores.

At the outbreak of war the Operations Room was a wooden hut protected by sandbags manned in six hour periods by three watches. However, during October 1939, a new Operations block came into use (Bldg 22: 1938 design).

The following airfield plans (1918, 1929, 1939 and 1945) were drawn by Alan Gardener and reproduced with kind permission of Ordnance Survey.

---

[2] Smith, David J. p70.
[3] Ibid. p74.

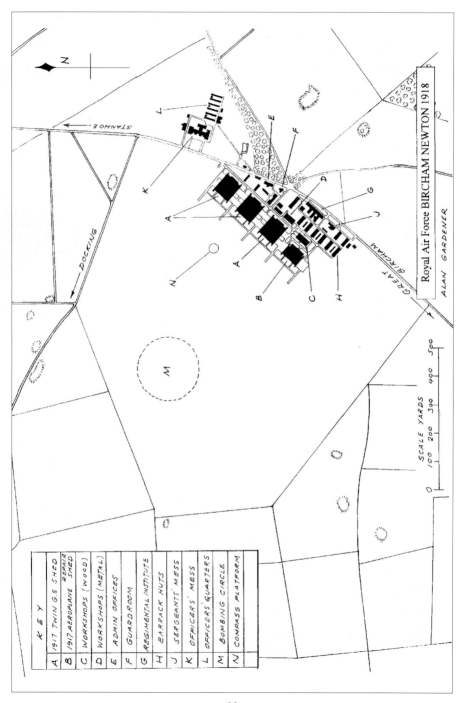

Royal Air Force BIRCHAM NEWTON 1918

ALAN GARDENER

KEY

A	1917 TWIN G S SHED
B	1917 AEROPLANE REPAIR SHED
C	WORKSHOPS (WOOD)
D	WORKSHOPS (METAL)
E	ADMIN OFFICES
F	GUARDROOM
G	REGIMENTAL INSTITUTE
H	BARRACK HUTS
J	SERGEANTS' MESS
K	OFFICERS' MESS
L	OFFICERS QUARTERS
M	BOMBING CIRCLE
N	COMPASS PLATFORM

SCALE YARDS
0   100 200 300 400 500

N

STANHOE

DOCKING

GREAT BIRCHAM

Bircham Newton c.1918. (RAF Museum Photograph: Ref PO12600)

Aerodrome c.1924, facing north-west. (Mrs Prue Riddiford / CITB)

Aerodrome, September 1927. (P.H.T. Green Collection)

Aerodrome in 1929. (CITB)

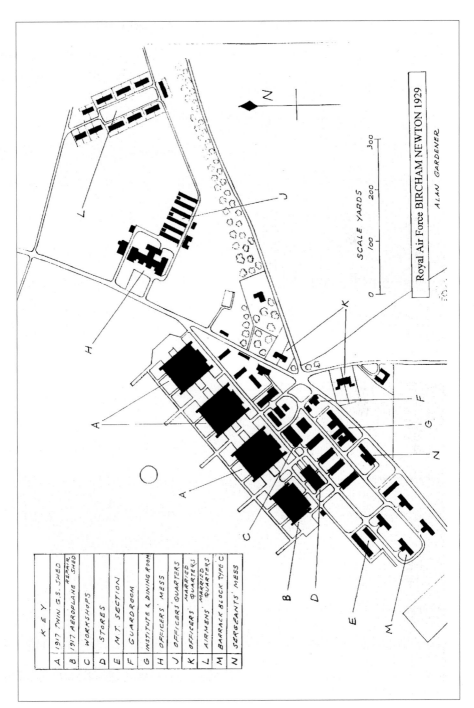

KEY

A	1917 TWIN G.S. SHED
B	1917 AEROPLANE REPAIR SHED
C	WORKSHOPS
D	STORES
E	M.T. SECTION
F	GUARDROOM
G	INSTITUTE & DINING ROOM
H	OFFICERS' MESS
J	OFFICERS' QUARTERS
K	OFFICERS' MARRIED QUARTERS
L	AIRMENS' MARRIED QUARTERS
M	BARRACK BLOCK TYPE C
N	SERGEANTS' MESS

Royal Air Force BIRCHAM NEWTON 1929

ALAN GARDENER

SCALE YARDS

0   100   200   300

N

Aerial photo of Bircham Newton taken from Anson K6204 1937/1938 showing some of the remodelling of the aerodrome, including one of the new Type 'C' hangars (extreme left). By the start of the war a total of three Type 'C' hangars would supersede the General Service Sheds of World War I vintage. (L.A. Smith)

Aerial photo of CITB late 1980s (for comparison with previous photo). Three Type 'C' hangars still in place, and remodelling of the aerodrome completed by 1939 still visible SE of the main road. (CITB via Peter York)

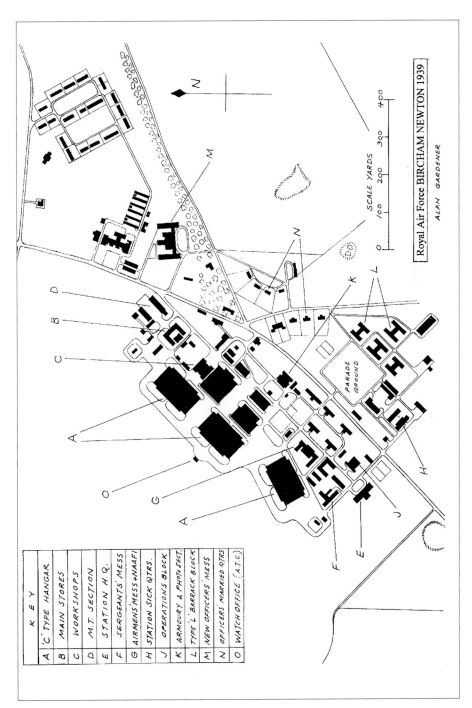

Royal Air Force BIRCHAM NEWTON 1939

ALAN GARDENER

SCALE YARDS

0   100   200   300   400

N

M

N

L

K

D

B

C

A

O

G

A

F

E

J

H

PARADE GROUND

KEY

A	'C' TYPE HANGAR
B	MAIN STORES
C	WORKSHOPS
D	M.T. SECTION
E	STATION H.Q.
F	SERGEANTS' MESS
G	AIRMENS' MESS + NAAFI
H	STATION SICK QTRS.
J	OPERATIONS BLOCK
K	ARMOURY & PHOTO SECT.
L	TYPE 'L' BARRACK BLOCK
M	NEW OFFICERS' MESS
N	OFFICERS' MARRIED QTRS
O	WATCH OFFICE (A.T.C.)

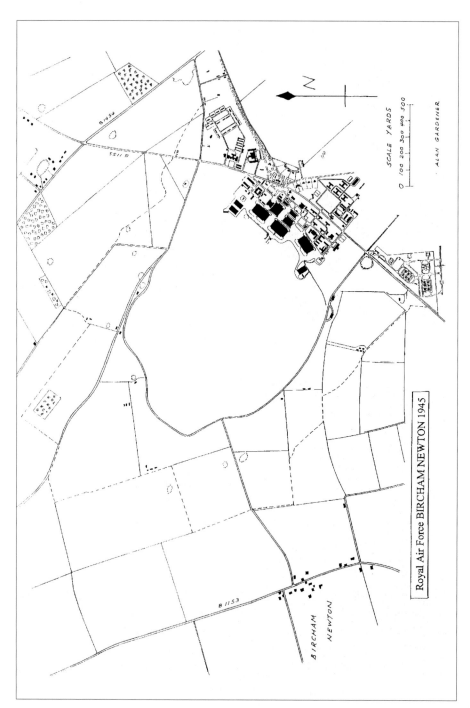

Royal Air Force BIRCHAM NEWTON 1945

SCALE YARDS

0 100 200 300 400 500

· ALAN GARDENER

B 1153

BIRCHAM
NEWTON

Construction Industry Training Board c.1991. Note the bases of the former General Service Sheds of World War I vintage. (CITB)

Former Guard House (Barclays Bank - later CITB Shop) 1991. (Bldg No. 101 - 166/23). (author)

Two of the former Barrack Blocks Type 'C', Dec. 2001 (Bldgs 45-48 - 1100/28). (author)

Watch Office with Tower, 'Fort' type, Dec. 2001 (Bldg No. 84 - 1959/34). (author)

Aircraft Shed Type 'C' (Hipped), 1991 (Bldgs Nos 14, 82, 116 - 2029/34 & 6438/37). (author)

Bircham Newton's water towers (photo 1991). On left standard Braithwaite tower from World War 2. Old circular one to right. At airfields laid down in mid-1930s water tanks were enclosed in tall brick encasements. Designs for these were submitted to the Royal Fine Arts Commission, and also opinions of the Society for the Preservation of Rural England were sought. (author)

CHAPTER 5

THE PHONEY WAR
September 1939 to March 1940

'In 1939 the war, to us, was inevitable and we had no doubts at all about our own unpreparedness.'
(Vernon Buckman, No. 206 Squadron at Bircham Newton, September 1939)

At the outbreak of war Bircham Newton and its squadrons represented only one small cog in a very large machine, so it would be appropriate to examine its part in the wider strategy of Royal Air Force Coastal Command at this time.

Air Marshal Sir Frederick W. Bowhill KCB, CMG, DSO was the AOC-in-C Coastal Command (HQ Northwood, Middlesex) from 16 August 1937 until 14 June 1941 and he had four groups under his command of which Bircham Newton's was No. 16 (General Reconnaissance), in turn commanded by Air Commodore R. L. G. Marix DSO, with HQ at Chatham. Other aerodromes besides Bircham Newton in the No. 16 Group area were Thorney Island on the south coast and Detling in Kent. With only five squadrons on the Group's strength at this time, two of which (Nos 42 and 206) were at Bircham Newton, it is not difficult to see how overstretched Coastal Command's resources were in this vital area of the North Sea and English Channel. Looking at the overall picture of the Command in 1939 there were 19 operational squadrons with 298 aircraft of which 171 were available for operations.[1] Putting that alongside the fact of the obsolescence of the Ansons and Vildebeests that were the backbone of the available units it is clear that the odds were going to be heavily stacked against Coastal Command. The fact that the Royal Air Force possessed 2,451 first-line aircraft illustrates how impoverished Coastal Command was in terms of air strength as a whole, particularly compared to Bomber Command which was allocated the major share of available multi-engined aircraft. It was freely admitted that Coastal Command was unlikely to perform a more ambitious role than that of reconnaissance, the offensive operations in the main being conducted by the bombers. The formidable task awaiting the Royal Air Force and Coastal Command in particular is amply demonstrated by the strength of the Luftwaffe at the outbreak of war, with some 4,204 aircraft ready to be deployed.

The first day of the war saw the aircraft of the two resident squadrons, Ansons of No. 206 Squadron and Vildebeests of No. 42 Squadron, dispersed around the edge of the airfield. For No. 206 Squadron, the squadron number on the side of the aircraft had been replaced by the code letters 'WD' from September 1938 (the time of the Munich Agreement) until the outbreak of war. Then the code letters became 'VX'. Other units present were 'C' and 'D' Flights of No. 1 Anti-Aircraft Co-operation Unit (1 AACU)

---

[1] Ashworth, Chris: *RAF Coastal Command 1936-1969*, Patrick Stephens Ltd 1992 (an imprint of Haynes Publishing, Sparkford, Yeovil, Somerset).

which were shortly to leave for Weston Zoyland in Somerset and Cleave in Cornwall respectively, with their assortment of aircraft which included the Westland Wallace, Fairey Gordon, Hawker Henley, Miles Magister, de Havilland Tiger Moth and Westland Lysander.

By this time the airfield had taken on the appearance in buildings and layout it retains up to the present day, including the three large 'C' Type hangars, the new Station Headquarters, a new Institute, Sergeants' Mess and Quarters, NAAFI and Sick Quarters. The Operations Room at this time was a wooden hut protected by sandbags manned in six hour periods by three watches, each including a Controller, Navigation Officer, Cypher Officer and Plotting Officer.

By the end of the first day of the war No. 206 Squadron had carried out its first operation, with three Ansons on an anti-submarine sweep. With detection relying on purely visual sighting it was not surprising that no enemy U-Boats were sighted and the aircraft returned safely. The following day navigators from the squadron guided aircraft of Bomber Command on the first RAF bombing raids of the war against naval targets in Kiel and Brunsbüttel. One of those seconded was Sergeant (later Squadron Leader) Ernest Fitchew who was attached to No. 83 Squadron Bomber Command, and took part in that first raid of the war. He recalls that the Kiel raid was aborted due to bad weather, making it impossible to identify the target and avoid civilian areas. He was absent from No. 206 for several days, at Scampton, Feltwell, Honington and Marham on standby navigational duties for further raids against the German fleet.[2]

On the 5th, the third day of the war, Pilot Officer R. T. Kean and his crew in Anson K6187 'E' of No. 206 Squadron sighted and attacked an enemy U-Boat 85 miles north-east of Lowestoft, the first attack of the war by an RAF aircraft on a U-Boat. Two 100 lb bombs were dropped just as the submarine had submerged but it was impossible to estimate any damage. During the attack Kean flew so low that a column of water from the explosion of one of the bombs split the aircraft's tail. This experience seemed to confirm the misgivings about the inadequacy of the bomb load capable of being carried by the Anson, especially as U-Boats on the surface could survive even a direct hit of a 100 lb bomb.

On the same day No. 206 suffered its first loss, Anson K6183 'B' with Pilot Officer L. H. Edwards, a New Zealander, and navigator Sergeant Heslop, LAC Quilter and AC1 Sheffield. The aircraft was reported missing after being shot down by a Heinkel He115 floatplane. A sea search was carried out by four Ansons the same day but no trace was found of the missing aircraft. However, a few days later it was learned from a German broadcast that Pilot Officer Edwards had been picked up by a German flying boat and was now in hospital at Bremen, the first officer of any of the services to become a prisoner-of-war in Germany.

The transition from peace to war was a gradual one at Bircham Newton, at least as far as No. 206 Squadron was concerned, with a continuation of the same squadron routines of convoy patrols and anti-submarine sweeps. The station had the responsibility

2 Fitchew, S/Ldr Ernest: letter to author 12/2000.

to provide air cover for convoys between Flamborough Head and Orfordness, handing over to aircraft based at Thornaby (north) and Detling (south). Life was given perhaps an added edge with extra security in evidence, the blackout (which made for more tricky driving at night) and petrol rationing. During the phoney war period food rationing was not severe as yet and excellent food continued to be served in the Mess. With the local pubs thriving at nights the threat of bombing from the air had not yet materialised.[3] It was almost as if there was a gentleman's agreement between the opposing sides not to make life too inconvenient at this stage. The most aggressive form of action on the part of RAF Bomber Command seemed to be the dropping of propaganda leaflets over enemy territory, interspersed with attacks on German naval bases like Wilhelmshaven and Brunsbüttel. Probably the most visible change on the station was the appearance of many more personnel, mostly reservists called up for the emergency. On 30 October a unit of the recently formed Women's Auxiliary Air Force (WAAF) arrived for duties as cooks, accountants and clerks. The officer and nine other ranks were accommodated in the old sick quarters. Of 60-70 officers in the mess around one third were from Australia, Canada, South Africa and Rhodesia, with a sprinkling from the United States.[4]

Regulars in the RAF like Sergeant Vernon Buckman found that many of the reservists, while being keen, lacked formal training. Others were Class C reservists who had left after the Great War and the electricians in this group found the complexities of the Anson difficult to understand.[5] AC2 Mike Applegarth of No. 42 Squadron had a similar experience, as many of the officers and NCOs he encountered on his arrival at Bircham Newton in October 1939 were sporting Royal Flying Corps pilot's wings and medal ribbons! Even the terminology of the 'Dawn Patrol' brought back echoes of a previous war.[6] Admittedly, the Vildebeest biplanes of No. 42 Squadron were, even by the standards of the day, already obsolete with a design dating back to 1928.

Fully trained airmen like Vernon Buckman were kept busy training the new intake who were then posted and replaced by fresh 'greenhorns' and the process began all over again. At other times there was continual repainting and camouflaging of the aircraft and almost anything else that moved! In Vernon's opinion all this achieved was to add considerable weight to an already low-powered machine.[7]

On 8 September, two Hudson aircraft of No. 224 Squadron flew to Bircham Newton from Leuchars in a search for a German convoy from Rotterdam. That unit had been the first to replace its Ansons with Hudsons at Leuchars, closely followed by No. 233 Squadron and the former Bircham Newton-based squadron No. 220 now based at Thornaby. It was, however, to be March 1940 before No. 206 Squadron converted to this type.

[3] Spooner, Tony, DSO, DFC: *Coastal Ace* (William Kimber 1986).
[4] Brown, Ron: *All Round the Compass* (Janus 1993).
[5] Buckman, Vernon: *Memories of Life with 206 (GR) Squadron.*
[6] Applegarth, M.J.: letter to author 18/7/91.
[7] Buckman, Vernon.

Anti-submarine patrols continued and on 9 September Pilot Officer R. T. Kean and his crew were forced to ditch their aircraft K6187 by the Dyck light vessel four miles off the coast from Calais. They had jettisoned their bombs after getting lost in the blackout on return to the airfield. The French crew of the Dyck looked after the RAF fliers in regal style before they were transported to Folkestone. Later a letter of thanks was sent to the French skipper of the Dyck, in French of course!

Routine patrols included searching for suspected mines off Aldeburgh on the 11th, convoy escort duties and anti-submarine patrols. On one of the latter occasions, 16 September, a No. 206 Squadron Anson sighted a submarine and dropped bombs, only to realise from the recognition signals five minutes later that the submarine was British! On 17 September the SS *City of Paris* foundered off Aldeburgh after what the Admiralty believed to be German use of magnetic mines, a fresh threat to our shipping. These deadly weapons could be set to explode under the third or fourth ship in the convoy. They were usually laid by Dornier Do18 flying boats and the shallow waters off the east coast were ideal for the purpose. Ansons from Bircham Newton were sent on sea searches of the area for such mines but without avail. Other sea searches were organised during the month for the crews of downed aircraft, such as that for a Handley Page Hampden on the 29th, again without result.

Contingency planning was essential for aircraft crippled due to enemy action or for deteriorating weather in the area. Therefore, the aerodrome at Sutton Bridge in Lincolnshire was being considered for use as a possible emergency landing ground. On a lighter note, a new sports field came into use at the station and it was reported that the cinema was a popular venue as the number of performances were increasing.

During October No. 206 Squadron was well established in its routine work, flying 123 operational sorties during the month. Convoy air escort duty was sometimes carried out along with the Vildebeests of No. 42 Squadron. A new duty was fishery protection patrolling towards the end of the month with two aircraft at a time on flights of up to three hours' duration. On the 28th the Ansons of No. 206 Squadron were joined in this task by three Hudsons of No. 224 Squadron from Leuchars and six Blenheim fighters from No. 23 Squadron based at Wittering. There were brief detachments to Carew Cheriton in Pembrokeshire and Hooton Park in Cheshire by 206's Ansons, for the purpose of convoy patrol work and to guard the approaches to major ports.

The other squadron at Bircham Newton, No. 42, under the command of Squadron Leader H. Waring, was playing a full part in the operational life of the station. Its motto 'Fortiter in re' ('Bravely in action') seemed appropriate for its maritime work, given the antiquated Vildebeest biplanes in which its aircrew had to operate. To the other resident squadron, No. 206, this unit appeared like a poor relation in spite of the fact that most of its sixteen aircraft on strength were the later Vildebeest Mark IV types, a distinct improvement on the Mark III version of which there were only three on the squadron. The Mark IV was fitted with a Perseus sleeve-valve engine (in 1937 the first such type in the RAF) with a fixed pitch metal three-bladed Rotol airscrew.[8]

---

[8] Applegarth, M.J.

AC2 Mike Applegarth joined No. 42 Squadron at Bircham Newton in October 1939 as a flight mechanic (engine) having just completed training in his trade at St Athan. On the first morning he made his way towards the No. 42 Squadron hangar. One solitary Vildebeest stood on the grass outside the building but he was surprised that there was no one else around. Nearby there was a small tree with a painted sign on which was written '42nd Street', a squadron tradition, apparently. On entering the hangar by a small door he soon met up with other NCOs and flight mechanics, some of whom were of mature age and wearing Royal Flying Corps pilot's wings and medal ribbons. Mike Applegarth was eventually assigned to Flying Officer Barrie-Smith's aircraft K8087 'N', replacing a previous fitter AC Westgarth, who had apparently fallen from an aircraft to his death in the Sandringham area while under training as an air gunner.[9]

Squadron routine consisted of convoy escort duties, with 'A' and 'B' Flights rotating, each aircraft armed with eight 100 lb bombs in patrols of around four hours' duration. The first aircraft would take off at first light, the last returning at around 8 p.m., with eight patrols taking to the air daily.

WAR PICTORIAL

In lieu of actual photographs, which are, of course, impossible to obtain, this brilliant artist's impression clearly shows how the Nazi mines are laid by parachuting them from seaplanes

Heinkel He115 floatplane dropping a magnetic mine in the Harwich area, Nov. 1939 (artist's impression). There were frequent duels with Anson from Bircham Newton along the east coast.

---

[9] Ibid.

Wreckage of the He115 which crashed at Sheringham, 6 December 1939. Lt Emil Rödel's body was the only member of the crew found.

Funeral of Lt Rödel at St. Mary's Churchyard,   *The same scene today. (author)*
Great Bircham. (Don Nelson)

There were frequent duels with Heinkel He115 floatplanes and Dornier Do18 flying boats as they shadowed our convoys, usually without loss on either side, although on 8 November Flying Officer Featherstone's Anson was attacked by an He115 which was then downed by his gunner. There was no connection between this and a report by Cromer police on 6 December of the wreck of an He115 washed up on the beach at Sheringham. The aircraft belonged to a Sylt-based mine-laying unit which had encountered bad weather and icing, crossed the coast in error and crashed into the sea. A crash party from Bircham Newton was sent out and the body of a German airman recovered, identified as Leutnant Emil Rödel. The rest of the crew were never found. Subsequently a funeral was held at Great Bircham churchyard accompanied by full military honours, with the German national flag covering the coffin and six Sergeants from Bircham Newton acting as pallbearers.

By the middle of November the weather was beginning to close in, with fog being the main enemy. Operational routine continued into the New Year, 1940, with Ansons on anti-submarine searches and fishery protection or 'Kipper' patrols. Sometimes the aircraft were able to direct the fishermen to the most promising shoals by waggling wings and flying off in a certain direction. The success produced by this team effort resulted in the August to December fishing season being the best ever enjoyed, thanks to the RAF assistance. A bonus for Bircham Newton's help was that Ron Brown, Intelligence Officer, was invited to collect enough kippers for everyone on the station (nearly 2,000). He duly drove down to the coast in his 1934 Hillman Minx and had to exercise considerable endurance in the drive back to base due to the strong smell of his cargo! Subsequently, all aircrew who had assisted the fishermen on patrol were invited to a grand end of season party at a large Great Yarmouth hotel.[10]

In addition to these duties, a watch had to be maintained for enemy minesweepers, minelayers and other patrol vessels. There was also a requirement to monitor the movements of German warships in the North Sea, should there be any attempt to sail around the north of Scotland into the Atlantic Ocean. One such episode was on 14 December when six Ansons took off on a parallel search for five German cruisers. A flotilla of British destroyers was located but there was no sign of the cruisers. Vildebeests of No. 42 Squadron maintained escort duty for northbound and southbound convoys. One loss during December was Anson K6189 of No. 206 Squadron which failed to return from a patrol on 6 December.

Anson on convoy patrol late 1939/early 1940. (Imperial War Museum photograph: Ref HU63066)

---

[10] Brown, Ron.

The following day Pilot Officer R. H. Harper in Anson K6184 coded VX-P dive-bombed what he had identified as a U-Boat on the surface. He claimed a hit at the base of the conning tower but the sub dived and disappeared. It turned out that HMS *Snapper* had been the unlucky target but fortunately the only damage done had been to four light bulbs inside the vessel. There was a marked increase in the signal communications between the Admiralty and Coastal Command as a result, but the incident illustrates the fact that only one per cent of attacks on submarines by aircraft during this period of the war caused any damage, thanks to the relative ineffectiveness of the standard weapon, the 100 lb anti-submarine bomb. It was to be 1942 before No. 206 Squadron destroyed its first U-Boat. More success was achieved against enemy aircraft, such as the destruction of an He115 by Pilot Officer S. R. Henderson in early January 1940, in the same sortie damaging a second aircraft and attempting to attack a third, daring exploits for which he was awarded a Distinguished Flying Cross (DFC). At around the same time Pilot Officer Harper's crew in K6190 sighted a Dornier Do18 on the water and bombed it. This action also earned Pilot Officer Harper the award of a DFC.

A change of command had occurred on 13 December 1939 when the station commander Group Captain C. L. Scott DSC was replaced by Group Captain W. H. Primrose DFC. The new CO's nickname was 'The Flower of the Desert' after his service in Mesopotamia (now Iraq) where he had become an expert in maintaining order by means of a few armoured cars and a handful of de Havilland biplanes.[11] He was to remain at Bircham Newton until March 1941.

Photo of Armstrong Whitworth Whitley V (N1377) DY-P of No. 102 Sqn showing damage due to a lightning strike in operations over Germany, 28 Nov. 1939. (Imperial War Museum photograph: Ref. C48)

[11] Brown, Ron.

Close-up of the damage to the aircraft. (RAF Museum photograph: Ref. PO16019)

The easterly, coastal location of the airfield made it suitable as an emergency landing ground for aircraft damaged, short of fuel, or simply lost on return from operations over Germany. This happened with growing frequency, as on 28 November when a badly damaged Whitley bomber DY-P of No. 102 Squadron based at Driffield in Yorkshire forced-landed in the early hours with extensive mainplane damage due to severe weather conditions over the Cuxhaven/Heligoland area. The pilot, Flying Officer Ken N. Gray, and fellow New Zealander Pilot Officer F. H. 'Tiny' Long and the crew were unhurt, having struggled back the 340 miles from the target area. For this daring airmanship Ken Gray and 'Tiny' Long were awarded the Distinguished Flying Cross and the rest of the crew Distinguished Flying Medals. The epic story was broadcast over the BBC in early December, in Ken Gray's own words. Tragically, Ken Gray was killed the following April in a Whitley crash near Dyce, Aberdeenshire.[12] 'Tiny' Long, back at his home station of Driffield was 'tutor' captain to novice Pilot Officer Leonard Cheshire (later Group Captain, VC, DSO, DFC) on the latter's first posting to an operational bomber squadron in the summer of 1940. Sadly Long was killed in March 1941 when his aircraft was hit by flak over Holland en route to bomb Berlin.[13] In the course of the war many Allied bombers were to find a welcome landfall either at Bircham Newton or at the Docking satellite. It was found that in the severe winter weather from late December 1939 a snow-covered grass field was better for emergency landings than a conventional runway.

---

[12] Gray, G/Capt. Colin, DSO, DFC: *Spitfire Patrol* (Hutchinson 1990) pp17-21.
[13] Info from *Cheshire*, the biography of Leonard Cheshire VC, OM, by Richard Morris (Penguin Books 2001) pp38-9 & 72.

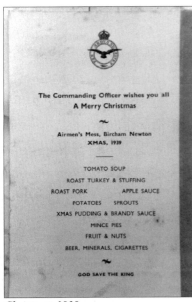

The Commanding Officer wishes you all
A Merry Christmas

Airmen's Mess, Bircham Newton
XMAS, 1939

TOMATO SOUP

ROAST TURKEY & STUFFING

ROAST PORK   APPLE SAUCE

POTATOES   SPROUTS

XMAS PUDDING & BRANDY SAUCE

MINCE PIES

FRUIT & NUTS

BEER, MINERALS, CIGARETTES

GOD SAVE THE KING

Christmas 1939.

During the last week of December snow, fog and freezing conditions were paralyzing operational flying, conditions which persisted into February 1940. In the worst of the weather even some of the approach roads were blocked. Mike Applegarth of No. 42 Squadron recalled the hardships faced by ground crews in starting and running up the iced-up Vildebeests for the first patrol of the day as winter dawn was breaking. To make matters worse, it appeared that parades and messing procedures were still geared to peacetime routines, as the cookhouse refused to serve a late supper for the fitter and rigger on stand-by duty to cover the final 1630 to 2000 hrs patrol of the day, unless a signed chit was presented. The last aircraft to land had to be refuelled with 157 gallons of petrol and made ready for the first patrol next morning, an elaborate and hazardous job given the lofty dimensions of the Vildebeest and its wingspan of 49 feet, as well as the normally soaking conditions of the mainplane which had to be covered overnight. Mike recalls 'seeing the huddled frozen figure of the pilot writing in a page torn from his logbook the words: "To NCO i/c Cookhouse: Please supply the

AC1 Mike Applegarth, aged 18, in cockpit of a Vildebeest MkIV of 'B' Flt No. 42 Sqn, Bircham Newton c. Feb. 1940. (M. Applegarth)

79

Vildebeests of No. 42 Sqn in formation, 1940. (Ray C. Sturtivant)

undermentioned airmen (named) with a late supper as they have been detained on operational duties. Signed.....'' ' All that happened then were critical remarks from the cook on duty![14]

Squadron and unit movements to Bircham Newton in December 1939 included Blenheim IF and IVF fighters of 'D' Flight, No. 233 Squadron, to become the basis of No. 254 (GR) Squadron which operated from the airfield until April 1940.

One aircraft from this unit forced-landed in bad weather at Brancaster on 6 January after an anti-submarine patrol to the Dutch coast, no casualties being reported and on 10 January No. 42 Squadron lost its first aircraft when a Vildebeest IV K6411 crashed on the airfield, fortunately again without casualties. Freezing fog and snow storms continued to hamper operations throughout January. On the 26th Anson VX-U of No. 206 Squadron crashed in a field at Morston after an unsuccessful search for a reported enemy U-Boat, having experienced snow storms on the return flight. Once again the the crew were lucky to emerge unhurt.

One of these episodes during that winter had a lighter side as recalled by Vernon Buckman of No. 206 Squadron. As crash NCO he and his party were called out one night to an Anson which had come to grief during a snow storm and crashed in a field near Cley-next-the-Sea. A guard was posted and Vernon returned in daylight to drain the tanks and prepare for the recovery team. He was amazed to find the aircraft just 20 yards from the church steeple, and found it impossible to believe that it could have got there avoiding the steeple. Also, there was no fuel in the tanks and no sign of leaks or tampering. They should have been full. The local landlord gave the recovery team all possible hospitality but nobody could shed any light on the mystery. It happened that a year later Vernon was invited by the same landlord to a duck shoot, and he casually

[14] Applegarth, M.J.

asked how fuel was obtained for the boats. The landlord gave a wink: 'from heaven in a snowstorm'![15]

In March 1940 the Ansons of No. 206 Squadron were continuing to operate alongside the Blenheims of No. 254 and the Vildebeests of No. 42. No. 254 Squadron spent part of the spring on detachment at Lossiemouth, extending its range to the Norwegian coast. At the same time, various events of interest interrupted station routine, as on 5 March when a full parade was held on the new parade ground with march past on the occasion of LAC L. J. Britton being decorated with the Distinguished Flying Medal[16]. On the 16th liaison visits were paid by lifeboatmen from Sheringham, with visits by officers from the station to Wells lifeboat station. Lord Trenchard, now Inspector-General of the RAF, along with the Air Officer Commanding No. 16 (GR) Group, Air Vice-Marshal J. H. S. Tyssen, arrived to inspect the station and stay overnight on the 27th. This was probably the occasion recalled by LAC S. J. 'Robby' Robilliard when Lord Trenchard came to the camp cinema in the old Pump House to address the personnel. The roof leaked so badly that half the seats were full of water![17] Lord Trenchard took his role as Inspector-General very seriously and, typical of a man with such a formidable reputation for attention to detail, took particular note of the correct storage of aircraft 'dope' which was used in repairs on canvas and wood. He also enjoyed an epidiascope show of photographs of World War One aircraft, an instrument which was useful in aircraft recognition training.[18]

Early in 1940 came the first signs of improved prospects for No. 206 Squadron with the beginning of the conversion to the American-built Lockheed Hudson. Vernon Buckman and a few other senior NCOs were sent on detachment to Speke, near Liverpool, to work alongside a team of Lockheed engineers in preparing the first Hudson Mark Is for RAF service. The work was hard, involving the towing of aircraft behind Fordson tractors through the city of Liverpool for their final assembly at Speke, followed by flight testing and collection for delivery to squadrons by Air Transport Auxiliary (ATA) pilots. The teams of RAF personnel and twenty Americans worked night and day with only short breaks in the Adelphi Hotel for food, drink and sleep. Four aircraft per day were assembled, tested, certified and collected.[19]

The first two Hudson Is arrived at Bircham Newton for No. 206 Squadron on 26 March from Silloth in Cumberland. Over the next few weeks the numbers gradually built up until the full complement of approximately 16 aircraft was reached. Ansons continued to operate until the beginning of June on anti-submarine patrols when they were finally removed from squadron charge, but there was no doubting the improvements brought about by the new aircraft, both in terms of technology and handling characteristics. The statistics were impressive, according to Vernon Buckman. While the Anson had barely

---

[15] Buckman, Vernon.
[16] LAC Britton was posted missing on 22 May.
[17] Robilliard, S. J. 'Robby': letter to author 27/8/91.
[18] Brown, Ron.
[19] Buckman, Vernon.

Hudsons of No. 206 Sqn in the Brancaster area 1940. (Chaz Bowyer via S.J. 'Robby' Robilliard)

a mile of electric cable, the Hudson had over ten miles, a potential nightmare for the reservist electricians who were being trained on the new systems. While the Anson had been a roomy aircraft for crews, the Hudson, with its civil airline background, was luxurious. From the safety angle, a rapid exit was possible with the passenger door capable of being jettisoned complete with built-in dinghy. One possible problem was that the Hudson was less suited than the Anson to grass fields like Bircham Newton, preferring the conventional runway. Also, the gun turrets did not arrive for three months, leaving only a front gun for defence and a single Vickers K hand held gun where the turret should have been. The first ASV (Air-to-Surface Vessel) radar Mark I arrived with the Hudson, making it possible for the first time to detect and locate submarines on the surface at night or in poor visibility. Aerials were fixed on either side of the fuselage but the system was not very reliable at first and it was some time before the initial problems were rectified. Another new device was IFF (Identification Friend or Foe), which detected friendly radar and returned an enhanced echo thus indicating to the ground radar that the aircraft was friendly. To prevent the instrument falling into enemy hands it was fitted with a destructive charge operated by an inertia switch. The problem was that in testing the apparatus the charge could easily be set off and crews were warned eventually that they might have to contribute to the cost of IFF in the case of accidental destruction. Vernon Buckman wondered how many sets were plugged in after that threat![20]

On the performance side, the Hudson could boast an increased range and well over five hours' endurance which brought the north German coast well within operating distance. This meant that more hazardous operational tasks were selected and enemy fighters would become more of a threat. In general terms, the change from the Anson was like 'switching from an Austin 7 to a Ferrari'.[21]

The new aircraft had arrived just in time because as March gave way to better weather in April, German forces in the west were poised to strike a blow, first in Scandinavia and then in France. The Phoney War was over for Bircham Newton. The offensive war was about to begin.

---

[20] Ibid.
[21] Spooner, Tony, op. cit.

CHAPTER 6

AIRFIELD DEFENCE AND THE HOME FRONT

'Disguise fair nature with hard-favour'd rage....' (*Henry V*)

'......We shall fight on the beaches, we shall fight on the landing grounds........'
(W. S. Churchill, 4 June 1940)

The First World War had witnessed the birth of air power as a significant military weapon and events since then confirmed the threat it posed to civilian populations in towns and cities, as in the destruction of Guernica during the Spanish Civil War and the bombing of Shanghai at the start of the Japanese invasion of China in the late 1930s. Earlier in the decade there had been dire predictions of what might happen in a future war, for example in a novel entitled *The Gas War of 1940* by S. Southwold, published in 1931, which described in lurid detail the destruction of London by air attack. The lessons were not lost on politicians at home. In a House of Commons debate on disarmament in November 1932 Stanley Baldwin put into words the sentiments felt by many at the time:
'I think it is well also for the man in the street to realise that there is no power on earth that can prevent him from being bombed. Whatever people may tell him, the bomber will always get through. The only defence is offence......'[1]
In spite of his pessimistic outlook, events have confirmed that Baldwin was correct in predicting that defences against air attack could never be one hundred per cent effective. Thus, many imaginative minds went to work concocting schemes which would provide some additional security in the coming war and one of these was to utilise the methods of Mother Nature herself, decoy and deception. Given the heavy reliance in those days of visual interpretation of landmarks from the air, there was scope for using camouflage and concealment as well as decoy sites in the attempt to confuse enemy airmen. Important lessons in these techniques had been learned in the First World War and in more recent years the film industry had much experience in using mock-up constructions of buildings for indoor film-sets, where there would be some shelter from the ever-uncertain British weather. In 1939 a Colonel John Turner was given charge of this work, and with its headquarters at Sound City Film Studios at Shepperton, the organisation became known as 'Colonel Turner's Department'.[2]
German intelligence had been at work even before the war had broken out in mapping and photographing from the air large parts of the British Isles, as evidenced by the detailed photographic record captured after the war. Britain was particularly vulnerable to air attack, due to the concentrated nature of its population, especially in the industrial areas, so 'Starfish' sites were set up to attempt to draw enemy bombers away from cities

---

[1] Quoted in J. Terraine: *The Right of the Line* p13.
[2] Fairhead, Huby: *Colonel Turner's Department* pii.

and towns, utilising dummy buildings, fires, lights, and anything that would suggest a built-up area, albeit in the middle of agricultural land! Another prime target for the enemy were the airfields, especially in East Anglia with its extensive network of aerodromes and its proximity to the enemy coastline in the Low Countries and Scandinavia. This was indeed a Home Front and urgent measures were taken to ensure maximum protection with airfield defences and decoys wherever possible.

The first decoys were 'K' sites with a full range of dummy aircraft and buildings and mock bomb-dumps, old vehicles, tents, and anything else that would assist in

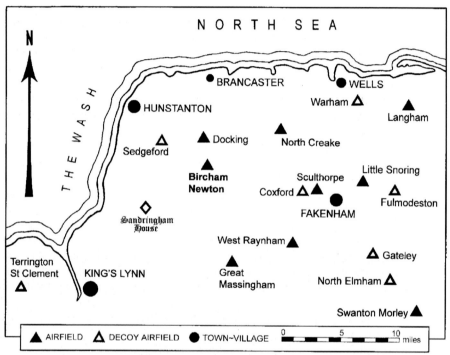

Airfields and decoy sites in North-West Norfolk 1939-45. (Drawn by Anthony Maynard. Reproduced by kind permission of Ordnance Survey. © Crown Copyright NC/02/3268)

MAP LOCATION REFERENCES

1. Decoys		*2. Airfields*	
		BIRCHAM NEWTON	***TF790341***
Coxford	*TF825310*	*Docking (Sunderland Farm)*	*TF787393*
Fulmodeston	*TG009305*	*Great Massingham*	*TF805235*
Gateley	*TF956243*	*Langham*	*TF989420*
North Elmham	*TF985205*	*Little Snoring*	*TF961334*
Sedgeford	*TF730365*	*North Creake*	*TF898385*
Terrington St Clement	*TF5623*	*Sculthorpe*	*TF860315*
Warham	*TF9443*	*Swanton Morley*	*TG009185*
		West Raynham	*TF850245*

confusing the enemy by day. At night, 'Q' sites were established sometimes on the same site as the daytime decoy with lighting in place to simulate landing lights. One can only admire the courage of the men who manned these sites, and also the landowners and farmers who made the sites available from private land knowing they were meant to be in the front line of any attack.

Eventually there were at least 630 decoy sites throughout the United Kingdom, of which about 230 were decoy airfields. Norfolk alone had around 33 decoy airfields and judging from the number of attacks recorded on these they could certainly be judged to have been a success.[3]

On operational aerodromes every means was used to camouflage the real purpose of the site, including suitable colour schemes on buildings, some of which can still be seen, and Bircham Newton was one among many which had camouflaged hangars and dummy hedges installed around the perimeter. A site for a dummy aerodrome was chosen at Coxford Heath on 19 September 1939 at a position three and a half miles south-east of Bircham Newton. At this stage of the war and in the Phoney War period which followed, enemy air activity at home was more imagined than real but the lull did not last long as 1940 progressed.

On the outbreak of war defence against low flying attacks was provided by machine gun posts comprising eight Lewis guns manned by one officer and 38 men of 'C' Company, 7th Battalion, Royal Norfolk Regiment. This unit was replaced on 27 September by an officer and 36 men of the 5th Battalion. Meanwhile, a strict blackout was in force. Mike Applegarth of No. 42 Squadron recalls that a Vildebeest was detailed from time to time to fly over King's Lynn, inspecting the blackout.[4] On 1 January 1940

Oblique, looking east, 31 March 1940. Dummy hedges have been painted on the airfield and the hangars have been camouflaged. (P.H.T. Green Collection)

[3] Ibid. ppii-iii.
[4] Applegarth, Mike: letter to author 18/7/91.

four Ansons from No. 206 Squadron reported an ineffective blackout over the town, no doubt spoiling the aftermath of somebody's New Year celebrations!

Ground defences were strengthened on 31 October by the arrival of two officers and 34 other ranks of the 114th/26th Regiment Light Artillery, who were now to man four re-sighted gun positions each consisting of two Lewis guns. The Royal Norfolk Regiment contingent was now increased to a total of 58 men, mostly for sentry duty and anti-sabotage security. For added protection against enemy aircraft, fighter squadron detachments of Blenheims from No. 600 Squadron based at Hornchurch and Defiants of No. 213 Squadron from Wittering arrived at the airfield during December 1939, the latter unit returning again in the spring of 1940.

On 20 January 1940 local police telephoned the station to report that a man dressed as an RAF officer was seen in the Honington area, presumably acting suspiciously, before heading off in the direction of Bury St Edmunds. There is no indication whether this was a scare story based on rumour or something more substantial - most probably the former, on this occasion.

With the approach of spring, the Germans resumed their offensive in the west in a surprise attack on Norway on 9 April in spite of the neutrality of that country. Clearly, it was only going to be a matter of time before Britain was once again to be in the forefront of the battle. Every airfield was on full alert and nobody quite knew where the next blow was going to come from. This state of affairs is amply illustrated by the experiences of 19 year-old AC2 W. H. H. Lewis who was posted to Bircham Newton after 'square-bashing' at Morecambe on 5 April 1940. Bill Lewis was awaiting training on a wireless operator's course and in the meantime was detailed for general duties at Bircham Newton.

On Bill Lewis's first morning, Saturday 6 April, the Station Warrant Officer addressed the parade in no uncertain terms that they were the nearest station to the continent, where collapse seemed imminent, and therefore all personnel would be on duty 24 hours per day. However, Bill managed to get some time to do some local walking, to the 'Norfolk Hero' Inn at Stanhoe and the 'Plough Inn' at Docking. Fortunately, he obtained the post of orderly in the Operations Room, the 'most secret room in the whole aerodrome' as he was warned - although his duties mainly consisted of making the tea and cleaning up. He witnessed the harassed aircrew coming in after operations, and, working two nights out of three on night-shifts from 8 p.m. to 8 a.m., he still found time for local walking to Burnham Market, Syderstone or Docking, or going to Hunstanton and King's Lynn by station transport. 'I found it impossible to interest my tired colleagues in my activities which therefore I pursued alone. The sleepy countryside appealed to me a lot, even although all the signposts had gone.' Bill was unable to see much of the 'big picture' as he worked in a lowly capacity but he recalled looking at a huge map of Coastal Command in the Ops Room one day, only to be castigated by Flight Lieutenant Cunningham, the duty Intelligence Officer, with the words: 'It is not your job, orderly, to look at that confidential map.' All that Bill remembered about the map was that 'balloon' was spelt only with one 'l'!

Bill Lewis was in the Ops Room when the King visited on 26 May along with the AOC No. 16 (GR) Group, AVM J. H. S. Tyssen, and the station commander. On Tuesday 26 May, King Leopold of the Belgians capitulated and Bill and others were ordered to spend the night at Station HQ to keep watch for enemy parachutists which he did from the roof of the building from 0330 to 0430 hrs, armed with a rifle. That was the end of 'off-duty' for a spell. He continues: 'You can imagine our apprehension. We were now (France having not yet fallen) the nearest operational RAF station to occupied Europe. We had a real fear that Jerry might drop out of the sky....We were succeeded by fully trained RAF Ground Gunners, later to become the nucleus of the RAF Regiment......There were at the time many rumours of unidentified (possibly German) characters, cycling around the neighbouring villages.'[5] There were many reasons for the high level of security in an area so close to an extensive coastline facing enemy occupied territory, not least amongst which was the presence of King Haakon VII and the exiled Norwegian Royal Family at nearby Appleton House, on the Sandringham Estate.

The fall of France and evacuation of the British Expeditionary Force (BEF) from Dunkirk heralded the opening of the German offensive against the home front in Britain. With the advantage of the newly captured airfields in Norway and the Low Countries it was not surprising that the Luftwaffe would carry the offensive to British home shores. And so it proved. Aerodromes were among the top priority targets and Bircham Newton was one of those singled out. The first recorded bombing raid on the station took place on the night of 5/6 June 1940, when one or two enemy aircraft flying at 15-20,000 feet dropped some 200 incendiary devices, but no damage occurred. AC2 Bill Lewis recalled some of these incidents and the dozen or so air raid warnings received by Bircham Newton every week during June. What particularly sticks in his memory, though, were not so much the raids which mostly resulted in little damage, but the heavy losses endured by the aircrew, which were brought home to him after a casual meeting with a young LAC Air Gunner he met in the NAAFI one evening: 'This was before all aircrew became sergeants. He seemed such a nice chap with many interests the same as mine, but I do not even remember his name. Less than 48 hours later I heard and recognised it; someone mentioned in my hearing that that ".....(the man's name) went for a Burton last night!" I was horrified. The life of an aircrew member seemed very cheap in those days and their heroic deaths were often hardly a matter of casual conversation.'[6]

It was the turn of the decoy airfield at Coxford Heath on the night of 7/8 June when bombs were dropped to the south-east of the site. At the same time, there were air raid warnings at Wolferton and Dersingham and on the 18th another attack in the vicinity of Coxford Heath. More attacks on Coxford Heath followed on the night of 21/22 and 25/26 June, testifying to the success of the dummy airfield strategy. The site was classified a 'K' site for day use, that is with dummy Hudson aircraft and hangars deployed south of Coxford Wood and dummy bomb dumps, vehicles and buildings to make

---

[5] Lewis, W.H.H.: letter to author 30/9/91.
[6] Ibid.

everything as realistic as possible. For night use, a 'Q' site was created, using lights to represent runways and a flashing beacon. Mock fires were sometimes lit to simulate the destruction of aircraft and when raiders were reported in the area, Hudson aircraft from Bircham Newton were sometimes tasked by coded radio signals to make approaches, followed by the lights being dimmed as the aircraft climbed away. There was much evidence that this technique was successful during the tense days of 1940, as even 'Lord Haw-Haw' broadcast on German Radio on one occasion that Bircham Newton had been bombed!

The Coxford site was manned by eleven men and an NCO, plus a dog as mascot, with a five-hundredweight canvas-back truck. The personnel were billeted in a requisitioned gamekeeper's cottage close to the site. Later in the war, the site became the 'Q' site for Sculthorpe and on one occasion an enemy aircraft was claimed to have been shot down by a Coxford gunner.[7] The site at Coxford was said to have collected some 60 enemy bombs during 1940 as against 28 on Bircham Newton itself![8]

The former Great War aerodrome at Sedgeford became another decoy site for Bircham Newton, using some of the existing buildings and hangars as a 'K' site. Some dummy aircraft were dispersed around the site and a flarepath was installed for night

Remains of underground bunker at former decoy airfield at Sedgeford. (author, with kind permission of William Barber)

---

[7] Fairhead, Huby: *Decoy Sites* pp22-3.
[8] Brown, Ron: *All Round the Compass.*

use as a 'Q' site. Power for the lights was provided by a generator housed in an underground bunker where the personnel were billeted.[9] It appears that this decoy site was only attacked on one occasion.

One notable event during these tense days was an invasion scare in the early hours of 29 June. 80 vessels escorted by E-Boats were reported north-east of Great Yarmouth, confirmed by 18th Division based at Norwich. Albacores and Blenheims at Bircham Newton were put on stand-by, but within a few hours the report was withdrawn as a false alarm.

During July there were continual air raid warnings, with enemy air activity very much in evidence throughout the area. On the 7th Coxford Heath was attacked again, this time by an aircraft identified as a Heinkel He111. Bombs were dropped in the wooded area on the edge of the site. On the 10th an unidentified aircraft made three circuits of the airfield at Bircham Newton, later thought to be a captured French aircraft on a photo-recce sortie.

It was during the month of July that a satellite airfield opened at Docking, at Sunderland Farm, just over three miles to the north of Bircham Newton and two and a half miles from Docking village. The site started life operationally as a decoy for Bircham Newton, a 'Q' and 'K' site, and around a dozen dummy Hudsons were set up around the perimeter. Eventually its usefulness as a dispersal field for the main airfield was proved by the fact that it was targeted by the Luftwaffe on several occasions. It also became an emergency landing ground for aircraft in trouble or unable to reach their home stations. Later, it became an airfield in its own right with its own decoy site at North Creake.

Yet another satellite and dispersal field was provided in 1940 at Langham, towards the north Norfolk coast, five and a half miles north-west of Holt, which acted in that capacity until it achieved independent status in 1942. Thus a vast effort was being made to render the task of the Luftwaffe as difficult as possible, just in time for Hitler's offensive to be aimed right at the heart of Britain, and Norfolk's airfields were very much in the front line of that battle.

August 1940 saw an intensification of enemy air activity. The 21st saw one of the worst raids to date, when, just after 8 a.m. and in under 15 minutes enemy aircraft bombed Bircham Newton, damaging aircraft and buildings, including the married quarters. A total of 22 casualties resulted, one of which was fatal.

Docking was hit by incendiary bombs on 12 September, although damage was slight, and on the 15th bombs were dropped west of Sedgeford. There were continual reports of enemy aircraft in the vicinity which kept all the air defences on full alert throughout the month and into the autumn. On 1 October incendiaries were dropped around Docking, the same day on which Albacores from Bircham Newton were bombing Rotterdam. On the 20th a land mine was dropped at Docking by parachute, landing near the flarepath but it was destroyed by a naval party before any damage was done. There were also reports during the month of enemy intruders in the Docking area, as on the

[9] Fairhead, Huby: *Decoy Sites* p32. See also photograph on previous page.

Control tower at Docking satellite airfield. Faded lettering 'ALL VISITING PILOTS REPORT HERE' barely discernible now. (author, with kind permission of R.W. Perowne)

24th, when a Beaufort from Silloth was attacked over the airfield by a possible Heinkel He111, resulting in the petrol tank being shot through by a cannon shell but without serious damage or casualties. Another attack took place in the same vicinity on the 25th by an aircraft thought to be a Messerschmitt Me110. There were many other reports of enemy intruders, often unidentified, which were bound to keep everyone on their toes during this tense period of the war.

Other aerodromes in Norfolk were receiving the attention of the enemy, especially West Raynham, Great Massingham and Marham. There was plenty of scope for a determined Luftwaffe offensive in the autumn of 1940. However, with a few exceptions it seems that these attacks resulted in little permanent damage or loss, and certainly had

Hawker Henley III L3353 of No. 1AACU on 6 January 1941, showing airfield bomb damage. (P.H.T. Green Collection)

an almost negligible effect on the operational efficiency of RAF stations in the area. The attacks were usually carried out by single or perhaps two aircraft at a time and had all the hallmarks of opportunism rather than a clear strategic objective. It was all part of the war of nerves designed to create maximum confusion and uncertainty.

Coxford's turn came again on 27 October when an enemy aircraft, thought to be an He111, machine-gunned dummy aircraft on the ground before heading in the direction of Docking. A gunner succeeded in firing thirty rounds with a Lewis gun but no hits were claimed. In November there were further attacks in the area including Docking and reportedly, a machine gun attack by an enemy aircraft at Burnham Market on the 16th.

As the weather deteriorated in December 1940 aerial activity on both sides was restricted, but this did not prevent an attack on Bircham Newton on 21 December when an aircraft, possibly a Heinkel He111, dropped seven incendiaries in line west to east 50 yards in front of the Watch Office. There was no reported damage on this occasion although the married quarters were narrowly missed.

The new year, 1941, saw the area in the grip of snow at the start of January, but on the 6th an enemy aircraft, possibly a Dornier, made a bomb and machine gun attack on Docking. The only reported damage was to a grid cable. The ground defences at Bircham Newton were in action during the month and in early February but with no confirmed 'kills' reported. On the 14th an aircraft, at first mistaken for a Blenheim, was caught in searchlights over the airfield but the mistake was realised when a stick of eight bombs fell on the northern perimeter area. A further attack was on the 27th when a Dornier Do17 flew across the airfield firing several machine gun rounds at buildings, resulting in windows being broken and a Blenheim on the ground damaged. On the same day incendiaries and high-explosive bombs were dropped near Coxford but the only casualties of the day were reported to be two seagulls.

'The Hero at Home' and 'The Hero at Camp' (both drawn by S.J. 'Robby' Robilliard, No. 206 Sqn Bircham Newton 1940/41)

During March it was very much the same pattern with attacks on Bircham Newton on the 8th, Docking on the 11th and a machine gun attack on the Langham flarepath on the 12th. There was also much intruder activity, as when a No. 221 Squadron Wellington was attacked and damaged by an Me110 when coming into land at Langham on the 15th. The month of April saw further intruder activity at Langham, the most serious incidents being on the 8th when a No. 206 Squadron Hudson was damaged during night flying practice by a Junkers Ju88, and then on the 10th with the destruction of a 221 Squadron Wellington also by a Ju88, as the aircraft was returning from a sortie. All the crew were killed. The increasing use of Langham as a satellite for Bircham Newton brought it to the notice of the Luftwaffe intruders. Captain Eric Starling, then of No. 221 Squadron, recalled several of the intruder incidents:

'We used to be bothered by a German intruder. He obviously had pre-war flying experience of the Eastern Counties because he only came over when the clouds were really low. One day he came over and dropped a stick of small bombs down the runway. He was so low when he dropped them that they hit the ground flat and didn't explode.

Junkers Ju88. A frequent unwelcome visitor to the east coast.

We watched at a safe distance while the armament officer defused them. When he had defused the last one, as a gesture he held it above his head and threw it to the ground....On another day we were having lunch in the Officers' Mess. Some big shots from Coastal Command were being entertained. The Group Captain was explaining that on very low cloud days as we were having that day, we were being bothered by intruders. Almost as he said it we heard Hell let loose as every gun in the field opened up. We all dropped to the ground until there was silence once more. A few minutes later the Intelligence Officer entered with a broad smile on his face and holding above his head a large piece of bomb-door. The joke - to us only - was that having had his bomb-doors knocked off by us, he went and dropped his bombs on a neighbouring airfield.....I was living out at Thornham and one day my wife was pushing our year-old son down the main street in his pram when the intruders came over spraying the street with machine gun fire, fortunately hitting no one. Those were the days!'[10]

Further raids took place in May 1941 when once again bombs were dropped near the Watch Office at Bircham Newton and attacks were reported at Coxford. The worst incident occurred at Docking on the 16th when the farm house was hit and crew sleeping quarters demolished, resulting in the deaths of three airmen with 15 being wounded. The events were recalled by A. Cockle of No. 59 Squadron, who was a ground wireless operator:

'On this night I was duty wireless operator in the dispersal hut which was right over on the other side of the airfield opposite the control tower at Bircham Newton. We got a call to say that one of our aircraft which had landed at Docking had broken a tail wheel. Now it was the practice for our aircraft before they went on a strike or mission to take off and land at Docking. When the time came they would take off, complete the operation, and return to Docking, flying back to Bircham Newton the next morning. This was designed to avoid being followed in by enemy aircraft resulting in Bircham Newton being bombed. So when we had received the call, a couple of fitters, the duty electrician and myself got a van and went over to Docking. It was nearly dark when we got there and we found the aircraft, put our macs under the tail, lifted the aircraft and the new tail wheel was fitted - job done! While we were waiting for transport to pick us up and take us back to Bircham an aircraft came in to land, with full landing lights on. As he taxied he swung around and illuminated all the aircraft lined up on the field. Another aircraft was flying around at the time and somebody said: "He's got a ropey engine!". Well of course it was a Jerry and he came in to attack. We all scattered and I know I ran like blazes. He released his bombs which passed overhead, missed the hedge and line of trees behind us and hit the farmhouse where some of the personnel were living. It caused havoc with the farmhouse, the stables caught fire and several people were injured, one man very seriously. When we were searching through the rubble somebody said: "Get away from there, mate, you're standing on a sixty-foot well!". Whether that was true or not I don't know but I got away from there quickly!'[11]

---

[10] Starling, Capt. Eric: letter to author 5/12/92.
[11] Cockle, A.: audio tape sent to author 1993.

Every possible means had to employed to provide airfield defence, as AC2 Gordon C. Dick recalled:

'I was posted to Bircham Newton in late 1940 or early 1941 with a few others, as UT (Under-Training) aircrew. We were give a course on various weapons - notably the OERLIKON 20 mm cannon, several of which were placed in sandbagged emplacements around the airfield perimeter. They were manned by us UT aircrew who were given badges to sow on to our uniforms with the letters 'GG' (*presumably 'Ground Gunner'*) entwined and surrounded by laurel leaves! Needless to say on visits to King's Lynn we had our legs pulled unmercifully about 'Girl Guides' etc etc. I have never seen or heard of the badges since those days.....Our instructor at the time was a Flight Sergeant Hadlow - we all hated him - but he was a very brave man who would rush out of his office hut and man a Vickers gun mounted on a pole against any enemy aircraft - minus his tin-hat! It has occurred to me, since the RAF Regiment was formed in 1941, that we few rookies may well have been the founder-members of that illustrious body of men!'[12]

By the middle of the year there was a notable scaling-down of Luftwaffe operations over Britain. The indefinite postponement of the invasion of Britain reduced the immediate urgency, combined with the fact that our fighters and bombers were increasingly on the offensive and the Luftwaffe could not claim total aerial superiority. Also, Hitler was turning his eyes towards the invasion of Russia, so that by June 1941 many Luftwaffe units had been moved east. However, there was every reason to maintain a continual watch for attacks that might still come at any moment, especially by enemy intruders lurking in the skies around the airfields and hoping for the easy meat of tired aircrews returning from long and dangerous operations over occupied territory. A typical example was an attack on a No. 500 Squadron Blenheim on 7 July 1941 as it came into land at Docking. All the crew were killed.

In August and September, Docking was bombed on two occasions but this time with little damage done. In October, attacks were reported at Sedgeford and Langham. Towards the end of 1941 the weather once again became the ally of home defence, combined with the decreasing capability of the Luftwaffe to continue a sustained offensive against the airfields.

But if the Luftwaffe was 'down' it was certainly not 'out', for in April 1942 Hitler ordered the so-called 'Baedeker' raids[13] on cities of architectural importance in direct retaliation for the destruction of Lübeck by Bomber Command, and on two successive nights on 27/28th and 29/30th Norwich was the target, causing considerable death and injury. King's Lynn suffered its worst raid to date on Friday 12 June when a lone Dornier Do17 dropped a stick of bombs hitting the Eagle Hotel in Norfolk Street with the loss of 42 lives, including not only civilians but many RAF servicemen enjoying a welcome night out.[14]

---

[12] Dick, Gordon C.: letter to author 22/7/91.
[13] Named after the Baedeker guide to the British Isles, a pre-war guide book.
[14] Wilson, Ray: *Red Alert - Lynn* (Panda Books 1985).

Dorniers attacked Docking on 27 July 1942, destroying a Wellington and damaging buildings and three cottages. There was no report about casualties among personnel on this occasion. It was during that summer that a new apparent threat to airfields began to concentrate the minds of the powers that be, as Flight Lieutenant Don Rogers, then Station Navigation Officer, relates:

'Group Captain Mason, the station commander, called me in one day and told me that I was being appointed Station Defence Officer as the Army, who had always controlled the defence of RAF stations, were moving out as they had other priorities. Apparently a new RAF Regiment was going to be formed but for the time being station defence was going to be left in the hands of station personnel. An Army major from the Suffolk Regiment was going to liaise with me and we were going to take over all the pillboxes and other fortifications which the Army had built around the camp. I was chosen for this job because of my Certificate 'A' when in the Officers' Training Corps at school and it was felt that that was a sufficient qualification.

'I had all the Station HQ personnel on parade one day and what a motley crew they were too. Most of them had never fired a rifle in their lives. I formed them into squads and they were issued with rifles and ammunition and ordered to the rifle range for practice under some Army NCOs who were drafted in to give some basic training. I was very thrilled to find that I was given a Thompson machine gun which, with ammunition, I had to keep with me at all times and at night it was under my bed. I was also issued with a .38 revolver and ammunition.

'Although we started this station defence before the Dieppe Raid (19 August 1942), I think the Air Ministry had decided that all RAF stations near the east coast would be vulnerable to German Commando attacks and that is why they took these rather draconian emergency steps, so that we could defend ourselves if attacked. The aircrew and squadrons thought the whole thing was hilarious, seeing the station barber and the cooks and clerks being marched about carrying rifles and wearing tin hats. In the summer I spent a lot of time with the liaison officer going around the camp and discussing where we would site machine guns and deploy our forces if attacked. One night the Army carried out a mock attack on the station and all the SHQ personnel were in the trenches and dugouts trying to spot the attacking enemy. It was quite a good night's party!'[15]

As late as June 1943 there was an airfield defence exercise called 'Great Binge', which included an attack on the camp by an invading party. Gas attack alerts and rumours about Fifth Column activity were all designed to create an atmosphere of crisis. It is not recorded whether this was for the purpose of serious training or an excuse for youthful high jinks!

However, during 1942 and 1943 there was no question of relaxing the guard at any time, as Luftwaffe attacks always remained a high probability. As mentioned earlier, airfield camouflage could be very effective as Syd Roberts remembered of his time at Bircham Newton during 1942:

---

[15] Rogers, Don: *Wartime Recollections.*

'I had the good fortune to be given a "flip" over the camp, and because it was a grass "drome" and well camouflaged it disappeared at 2,000 feet!'[16]

Corporal R. G. Cardew of No. 279 Squadron also recalled the airfield appearance in 1942:

'Black paint or some substance was used to camouflage the airfield imitating hedges and ditches. There was no concrete runway so it was probably quite effective.'[17]

There could not be one hundred per cent security against the threat of attack by Luftwaffe aircraft acting independently or in small formations, as the tragedy at Docking in May 1941 amply demonstrated. Every effort had to be made to disperse air and ground crew around the area in local villages and country houses while at the same time guaranteeing the operational efficiency of the station. The pressure on accommodation in a busy station like Bircham Newton was another factor. Large country houses like Heacham Hall were ideal for the purpose (although the property was burned down accidentally in November 1941). It would be the first and possibly the last time that personnel of all ranks would experience a style of gracious living that had echoes of the nineteenth century. Fring Hall, about six miles from Bircham Newton, was brought into use during the summer of 1942, as Syd Roberts recalled:

'On another occasion a Polish squadron (*sic*) arrived on the camp, for whom no accommodation had been arranged. What a panic! All of our section had to move out of our billet and take up sleeping quarters in various places, and others in the guardroom, stores, library etc.! This was my first experience of the super-efficiency of the RAF administration and the happy result of this was the fact that we were in the party that had to take up residence in Fring Hall for sleeping only. This was a lovely country estate belonging to Lord Llewellyn. We were issued with new bicycles and were allowed half an hour's grace for breakfast. Three of us, on a rota basis, were supposed to stay at the Hall, one to clean the baths and hand basins, one to clean and tidy the dormitories and the other to prepare a midday meal.'[18]

Hugh Wilkins of No. 279 Squadron had a similar experience: 'In the summer of 1942, with the idea of dispersing personnel as a precaution, a lot of us were issued with bicycles and billeted at Fring Hall. This was a pleasant diversion but it involved rising early to ride and report for breakfast at Bircham!'[19]

However, the main focus was no longer on the Home Front but elsewhere as the war was being carried to the occupied territories and to enemy shipping, a task in which Bircham Newton squadrons played no small part as we shall see. Further afield, the Axis powers had been defeated at El Alamein in the Western Desert (October to November 1942) and on the Eastern Front the advance of the German armies had been slowed to a crawl, even stalemate, as the Soviets prepared for a long war of attrition.

---

[16] Roberts, Syd: letter to author (undated).
[17] Cardew, Geoffrey: letter to author 30/7/91.
[18] Roberts, Syd.
[19] Wilkins, Hugh: letter to author 10/9/91.

CHAPTER 7

TAKING THE WAR TO THE ENEMY
April to December 1940

'Of all the flying I had to do during the war, I disliked our twenty-nine Bircham Newton operations the most. Each trip across the North Sea was as frightening as the last.'
(Charles Lamb, *War in a Stringbag*)

The German assault against Denmark and Norway on 9 April 1940, both traditionally neutral countries, and the invasion of Belgium and Holland on 10 May, opened up a new deadly phase in the war where the struggle for sea and air superiority was going to be decisive. The strength of the Royal Air Force in general and Coastal Command in particular had not significantly increased in the months since the outbreak of war[1] but the Luftwaffe was able to deploy some 500 combat aircraft in the invasion of Norway, and 571 Junker Ju52s for the transport of troops and supplies.[2] In the invasion of France and the Low Countries the Luftwaffe figures were even more daunting, 3,530 aircraft of which well over 1,000 were fighters.[3]

The establishment at RAF Bircham Newton at the beginning of April 1940 consisted of the station commander Group Captain W. H. Primrose DFC, with resident squadrons No. 206 commanded by Wing Commander N. H. D'Aeth and equipped with its new Hudsons and a few remaining Ansons, Blenheims of No. 254 commanded by Squadron Leader G. K. Fairclough and the Vildebeests of No. 42 Squadron commanded by Squadron Leader H. Waring. During March and April another Coastal Command unit No. 48 Squadron, equipped with Ansons, was on detachment from Thorney Island.

On 7 April, No. 254 Squadron Blenheims were carrying out mine-laying and convoy escort duties. Ansons of No. 206 Squadron and Vildebeests of No. 42 escorted northbound and southbound convoys. One Blenheim of No. 254 Squadron was damaged by hostile fire from a trawler which it was attempting to identify at low level, but the aircraft returned to base safely. By the end of the day No. 42 Squadron ceased to be operational preparatory to leaving for Thorney Island on the 27th and re-equipment with the greatly improved Bristol Beaufort torpedo bombers. This squadron had been officially designated a torpedo bomber squadron but on only one occasion had a Vildebeest been armed with a torpedo at Bircham Newton. With the extra loading of 1800 lbs the Vildebeest Mark III had required a protracted take-off and the experiment was not judged a success and not repeated![4]

On 10 April No. 254 Squadron extended its range to the Norwegian coast and bombed the airfield at Stavanger, the prelude to many offensive operations to come.

---

[1] See figures on p70.
[2] Terraine, John: *The Right of the Line* p115.
[3] Ibid. p124.
[4] Applegarth, M.J.: letter to author 18/7/91.

A new unit to arrive on 8 April was the first of the Fleet Air Arm squadrons, No. 815 from Cardiff, with its Fairey Swordfish Mark I aircraft commanded by Lieutenant-Commander Simon Borrett and from the 17th Lieutenant-Commander Robin A. Kilroy DFC. The main task of the unit was to assist in laying magnetic mines before its planned embarkation in the new aircraft carrier HMS *Illustrious* in the summer. There was also an ambitious plan to mount an attack against German warships in the German port of Wilhelmshaven with torpedoes and magnetic mines for which considerable training had to be undertaken. Charles Lamb was a pilot on the squadron at the time and has outlined his experiences at Bircham Newton in his book *War in a Stringbag*.[5] A model of the port was kept under lock and key at Bircham Newton for crews to study and total secrecy was to be maintained. Married officers were permitted to rent houses in the vicinity of the station from a list provided by the station commander Group Captain Primrose, but single officers would live in the mess.

The Wilhelmshaven plan was a formidable one and overshadowed the time spent at Bircham Newton. The only crumbs of comfort were that the Germans would find anything as slow as the Swordfish difficult to hit and the attack would be at night!

Charles Lamb disliked the 29 operations he flew from Bircham Newton across the North Sea more than any other flying he did in the war. He got off to a bad start on his first trip to the Frisian Islands because his aircraft, flying in formation with the CO at 85 knots and at 100 feet above sea level, was picked on by a flakship. To make matters worse, he broke formation and attracted even more fire, ending up with several terrifying minutes and damage to his aircraft, which he nevertheless got back to the airfield. The lesson he learned from this episode was 'stick close to Father'.[6]

Charles and the senior observer Lieutenant-Commander Chapman with their wives shared the same comfortable mansion near Hunstanton called Woden House. At least this represented some normality at a time of great uncertainty and foreboding. As squadron stores officer, Charles drew at least a score of RAF flying jackets from the clothing stores called Irving Jackets which were lined with fur. Strictly speaking the Fleet Air Arm was not entitled to these and they were designated as 'temporary loans'. Unfortunately, these jackets were to be scattered far and wide, in prison camps, in other squadrons, even in the sea, but Charles was pursued by the naval authorities for their return for many months afterwards.

Among a few acquaintances at Bircham Newton was the station signals officer, Acting Squadron Leader Darby Welland, an Australian, whom Charles remembered from an RAF navigation course. There was much good natured banter between the RAF and naval men on the subject of the antique Swordfish which at that time was the mainstay of the Fleet Air Arm.

In the weeks that followed the squadron was at constant readiness for the projected attack on Wilhelmshaven. However, in that period most operations were for mine-laying, or 'planting cucumbers' to use the technical jargon, a task which required

[5] Lamb, Charles: *War in a Stringbag* (Cassell Military Paperback).
[6] Ibid.

very accurate navigation, the responsibility of Lieutenant-Commander Chapman. The route usually took them in the area of Texel and Borkum where there were the ever present flakships at the ready.

If a mine was detonated and a ship foundered, the gap had to be filled speedily. This would entail a telephone call in the middle of the night, a dark drive to the airfield followed by at least six hours over the sea in an open, cold cockpit with hostile fire from the enemy flakships to contend with.[7]

The task facing No. 815 and later No. 826 Fleet Air Arm Squadrons in laying mines in Dutch rivers and canals required not only considerable flying skill at a height not above 50-100 feet for accuracy but also much intelligence gathering beforehand. This job was the responsibility of the Intelligence Officer Ron Brown who had to find out about water depths, obstructions, trees and any other relevant details to pass on at the briefings. In those early days before the age of electronic and satellite surveillance and in the absence of accurate ground intelligence, the only source of information was the Cambridge University Library. Ron Brown had to use his old Hillman Minx and all available petrol coupons to go to Cambridge and obtain reference books such as pre-war books for amateur yachtsmen planning holidays in Dutch waters. As a trade-off with the Library, aerial photographs of the University and Library were promised![8]

In the meantime No. 206 Squadron's newly acquired Hudsons were becoming operational, the first patrol being carried out on 12 April by Hudsons N7312 and N7343 with convoy escort duties continuing throughout April. There was one mishap on the airfield on the 25th when Hudson N7312 crashed on the airfield. There were no reports of casualties. At least by now the Hudson was being equipped with the long-awaited Boulton and Paul electro-hydraulic gun turrets so that the aircraft could defend themselves against the increasing number of enemy fighters.

A new unit arrived at Bircham Newton for a brief spell from April to May, No. 2 General Reconnaissance Unit (GRU) with five Wellington DWI aircraft (Directional Wireless Installation) under the command of Squadron Leader Purvis. These aircraft (nicknamed 'Hoopla Wimpeys') were equipped with a magnetic 'halo' to detonate magnetic mines before they could damage our shipping. This was dangerous work involving the aircraft flying close to the water to explode the mines which threw up a column of water nearly 100 feet high. Later Purvis was to win the Distinguished Service Cross (DSC) for his work. [9] The Admiralty was desperate to find a remedy for this fearsome threat and No. 2 GRU was charged with this important task.

No. 206 Squadron stepped up its operations along the enemy coastline during May, made possible by the increased range of the Hudson. The squadron carried out its first attack on 1 May when Flight Lieutenant W. H. Biddell and his crew in N7351 bombed enemy ships just off the Frisian Islands. However, enemy fighters were bound to become a greater threat, as was proved on 3 May when Pilot Officer Kean in Hudson

---

[7] Ibid.

[8] Brown, Ron: *All Round the Compass.*

[9] Ibid.

N7319 coded VX-C was set upon by three Me109s and his gunner, LAC Ernest Townend, shot one down only to be killed himself †. The remaining two continued the attack but Kean managed to out-turn them and, although injured himself, flew at zero feet to escape disaster. It is related that the two enemy pilots acknowledged Kean's daring and skill by flying in formation and waving goodbye! Kean reached Bircham Newton but the navigator had to land the aircraft. Afterwards, the machine was found to have 242 bullet holes and 12 cannon shells.[10] Pilot Officer Kean was awarded the DFC as a result of this episode and his navigator Sergeant E. L. Deverill the DFM. LAC Townend's bravery went unacknowledged as only the Victoria Cross could be awarded posthumously. Sadly Pilot Officer Kean was killed on 5 August 1940.[11]

Grave of P/O R.T. Kean of No. 206 Sqn at New Hunstanton Cemetery, Norfolk. (author)

It was a deadly game, aerial combat in daylight hours during the early summer of 1940 over the narrow seas to the enemy coastline, with the Germans carrying all before them in Scandinavia and the Low Countries. The month of May was the worst month for losses for the Bircham Newton squadrons in the war so far, with six Hudsons of No. 206 Squadron downed, five due to enemy action and no fewer than eight Blenheims of No. 235 Squadron lost, three due to enemy action.[12]

On the 12th a Hudson of No. 206 Squadron, N7353, with Pilot Officer I. L. Gray and crew, failed to return from a reconnaissance flight along the Dutch coast and on the same day two Blenheims of No. 235 Squadron were shot down by Bf109s although an Me110 was claimed to have been shot down in the same dogfight. The Blenheims had been tasked to cover the evacuation of Queen Wilhelmina of the Netherlands. Pilot Officer N. A. L. Smith

and his crew in the first Blenheim were killed but the pilot of the second, Sergeant N. A. Savill, survived to become a prisoner-of-war in Stalag Luft III at Sagan although his two fellow crewmen were killed. Both Blenheims were later claimed by pilots of Luftwaffe unit II./JG27. The aircraft of Sergeant Savill was later salvaged by the Royal Netherlands Air Force in August 1967.[13]

---

[10] No. 206 Squadron 75th Anniversary history.
[11] P/O Kean is buried in New Hunstanton Cemetery, Norfolk.
[12] For fuller details see Appendix IV.
[13] Boiten, Theo: *Blenheim Strike* (Air Research Publications 1995) p242.

Accidents due to weather conditions, damage by enemy action, mechanical failure or even pilot error were an unfortunate aspect of life on any RAF station and Bircham Newton was no exception. Mike Applegarth recalls two crashes of Hudsons in landing shortly after No. 206 Squadron converted to this type. On both occasions the problem was caused by a heavy landing damaging the undercarriage mounting which was riveted near the wing petrol tanks. The result was that petrol from the ruptured tank deluged the hot engine and a fierce fire resulted. The fate of the crews concerned is unknown.[14]

Vernon Buckman confirms the undercarriage riveting hazard, a problem exacerbated by the grass field at Bircham Newton which could sometimes cause the Hudson to swing on landing or take-off, resulting in some five Hudson accidents in six months. An additional factor was the tendency of the airfield surface to develop gault holes, subsoil collapse due to clay or marl combined with steady pounding from above, which led to aircraft causing a minor ground collapse and sinking into the ground.[15]

For the Fleet Air Arm Squadron No. 815, the proposed Wilhelmshaven attack never took place and the squadron moved to Ford on the 16th, returning to Bircham Newton on the 20th for three days, before again flying to Ford until 6 June during which period it helped to cover the evacuation of the British Expeditionary Force (BEF) from the beaches of Dunkirk, Operation *Dynamo*, until the squadron's eventual embarkation to HMS *Illustrious*.

The evacuation of the BEF started on 26 May and No. 206 Squadron operated with No. 220 Squadron which had returned briefly from Thornaby, in cross-over patrols to prevent interference from German warships. These operations, codenamed *Sands*, continued until 3 June and the descriptions of the scene were vivid. Heavy enemy bombing of the beaches was reported on 29 May, by this time crowded with our troops. Nothing was spared, not even hospital ships. The Hudsons were met with heavy anti-aircraft fire from the shore in the vicinity of Dunkirk and Ostend, fortunately with no damage reported to the aircraft. A Heinkel He111 was attacked and shot down on the 30th, and in spite of fog and poor visibility the sea lanes in the Channel were reported to be crowded with boats. Dunkirk was in flames with the wreckage of boats visible in the harbour. On 1 June the patrols continued in improved weather. One No. 220 Squadron Hudson reported sighting 40 enemy aircraft and later in the day two Ju87s were reported shot down by the Hudsons, and Spitfires and Hurricanes were also in evidence. By 3 June the debris of war including hundreds of abandoned lorries were littering the beaches. The same day eight Hudsons from No. 220 Squadron made a bombing attack on Rotterdam, one aircraft being damaged but all returned safely.

Jack Holywell recalled his posting to No. 206 Squadron at around this time, after training as an air gunner at Penrhos in north Wales. With a dozen others for the journey to Norfolk they were given rations which included some tins of bully beef dated 1917!

---

[14] Applegarth, M.J.
[15] Buckman: *Memories of Life with 206 (GR) Sqn.*

However when the tins were opened they smelt all right in spite of the date. Jack took part in the operations covering the Dunkirk evacuation and its aftermath:

'I well remember the last flight to Dunkirk. The Channel was empty. We had been looking for stragglers making their way back on rowing boats, oil cans or anything they could get hold of. Normally we would have directed a naval boat to pick them up but on this flight it was all over; the sea was empty.'[16]

During the Dunkirk episode Flight Lieutenant W. H. Biddell of No. 206 Squadron in Hudson N7351 led his wingmen Pilot Officer Kean in N7333 and Flying Officer Marvin in P5133 into a formation of six Bf109s, shooting two of them down, an exploit for which Biddell was awarded the DFC. Later that month, the same officer was the pilot of the Hudson which evacuated General Sikorski and his staff from Bordeaux to England, where a Polish Government-in-exile was formed. It was an heroic exploit, with the Polish VIPs being rescued at the last moment from under the noses of the advancing German armies before being flown to safety in Northolt. Biddell was afterwards decorated with the Polish Cross of Valour by General Sikorski himself.

The comings and goings of squadrons and units during wartime on a busy operational station like Bircham Newton must have gone almost unnoticed by the

Crew of the No. 206 Sqn Hudson that rescued Gen. Sikorski from Bordeaux. Left to right: LAC Garrity (from USA), navigator; F/Lt W.H. Biddell, pilot; ? unknown; LAC W.D. 'Spike' Caulfield, WOp/AG. (Chaz Bowyer via S.J. 'Robby' Robilliard)

---

[16] Holywell, Jack: Memoirs of Life with 206 Squadron 1940-41 (206 Sqn Archives, RAF Kinloss).

F/Lt Biddell at the controls of his Hudson. (Chaz Bowyer via S.J. Robilliard)

personnel, but if a unit remained for any length of time bonds of friendship and mutual respect were bound to develop. Leading Aircraftman S. J. 'Robby' Robilliard of No. 206 Squadron recalled seeing a large crowd gather to see off one of the FAA Swordfish squadrons when they were posted, with 'bicycles and suitcases strapped to their wings'.[17]

The Fairey Albacores of No. 826 Squadron which had arrived at the station during May rapidly became operational, carrying out tasks like escorting southbound convoys as on 10 June. Meanwhile a new challenge emerged in the shape of Hitler's Operation *Sealion*, the planned invasion of Britain. The assembly of invasion barges along the enemy coast became a priority target for both Bomber and Coastal Commands. Although the Hudson was not designed for low level bombing, this was one of the additional tasks undertaken by No. 206 Squadron throughout the summer, as on 12 June when Terry Bulloch in Hudson P5162 dive-bombed barges in Boulogne harbour. There were also daily North Sea patrols to locate enemy warships and U-Boats and searches for aircrew downed in the sea.

On 18 June there was a low level attack by Hudsons on warehouses on the southern bank of the canal at Ijmuiden. Albacores of No. 826 were also engaged in attacks on enemy barges. On the 19th Hudsons of No. 206 dive-bombed a bridge north of Texel and the following day returned to attack harbours, warehouses and troop

---

[17] Robilliard, S.J. 'Robby': letter to author 27/8/91.

Blenheim IV of No. 235 Sqn over Bircham Newton, June 1940. (Drawing by Wing Commander John Stevens MBE, RAF Ret'd)

Blenheim Mk IVF aircraft of No. 235 Sqn at Bircham Newton dispersal during the summer of 1940. Note the squadron code 'LA' and the Spitfire and Wellington bomber in the background. (Ray C. Sturtivant)

concentrations in the area, with the Albacores of No. 826 concentrating on the aerodrome. Two of the Albacores 'P' and 'R' failed to return from this raid.

The Blenheims of No. 235 Squadron returned from Detling on the 24th to assist with the offensive and experienced a baptism of fire with a vengeance when on the 27th four out of six aircraft were shot down on a reconnaissance of the Maas and Scheldt estuaries and the south end of the Zuider Zee by a crack unit of Bf109Es based at Schiphol. In this disaster, the worst month in Bircham Newton's war thus far, 11 aircrew lost their lives and the only survivor, Sergeant Aubrey O. Lancaster, became a prisoner-of-war in Stalag Luft III (Sagan). During his years in captivity Aubrey Lancaster had much time to reflect on happier days in Norfolk, spending 'all too few hours in King's Lynn, in particular the dances held on a Saturday night in the "Globe." '[18]

Frequent Luftwaffe air raids against home airfields including Bircham Newton guaranteed no respite from the war for air or ground crew and there were other problems too. On 29 June there was an invasion scare when 80 vessels escorted by E-Boats were reported to be approaching the coastline north-east of Great Yarmouth. All the available crews of Hudsons, Albacores and Blenheims stood by for immediate take-off, but within hours the alert was proved to be a false alarm. However, a Hudson N7299 of No. 206 Squadron collided with a line of Albacores on landing, just at the moment when the flarepath was extinguished without warning. Fortunately the Hudson crew escaped without injury but the aircraft was destroyed by fire as well as two Albacores. It was a miracle that nobody was injured.[19]

At the beginning of July the Swordfish of No. 816 Squadron FAA arrived from HMS *Furious* for a brief detachment. In the meantime the campaign against enemy invasion preparations and troop concentrations continued with Texel, the Hook of Holland, and the Scheldt estuary on the list of targets. These offensive patrols along the Dutch coast were code-named *Rovers*. On the 29th six Hudsons attacked docks, shipping and an aerodrome in the Amsterdam area. With the increasing momentum of operations to cope with, a satellite airfield at Docking opened during the month to assist with the dispersal of aircraft and to act as an emergency landing ground. Surprisingly, the month ended without the loss of any aircraft on operations, although a No. 235 Squadron Blenheim had forced-landed at Horsham St Faith on the 22nd with engine failure. Damaged bombers from other squadrons continued to use Bircham Newton as an emergency landing ground if they were unable to return to their home base after operations.

Squadron Leader G. V. Donald joined No. 206 Squadron at Bircham Newton from July 1940, remaining until June 1942. He recalls the day and night reconnaissance patrols over the Dutch and Belgian coastal areas and in particular anti-invasion operations, convoy protection and anti-E-Boat patrols:

'Reconnaissance was largely the order of the day and night while attacks on German shipping were one of the best ways to dispose of the four 250-lb bombs carried. The Hudson was fitted with two .303 calibre guns firing forward through the nose, and it had a rear turret also with two .303 guns, and some versions were later fitted with a belly gun. For anti-E-Boat work I believe it was a Bofors gun of about 25mm fitted within the fuselage and based to fire downwards through a limited arc.[20] It was later believed that if the gun jammed the fuselage would burst.'

---

[18] Lancaster, Aubrey O.: letter to author 3/12/92.
[19] Buckman.
[20] See extract of Buckman (below).

Squadron Leader Donald remembered flying by day to the Docking satellite so that by night the flights would take off and land with less chance of interference from the Luftwaffe whose main attacks were directed against Bircham Newton itself. He continued: 'The anti- E-Boat patrols were quite interesting, in my logbook known as *Flares*. One Hudson would fly at about 1,500 feet over the North Sea particularly on the convoy route for UK shipping going north or south. They would unreel a wire rope curling several hundred feet behind and below, and a flare would be attached to this and trailed at the end, with the object of lighting up the E-Boats. Then a second Hudson with the pre-mentioned Bofors guns would formate on the flare and shoot the living daylights out of any located E-Boats. It was a difficult manoeuvre and probably created more of a distraction than effective damage to E-Boats.'[21]

Vernon Buckman also recalls the campaign against the E-Boats: '.....the E-boats were not only harassing coastal shipping in the North Sea but were also laying magnetic mines. Attacking them by machine gun was hopeless because long before the aircraft could get within range, they were subjected to fire from the boats' multiple cannons. Bombs were tried with limited success because the E-Boats operated at night and had great manoeuvrability. As they could be seen by the naval radar at Harwich which could also see the Hudson, it was decided to modify one Hudson with a captive flare capability - the flare being sent down a long cable to ignite and burn at the end - and to install in another Hudson a 3" Hispano cannon firing through the floor. For this we cut out a hole approximately eight feet long by two feet wide in the cabin floor and mounted the gun on a swivel which enabled the gunner to stand at the rear of the hole and fire forward, then to swing the gun over and fire to the rear whilst standing in front of the hole. A most dicey operation! The scheme was for Harwich to be in touch with both Hudsons by radio telephony (R/T).' It was hoped that Harwich would pass the location of any E-Boats to the two aircraft, which would then enable the 'gunship' to destroy the vessel. This ambitious scheme did not take into account the primitive nature of the radar available at the time or the short-range capability of the R/T, designed as it was for aircraft to aircraft communication and between aircraft and airfield control. Vernon became heavily involved with these trials, making frequent journeys to Harwich. The navy began to use more powerful radio almost to the point that it might have been heard all over Germany, while on the squadron more powerful R/T was fitted. In the end the trials were abandoned when a Lockheed engineer stated that if a cannon shell exploded prematurely the recoil, with as much force as seven tons, would have been sufficient to remove the rear half of the aircraft![22]

There was no relief in September for the hard-pressed crews, and it has to be remembered that not only were they facing the almost daily dangers of offensive operations over heavily defended enemy territory, but their home base was subject to frequent and damaging attacks by the Luftwaffe,[23] so no escape from the war was ever possible by day or by night.

---

[21] Donald, Graeme V.: letter to author 3/12/91.
[22] Buckman.
[23] See Chapter 6.

The attrition caused by accidents continued in the month as far as No. 206 Squadron was concerned. Three Hudsons came to grief in airfield accidents in early September. Vernon Buckman recalls one such incident:

'I was sitting in my hangar office at lunchtime when one of our aircraft was returning from Docking. As it was about to touch down, quite close to air traffic control, the pilot saw a light aircraft taking off underneath him. He was too low and slow to turn, so he attempted to drop behind the aircraft. Unfortunately he hit the ground very hard, bounced, and opened up, which caused him to stall at about 100 feet. The last I saw was the port wing dropping as the aircraft swung towards the station buildings where all were at lunch. The next thing I saw as I ran down through the camp was the inevitable pall of smoke. It transpired that, although out of control, the Hudson had flopped into the tennis court between the Sergeants' Mess and Station Headquarters without damaging the surrounding netting. All had leapt out - and there were many air and ground crew (complete with their bicycles) - only to discover that the gate in the tennis court surround was locked! When I arrived they (the crew) were running around trying to find a way out but eventually someone opened the gate. I do not recall whether bombs exploded but in this amazing incident there were no casualties.'[24]

An early loss was sustained by No. 826 Squadron on 2 September when an Albacore was shot down by flak on a bombing raid of invasion barges. On the 6th, Terry Bulloch of No. 206 Squadron was carrying out a dusk sweep of an area of the North Sea

WAIT FOR IT.

'Wait for it' (drawn by S.J. 'Robby' Robilliard, No. 206 Sqn Bircham Newton 1940)

[24] Buckman.

INLAND REVENUE,
VALUATION OFFICE.

• TGEV/EVL.
2457.

Barwick 239Pt.

Please quote..................on any reply.

Your reference is.............−...............

District Valuer's Office,
Tuesday Market Place,
King's Lynn,
Norfolk.

2nd October.........194 0 .

Sir,

<u>War Damage</u>.

I have now been notified of damage caused to a Sugar Beet crop by a forced landing on 3/9/40.

I enclose a Form of Claim, and should be glad to receive this back as soon as possible.

Would you kindly state the Ordnance number of the field where the crash occurred, and also note that a separate amount should be specified in respect of the damage done by the forced landing and that done by the salvage operations, if any?

        I am, Sir,

           Your obedient servant,

H. Peacock, Esq.,
    Sunderland Farm,
        DOCKING.

           District Valuer.

           <u>P.T.O.</u>

Result of the forced landing of Hudson N7351 of No. 206 Sqn on 3 Sept. after it had hit some trees.
(R.W. Perowne)

in his Hudson, on the lookout for enemy surface raiders attempting to slip into the Atlantic. During the patrol he spotted a Heinkel and engaged in a stern attack. The enemy hit the sea and Terry then droppped two of his 250 lb bombs on the aircraft with predictable results. For his various exploits with No. 206 in recent months, Terry Bulloch was awarded the DFC. The day after the Heinkel episode saw No. 826 Squadron dive-bombing dock buildings and railway sidings at Boulogne, a target already visited by No. 206 Squadron on the 5th. A combined attack by six Blenheims of No. 235 Squadron and six Albacores of No. 826 Squadron followed on the 11th, targeting enemy shipping at Calais. Me109s were engaged during the operation and three enemy aircraft shot down, but two Blenheims were lost along with their crews and one Albacore was shot down by enemy aircraft. Two of the crew of this aircraft, Lieutenant Downes and Sub-Lieutenant Mallex, were picked up later but Air Gunner Stevens was posted missing.

The 13th saw another accident, this time involving a No. 235 Squadron Blenheim L9393, which forced-landed at Grimston. In the meantime 'K' Flight of No. 1 Anti-Aircraft Co-operation Unit (1 AACU) had arrived from Cleave in Cornwall on 6 September, equipped with Hawker Henley target-tugs. Later in the month 'M' Flight of the same unit was formed at Bircham Newton, both units leaving later in the year for nearby Langham. The Henleys towed daily for the gunners at Weybourne range and also for the Bofors range at Stiffkey along with other gunnery ranges in East Anglia.

Also during this period Hurricane Mark Ics of No. 229 Squadron were on detachment, part of No. 12 Group based at Wittering. The fighters were present as a defensive measure against continued Luftwaffe attacks on the aerodrome and they remained there until the danger began to recede in September. Another unit on detachment, this time from North Coates, were the Beauforts of No. 22 Squadron, using the Docking satellite. Unfortunately, two of its aircraft crashed there on the 23rd and 27th, the accident on the 27th due to flak damage.

Operations continued through the month although storms, wind and heavy rain during the latter part of September added to the difficulties. There were patrols over Holland, Borkum, the Scheldt estuary, Ijmuiden and the Hook of Holland. On the 28th and 29th Albacores of No. 826 Squadron attacked Flushing and Rotterdam, but poor weather obscured the targets and on one of these occasions the bombs were not released out of consideration for the Dutch civilian population. On the 30th an Albacore was posted missing from a raid on Vlaardingen. On 1 October the Albacores returned to Rotterdam, presumably to complete the task started on the 28th. On 7 October the squadron moved to St Merryn in Cornwall.

Crippled bombers continued to use Bircham Newton and Docking as emergency landing grounds, as on 1 October when Hampden P4411 of No. 50 Squadron made a landfall after a raid on Berlin. The machine was destroyed but the crew were safe. The crew of Whitley T4137 of No. 58 Squadron coded GE-K, based at Linton-on-Ouse, Yorkshire, which crashed near Docking on the 8th on return from operations were not as lucky. The pilot, Pilot Officer R. A. Hadley† and his crew were killed.

There were also a number of incidents involving enemy intruders in the region as on 24 October when Blenheim P4858 of No. 17 Operational Training Unit (OTU) based at Upwood was attacked by a Heinkel He111 over Docking. The aircraft crash-landed but the crew were unhurt.

With the coming of November there was no doubt that the danger of invasion had receded, but there was a continuing need to carry the war right into the heart of the enemy. Accordingly, No. 206 Squadron initiated offensive attacks over enemy territory, codenamed *Race*, aimed at airfields, railway yards and other military or industrial targets in areas like Dunkirk or Gravelines. The first of these was flown on 14 November, the target being an airfield near Abbeville. The result of the sortie, by Pilot Officer Ward and his crew, was the destruction of an Me110 by the air gunner Sergeant Garrity. On 16 November three Hudsons of No. 206 and three Blenheims of No. 235 Squadrons took off for an airfield near Arras, but on this occasion the aircraft failed to locate the target. On the same day, on a different operation, a Hudson of No. 206 Squadron with Flight Lieutenant Dias and his crew sustained flak damage to one engine over the target and ditched in the sea off Birchington while trying to make for Manston. The crew waded ashore and the only injury was to the air gunner who suffered a sprained ankle and chill. Another Hudson ditched that day but the crew were rescued successfully. These offensive operations were the forerunners of the 'Intruders' which were so much a feature of RAF operations in 1941 and 1942.

Three units came into being during the latter part of November. Firstly, No. 221 Squadron was re-formed on the 21st under the command of Wing Commander T. R. Vickers. Equipped with the Wellington Ic, with ASV installed from the following January, the unit was tasked with anti-submarine work and was to remain at Bircham Newton until the following May. Eric Starling who joined the squadron at Bircham Newton in December 1940 recalled the events:

'Coastal Command was short of suitable aircraft for Atlantic patrols so Bomber Command had to give up some of their Wellingtons to Coastal. This was not a popular move especially when Coastal said they had no pilots who could fly Wellingtons and Bomber Command would have to train them. Eventually a compromise was reached. Coastal would find a few experienced pilots who would need little conversion and they could train the rest. This is where I came in. I was converted to Wellingtons by Bomber Command in just under seven hours which included night flying.'[25] Another pilot to be posted to the squadron was Tony Spooner who was destined to have a distinguished career in Coastal Command (later Wing Commander, DSO, DFC). Subsequently he became a notable writer on aviation history.[26]

At about the same time No. 252 Squadron re-formed with Blenheim IFs and IVs, but the squadron only remained at the station until its departure for Chivenor on 1 December, to become the first Coastal Command unit to be re-equipped with the Bristol Beaufighter. A third unit, No. 403 Meteorological Flight, was formed with three Blenheims to fly weather reconnaissance patrols over the North Sea. In March 1941 the unit was

[25] Starling, Capt. Eric: letter to author 5/12/92.
[26] Obituary of Tony Spooner, *Daily Telegraph* 31/1/2002.

renumbered 1403 Flight and the Blenheims were replaced by Hudsons. Later the Flight was absorbed by No. 1401 Flight and was redesignated No. 521 Squadron towards the end of 1942.

Meanwhile No. 235 Squadron was not left unscathed. On 23 November two Blenheims were hit by flak over their targets and made it back to Bircham Newton, both pilots being wounded. One Blenheim (coded LA-S) landed but one remaining bomb had failed to jettison and exploded on the impact. Fire broke out but the crew managed to escape. The second Blenheim (coded LA-Z) crash-landed but the crew also escaped with their lives.

The dangers faced by crews during this period was vividly recalled by Graeme Donald of No. 206 Squadron: 'You mentioned the Frisian Islands and its defences. I learned all about them on the night of 26 November 1940. This was quite a pleasant moonlit evening and we circled around Terschelling at about 1,500 feet, spotting several German ships there and finally selecting the biggest to bomb. Dropping the load at 600 feet, all hell was let loose and the barrage of light anti-aircraft fire appeared impenetrable. In escaping this it was necessary to dive very smartly to sea level. We ran a little too close to it and the rear belly gunner who insisted on firing back only shut up when he got covered in spray whipped up by our propellers from the sea. Settling down ten minutes later, he did observe a glow in the sky but there was no telling whether the attack had been effective or otherwise. Yes it was a danger area and I can well understand the number of bomber aircraft destroyed in that part of the world.'[27]

During the early part of December 1940 the weather closed in and operations were often cancelled or curtailed. On the 2nd, misty weather conditions combined with patchy sea fog led to the crash of a No. 235 Squadron Blenheim at the Holbeach range following a sweep over enemy territory. The crew escaped unhurt. On the 10th a Hudson of No. 206 Squadron bombed defences at the Hook of Holland and Rotterdam Canal. Another accident occurred on the 16th when a Blenheim of No. 235 Squadron crashed into the sea off Titchwell after a convoy escort of minesweepers, the crew being lost. This could well have been Z5754 which was reported diving into the sea from 1,500 feet off Brancaster at 1820 hrs.[28] On the 20th there was another loss, this time of Hudson N7333 of No. 206 Squadron coded VX-E, which crashed at 0405 hrs on take-off for an *EMRO* patrol.[29] The pilot, Pilot Officer R. Ward† and his crew were killed.

By the end of the year the rate of attrition of aircraft and crews was commented on by Vernon Buckman: 'Between the receipt of the first Hudson in April 1940 and the end of the year we had used up 17 Mark Is through accidents and operations. Preparing replacements placed a tremendous extra load on the servicing crews who still had to keep the operational aircraft available. Generally, within hours of an aircraft being written off or missing, a new one was delivered. No matter what time of night or day it arrived

---

[27] Donald, G.V.

[28] *Norfolk Crash Diary 1940* by Merv Hambling.

[29] *EMRO* patrols involved flying the entire length of the Dutch coast just before dawn to trace enemy shipping movements.

(and the ATA[30] delivered night and day), a team would descend upon it, install necessary equipment peculiar to the squadron task, calibrate the radios, paint identifications or camouflage, flight test it, bomb up and arm, swing the compass and hand it over to the appropriate flight. If we had lost a crew, there would be the formation of a new crew (as I recall, at that time Coastal Command crews were not formed at OCUs or OTUs[31]), and their initial flight together. All this would take no more than three days, generally.'[32]

Thus the second year of the war ended on a sombre note. The Battle of France was over. The immediate danger of invasion was over but Britain stood alone facing a hostile continent. What would the new year bring?

---

[30] Air Transport Auxiliary.
[31] Operational Conversion Units and Operational Training Units.
[32] Buckman.

CHAPTER 8

LITTLE RESPITE
January to May 1941

'It was beginning to snow hard and as I drove from one side of the country to the other, I thought back over the two most extraordinary months of my life and what had happened to me.............'
(Flight Lieutenant Don Rogers on leaving Bircham Newton, January 1941)

At this grim period of the war it must have been hard to retain any optimism about life in general and yet there were worse postings than Bircham Newton in 1940 and 1941, according to Flight Lieutenant Don Rogers of No. 500 Squadron (later Station Navigation Officer and Squadron Leader):

'Bircham Newton in 1940/41 was easily the best RAF station I had been in. It was the Officers' Mess which made the station so very comfortable. It was a large brick built pre-war mess with the most comfortable single bedrooms, beautifully heated and with plenty of bathrooms and excellent batmen. However it was the food in the Mess for which the station was renowned as it was quite exceptional. On one side of the airfield lay the estates of Sandringham and someone must have plagiarised Marie Antoinette and said: "If there is no meat, let them eat game." In that part of the world game was very plentiful and at Bircham Newton we dined several nights a week on pheasant, partridge or hare. There was always a four-course dinner: soup, a fish course, then probably game and a sweet. Once a week on dining-in nights we also had wine served with our meal......One afternoon as well as plates of brown bread and butter and cakes, there were heaped plates of delicious little brown shrimps, the local delicacy from the Wash.'[1]

Don Rogers recounted that a favourite recreation of the officers was nightly visits to the local country pubs, one favourite lying between Fakenham and Walsingham where the landlord had a packed cellar full of vintage wine of the 1920s and early 1930s, including burgundy, claret and some ports. Moreover, he was willing to sell at just two shillings per bottle. It was not long before the chairman of the Mess committee found out, visited the pub and bought every bottle for the Mess!

Other aspects of life could be more daunting, at least for certain honorary members of the Mess, where status and hierarchy ruled, as Don Rogers relates:

'A number of officers had dogs which lived with them in the Mess. The "King of the Castle" owned by the commanding officer (Group Captain Primrose) was a large, dirty, noisy, hairy springer spaniel called Stinker. Woe betide any new dog that entered the ante-room where Stinker held sway. He would immediately launch himself into an attack on any newcomer (most unbecoming for a gun dog), and invariably the newcomer was seen off. The only dogs therefore allowed into the ante-room were those thoroughly

---

[1]   Rogers, Don: *Wartime Recollections.*

subjugated by Stinker, some of whom on his approach would roll over onto their backs with their legs in the air showing their complete surrender. After a few growls Stinker would then return to his rightful place in front of the mess fire, much to the amusement of onlookers. On occasions a shoot would be organised on the Sandringham Estate and Stinker was expected to act as a gun dog, but proved impossible to control.'[2]

Don Rogers' squadron, No. 500 based at Detling in Kent, had just completed a short detachment at Bircham Newton but their aircraft would escort convoys in the area of the Thames estuary using either airfield as a convenient stopover between patrols. One of these was on 3 January when Don was ordered to pick up a southbound convoy north of the Thames estuary. He took off from Bircham Newton, completed the patrol and headed for Detling just as it was getting dark. As they neared the supposed location of the beacon at the airfield to guide them in, there was no sign of it. They searched around but there was still no beacon and as fuel was getting low after three and a half hours in the air Don ordered the crew to bail out, at 5,000 feet. At this point a very white-faced navigator pointed out that the aircraft had just been through a major inspection and no parachutes had been installed, and no one had thought to check. Thus they had no parachutes between them! Providence came to the rescue when the beacon was at last spotted and the aircraft landed after three hours forty minutes in the air!

Again on the 5th Don Rogers flew a patrol from Bircham Newton but the weather was appalling, with the cloud base at 5-600 feet and visibility in the Thames estuary at times not more than 800 yards. On the patrol Don came out of the mist and fog to encounter an armed trawler at the rear of the convoy. The vessel must have assumed the aircraft was about to attack the convoy and opened up with machine guns. They flew down the convoy until finally recognised by the destroyer captain at its head. There was a brief but robust exchange of views via Aldis lamp with the final remark that 'you should not have approached us from the seaward side'. After three hours with the convoy they returned to Bircham Newton to find that the aircraft had four bullet holes and the wireless operator had a slight rip in his trousers, having been 'nipped' by a bullet! Later, on listening to the six o' clock news, Don learned that the famous flier Amy Johnson had disappeared off the Thames estuary at around the time they were shadowing the convoy. 'What on earth she was doing over the Thames estuary as she was delivering an aircraft some 100 miles inland, no-one ever knew.'[3]

The next day, 6 January, Don was posted to No. 3 School of General Reconnaissance at Squires Gate near Blackpool. He had mixed feelings as he left Bircham Newton:

'It was beginning to snow hard and as I drove from one side of the country to the other, I thought back over the two most extraordinary months of my life and what had happened to me. I had pranged two aircraft, damaged a third in a taxiing accident after flying through a tree. I had been trained as a spy; I had wished to bail out and could not (and, I might add, that this was the only time in the whole war that I had to consider

[2] Ibid.
[3] Ibid.

bailing out); done a handful of boring ops and finally, finished up by having a row with a senior officer.'[4]

At the start of 1941 No. 206 Squadron still had a few months at Bircham Newton, after a stay which had lasted since 1936. Tragedy struck on the first day of the year, with the loss of a Hudson which crashed into a barn after low flying near Langham. All eight crew were killed. It was a sobering start to 1941.

Visit by King, Queen and Princesses to Bircham Newton 26 January 1941. Lined up for inspection are a No. 206 Sqn crew and Hudson. On extreme left Air Vice-Marshal J.H.S. Tyssen (AOC No. 16 Group). Crew lined up for inspection (L to R) G.V. Donald (pilot), F/O Tanner, F/Sgt Lewis, and F/Sgt Kelly. (Graeme V. Donald / No. 206 Sqn archives, RAF Kinloss)

On 26 January there was a ceremonial parade for a visit of the King and Queen with the two princesses, escorted by Air Vice-Marshal J. H. S. Tyssen, AOC No. 16 (GR) Group. Decorations and awards were presented to Bircham Newton personnel along with those from other local stations. The station commander Group Captain Primrose received a CBE and the famous flying ace Squadron Leader Stanford-Tuck was decorated with the DSO and a Bar to his DFC[5]. The event was recalled by Graeme V. Donald, a pilot with No. 206 Squadron at the time:

'During the visit I had the privilege of lining up my crew in front of our Hudson, supported by Group Captain Primrose who was at the time station commander. The King wore the uniform of Marshal of the Royal Air Force. It was fun showing the two young princesses over the aircraft. It must have been about the same time that *Flight* Magazine visited the Squadron and numerous photographs were taken, particularly at the satellite station at Docking where our mess was in a tent, all a bit cold and uncomfortable.'[6]

February brought snow showers but activity continued at as hectic a pace as ever. An early loss was a Hudson of No. 206 Squadron which failed to return from a patrol in the early hours of the 4th. The crew were posted missing. On the 6th operational flying was cancelled owing to fog. Further severe losses for No. 206 Squadron occurred on the 11th when three aircraft failed to return from a *Nomad* operation, the crews being posted missing.

It was No. 235 Squadron's turn on the 14th when two Blenheims crashed on a cross-country patrol, one north of Croxton near Fakenham, and the other near Thetford. Of the first aircraft, two of the crew were injured but the pilot, Pilot Officer E. R. Phillips, was killed†. The entire crew of the second aircraft were killed. On the same day a third Blenheim of No. 235 Squadron overshot the aerodrome on landing and crashed, the fate of the crew unknown.

No. 221 Squadron had in the meantime been continuing to train for its anti-submarine role and the work was progressing well, as related in the *221 Squadron History*:

'During December, January and February, the winter weather and shortage of aircraft prevented much flying, but a great deal of ground training was completed and the aircrews began to emerge in their final composition. While at Bircham Newton our NCOs and airmen were accommodated at Heacham Hall, a large derelict mansion situated ten miles away from the aerodrome. They were conveyed to and from work in very unreliable buses provided by a civilian contractor. It was not unusual for the entire squadron to have to push these ancient vehicles a considerable distance on the cold winter mornings. Heacham Hall consisted of a large number of small rooms with no central heating and totally unguarded fireplaces. Twice we set the place on fire and each time, by the Grace of God, the fire was put out without serious consequences. The only damage done was to the station commander's dignity, and in this connection we really

---

[5] S/Ldr Stanford Tuck was at this time based at Coltishall.
[6] Donald, Graeme V.: letter to author 28/11/91.

had our own back because when we left, Station Headquarters personnel moved in, and within three weeks the place was burned to the ground. The station commander, Group Captain Primrose, and his staff were extremely helpful to us during the days of our early teething troubles and we owe them a considerable debt for their assistance in getting us organised as an independent unit in double quick time.'[7]

On 3 March there was a minor mishap when Eric Starling of No. 221 Squadron did a wheels-up landing in Wellington N2840: 'This was the only wheels-up landing I have ever had to do. I had a hydraulic failure so I turned over to the emergency system. One had to hand pump the flaps and undercarriage down. I pumped and pumped and nothing happened. In my skimpy conversion I had not been told that it took about 15 minutes' pumping to get the undercarriage down. I landed on the grass and I must say that I have done heavier landings with my wheels down!'[8]

Meanwhile the Blenheims of No. 59 Squadron were active, with two aircraft on operations over Ijmuiden and the aerodrome at Knock on the 22nd. That same day five Blenheims were carrying out a sea search. On the 23rd two Blenheims of No. 235 Squadron were on a *Pirate* patrol and sighted three enemy vessels off the Hook of Holland. Hits were made on a flakship and E-Boat but the aircraft were attacked and both were shot down by Bf109Es. All six crew were killed.[9] A third Blenheim was attacked by enemy aircraft but returned safely.

Sleet and snow showers at the end of March and beginning of April added to the difficulties faced by the aircrew, but there was no let-up in operational activity. On 1 April No. 235 Squadron lost two crews in local accidents, the first when a Blenheim stalled and spun into ground near Hunstanton. In the second incident the aircraft crashed in the sea near Snettisham but the crew appear to have been saved. The machine had landed with undercarriage down but had turned turtle. Personnel were warned about mines on the beach when sifting through the wreckage.

A serious threat emerged at this time from enemy intruders over home airfields. A No. 206 Squadron Hudson was attacked over Langham at 800 feet while doing night-flying practice from the satellite airfield. The enemy aircraft were reported to be a Ju88 and a Dornier Do17 and the Hudson's rear gunner fired back. On this occasion the aircraft landed safely at West Tofts in the early hours of 8 April, with only some cannon damage to the tailplane. It was during this month that No. 206 Squadron began to receive some Hudson Marks II, later Marks III and V as related by Vernon Buckman:

'Early in 1941 we started to receive the Hudson Mk II and later Mks III and V. As far as I can recall there was little overall advantage. We had got on well with Pratt & Whitney Wasp engines and were not very happy with the Wright Cyclones, even if they were slightly more powerful. One of these marks (I cannot remember which) arrived with American radio, the Bendix TA2J. It was a beautiful piece of equipment but was

---

[7] *221 Squadron History.*
[8] Starling, Capt. Eric: letter to author 5/12/92.
[9] Sgts C. R. Evans, E.H. Harvey, G.S.M. MacLeod, P/O A.W.B. Newman, Sgts H. Willis and V.S. Key.

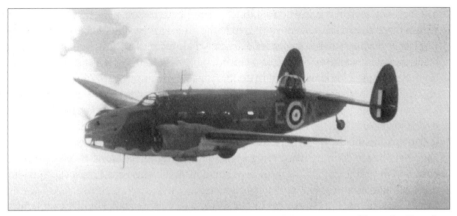

Hudson of No. 206 Sqn based at Bircham Newton, 1940/1941. Just visible is the Squadron wartime code 'VX'. (Crown Copyright: RAF Photograph)

crystal controlled with only eight channels. No crystals were available until later on so in addition to the other preparation tasks out came all the radio and in went the good old British T1154/R1155. I wonder whether the RAF policy that led to the use of the master oscillator controlled W/T had foreseen the problem of providing crystals?'[10]

Early May saw a strike and escort operation being carried out by three Blenheims of No. 235 Squadron and four from No. 59 Squadron. The latter formation attacked an enemy convoy from 200 feet resulting in dense smoke coming from the stern of one of the enemy destroyers. The escorting aircraft remained at 3,000 feet and witnessed three of the strike aircraft hit the water, the fourth setting off on a parallel course to the escorting aircraft. However none of the four No. 59 Squadron aircraft got back to base and later there was an intercepted message from the Germans that survivors had been picked up and the dead would be given military funerals.

Meanwhile, the early months of 1941 had seen a No. 206 Squadron detachment to Aldergrove, Northern Ireland, due to the need for increasing patrols in the light of the U-Boat menace. On 6 May, a second detachment went to St Eval in Cornwall (to be followed by the rest of the squadron at the end of the month) to attempt to locate the enemy battleship *Bismarck* and the heavy cruiser *Prinz Eugen* as they approached Brest. However, the battleship was to be hunted down and sunk later that month on an Atlantic patrol.

In the middle of the month *Pirate* patrols resulted in the loss of a No. 235 Squadron Blenheim which crash-landed on return to the airfield on the 15th. The following day, Hudson VX-N came down in the Thames estuary on a similar operation. A sea sweep by Blenheims of No. 235 Squadron on the 18th resulted in the sighting of some Danish fishing vessels of under 100 tons each. There was a suspicion that these were actually enemy ships, especially as on closer inspection German voices were heard over the

---

[10] Buckman, Vernon: *Memories of Life with 206 (GR) Squadron.*

R/T beginning with the word 'Achtung...'. But photographs were taken and no other action resulted, the aircraft returning to base. Towards the end of the month No. 206 Squadron received orders to split the squadron to re-form No. 200 Squadron. Vernon Buckman recalled the events:

'From the logistics angle "splitting" entails a lot of extra hard work, but it can also cause a lot of heartbreak from the personnel aspect. Although new members would be posted in, nevertheless the only fair way was to split the existing staff right down the middle to ensure that both squadrons would have, as near as possible, equal skills and experience. In this case, we were not to know until nearer the day that No. 200 Squadron was destined for West Africa. Few of my staff volunteered to go although in many cases a step up in promotion was offered. It was decided to stick to one Mark if possible for No. 200 Squadron and the Mark V was chosen. We had about six weeks to get them ready. This was a bad choice for me because it was the only Mark without the latest radio/telephony (R/T) so I had a major fitting task. By May all was ready and they left with Wing Commander Candy as their CO. The aircraft flew via Gibraltar where they did some escort duty. The ground crew went by sea but were torpedoed with heavy losses.'[11]

Graeme V. Donald was among the aircrew selected to be part of the re-formed squadron and duly left for Bathurst, Gambia. Thus the days of No. 206 Squadron at Bircham Newton were nearly over, as Vernon Buckman related:

'Unlike most Coastal Command squadrons, No. 206 had been left alone for a long time, having been at Bircham since 1936. However, after waving goodbye to No. 200 Squadron, we were posted to St Eval, probably so that we could build up our strength but also to give us a spell on runways. We took the place of a squadron which had had a hard time keeping a watch on Brest where the *Scharnhorst* and *Gneisenau* had been sheltering. Also they had suffered two or three severe night attacks on their undefended airfield with heavy aircraft damage. We did not mind the move - at least we could look forward to warmer winters.'[12]

No. 206's move was also recalled by Allan Monaghan who had come to the squadron only a few months before: 'The moving from Bircham to St Eval was one summer's night, weather marvellous, and most personnel and all equipment were loaded at Hunstanton station. It took until Sunday night to get to Padstow in Cornwall. We had a halt at Bristol due to an air raid.'[13]

A *Pirate* patrol on 28 May led to the loss of two Blenheims of No. 235 Squadron, Z5968 and V5453, due to attacks by Bf109s off Texel or Terschelling.[14] A third aircraft on the patrol returned safely. These were the final losses on operations of No. 235 Squadron at Bircham Newton, for on 4 June the squadron left for the more northerly airfield at Dyce, Aberdeenshire.

---

[11] Ibid.
[12] Ibid.
[13] Monaghan, Allan: letter to author 13/10/93.
[14] Crews were posted missing: P/O J.O. Fenton, Sgts R.H. Johnson, O.J. Dee, F/Sgt H.T. Naughtin, Sgts R. Oldroyd and S. Gordon.

Thus, the departure of No. 206 Squadron followed closely that of No. 235 Squadron, ending an historic era in the history of Bircham Newton. Their replacement was No. 500 (County of Kent) Squadron from Detling arriving on 30 May, charged with the task of maintaining the offensive from the east coast airfield.

A lighter side of life
Cartoons drawn by LAC (Ins/Rep) S.J. 'Robby' Robilliard, who was No. 206 Squadron cartoonist at Bircham Newton from 1940-1941. These pictures were originally from a set he drew for the Sergeants' Mess and have never been published before.

CHAPTER 9

OFFENSIVE OPERATIONS AND AIR-SEA RESCUE
June 1941 to April 1942

'The life of an aircrew member seemed very cheap in those days, and their heroic deaths were often hardly a matter of conversation....'
(AC2 W. H. H. Lewis, Bircham Newton)

Although the immediate danger of invasion was now past, Britain faced formidable dangers due to her isolation and the need to protect the transatlantic sea lanes on which her survival depended. On the eastern seaboard there was a need to deny the enemy superiority at sea, just as aerial supremacy had been snatched from the Luftwaffe during the Battle of Britain. This was an opportunity for defence to be translated into offence in the form of a revived anti-shipping campaign to disrupt the enemy transport system, especially as Hitler had launched Operation *Barbarossa* against the Soviet Union on 22 June 1941. In addition the sea routes from the German naval ports through the English Channel or the Northern Approaches around the north of Scotland were the means by which capital ships could enter the Atlantic and cause havoc with our convoys. Therefore, Coastal Command had a major challenge on its hands and Bircham Newton was ideally placed to be at the centre of this campaign with an area of responsibility stretching from Yorkshire and down the east coast as far as the Thames Estuary.

The 'Channel Stop' operations conducted by No. 2 Group Bomber Command earlier in the year was revived, to paralyse enemy shipping in the Channel. Local airfields like West Raynham and Great Massingham bore the brunt of this campaign with the heavy losses that resulted. In the period from 1 April to 30 June 1941 No. 2 Group flew over 1,000 anti-shipping sorties resulting in the loss of 36 aircraft, while Coastal Command in the same period made 143 attacks with the loss of 52 aircraft, a thirty-six per cent loss rate. So the price paid was a high one.[1] An informal arrangement was made with Bomber Command for their aircraft to conduct anti-shipping operations between Cherbourg and Texel, while Coastal Command had responsibility for the rest of the sea lanes around Britain - a formidable task, given the thinly spread resources available to the Command.

No. 500 (County of Kent) Squadron of the Auxiliary Air Force had arrived with Blenheim IVs at the end of May 1941 from Detling, commanded by Wing Commander M. Q. Chandler. 'A' Flight of the squadron had already been on detachment in Norfolk from late 1940 (then equipped with Ansons) and they found the conditions at Bircham Newton similar to those at Detling, with its cold climate and frequent fogs. However, due to the shortage of space they had to endure accommodation in the only available building, the pre-war decontamination block! On top of this there was the constant danger of air

---

[1] Ashworth, Chris: *RAF Coastal Command 1936-1969* p48.

attack, in particular a near escape one day from the marauding Heinkel He111 which sprayed part of the airfield with machine gun fire.[2]

This early detachment of No. 500 Squadron was recalled by John Stitt, then a Corporal Fitter Aero Engines. He remembers the relief at leaving their much-bombed airfield in Kent in spite of their anger at losing 62 personnel, several aircraft and nearly all their buildings. Bircham Newton by comparison looked substantial, friendly and undamaged. It was a relief to see a Hurricane outside the Watch Office on daily duty from its base at Sutton Bridge, as fighter protection in case of a sudden attack. He also recalled 'the number of of Bomber Command aircraft that just made it back to anywhere in Norfolk, the Wellingtons, Hampdens and Whitleys. They flew across the Alps to Turin and other cities. As Bircham Newton was Coastal Command and did not wish to illuminate a flare path, we saw bombers drop their own flares to light up the airfield and then land. Some of the crews were in a very sorry state.'[3] When No. 500 Squadron returned to Bircham Newton in May 1941, again from Detling, John Stitt had pleasanter thoughts on his mind:

'Having just unloaded our kit on the east side of the technical area and taken everything off the coaches, we were told to reload and climb aboard for our country retreat. The coaches rolled into the grounds of Heacham Hall and we could scarcely believe our good fortune - coaches for transport to work, the Wheatsheaf pub, local ladies providing sandwiches and a seaside resort within walking distance! Hunstanton offered us many pleasures that were lacking in the south - a good swimming pool, good food, girls from King's Lynn and the seaside.'[4]

Other units present during the summer of 1941 included a detachment of Blenheims from No. 59 Squadron, whose home base was at Thorney Island, from March until June. Later in June No. 248 Squadron arrived from Dyce commanded by Wing Commander S. G. Wise DFC, soon to be replacing its Blenheims with the formidable Beaufighter to enhance its 'strike' capability. A further unit on detachment, No. 608 Squadron, arrived from Thornaby in June and was also shortly to re-equip this time with Hudsons. In July the Blenheims of No. 53 Squadron flew in from St Eval to remain until October by which time they had also converted to Hudsons. Also operating at this time was No. 1403 Meteorological Flight with Blenheims, carrying out constant recce patrolling along the sea lanes. The Flight also possessed some Gladiators, and John Stitt of No. 500 Squadron recalled that 'first thing in the morning when you could not see your hand in front of your face, the aircraft would charge into the fog and become airborne in seconds. How they ever got back on to the ground again was a complete mystery.'[5]

Given the need for flexibility there were continual detachments to and from Bircham Newton, with Aldergrove in Northern Ireland, Carew Cheriton in Pembrokeshire, St Eval in Cornwall and Harrowbeer just outside Plymouth being on the list of locations.

---

[2] Brooks, Robin J.: *Kent's Own: The History of 500 (County of Kent) Squadron* pp65-6
[3] Stitt, John: letters to author 2/94.
[4] Ibid.
[5] Ibid.

At the end of May No. 500 Squadron had its first brush with the enemy from its new base, when a Blenheim set out on an air-sea rescue (ASR) operation for downed airmen. When the men had been located and a dinghy dropped, the aircraft was attacked by three yellow-nosed Me109s. In the ensuing fight, a 109 was damaged and then the others turned for home but this was only a foretaste of what was to come. On 8 June the squadron suffered its first fatalities with the loss of Blenheim V5689 which crashed into the ground in mist at Holme and caught fire[6]. In total during the month the squadron completed 100 sorties mainly in convoy patrols and ASR work.

With the improving weather and longer daylight hours of summer, the tempo of operations increased. No. 248 Squadron Blenheims (the unit not yet having converted to Beaufighters) were undertaking convoy patrols, mine searches and anti-shipping sorties to the Dutch coastline. On 2 July one of these aircraft, Blenheim IVF 'K' Z6171, crashed in the North Sea off Texel after being attacked by an enemy fighter. The crew were posted missing. On the 7th one of No. 500 Squadron's Blenheims, Z6041, was shot down by an intruder as it came into land at Docking, all the crew being killed.[7]

Frequent *Nomad* patrols[8] were being carried out by No. 53 Squadron, still with their Blenheims, as on 4 and 13 July, on the latter occasion one of the aircraft overshooting on landing and crashing into a hedge, luckily with no crew injuries. On the 15th a No.1403 Flight Blenheim failed to return from a recce flight and the crew, Sergeants Culley, Anderson and Elliott were posted missing.

There were constant reminders of the Bomber Command campaign with Bircham Newton, Docking and Langham being emergency landing grounds for bombers returning damaged or with near-empty fuel gauges and often with injured aircrew on board, examples being on 15 July when a Whitley from No. 102 Squadron, a Stirling and Halifax made landfalls after raids on Hanover. At the end of the month three Hampdens from No. 44 Squadron landed at Docking after a raid on Cologne. For those aircraft unable to reach their landfall frequent ASR operations were mounted, another task for the Bircham squadrons. One such successful operation took place in early August involving Nos 500 and 53 Squadrons and the Met. Flight, resulting in a launch picking up the downed crew. The arrival of so many aircraft from other squadrons which successfully made their landfall aroused much interest among the ground crews. John Stitt of No. 500 Squadron remembered 'dawn at Docking, which was always full of interest....I saw my first Stirling parked there one morning, which seemed like a giant of a machine after our Blenheims.' On another occasion at Bircham Newton he recalled 'the arrival of a sleek blue monoplane which was placed under armed guard! When it took off the pilot did a roll on one engine which left us speechless. We soon discovered that it was a photo-reconnaissance (PR) Mosquito and it must have been on one of the first such missions.'

---

[6]   Pilot: F/O F.W. Hall-Jones. †
[7]   Pilot: F/O A. Leeson. †
[8]   As the name suggests, a task which involved searching for targets of opportunity, in this case ships.

A *Nomad* anti-shipping sortie to the Dutch Frisians on 7 August led to another No. 500 Squadron loss, Blenheim L4899 coded MK-E, the crew being posted missing. On the 10th a No. 53 Squadron Hudson AM672 was shot down by a flakship off the island of Terschelling with the loss of the crew. Similar tragedies were suffered by No. 500 Squadron, one being the result of an ASR patrol on the 15th, when Blenheim Z6036 was shot down by a Bf110 in the North Sea with the loss of the entire crew. A further loss, this time on the 24th, was of Blenheim Z6039 which was shot down by flak from two harbour protection vessels off the Hook of Holland, yet again the crew being posted missing.[9]

In the meantime on 21 August three Beaufighters of No. 248 Squadron escorted by fighters attacked seven armed trawlers off Calais with cannon and machine gun fire. Considerable damage resulted with no reported loss on our side. At the end of the month No. 500 Squadron was yet again to register losses, on 30/31st of Blenheim V5525 which was shot down during a reconnaissance close to Schiphol and crashed near Amsterdam with the loss of its crew. On the same day Blenheim Z6164 set out on an offensive sortie to Soesterberg airfield and came down in the North Sea with the loss of its crew, the circumstances never coming to light.[10]

In September No. 500 Squadron began night intruder operations over Holland and bombing raids on dock installations along the enemy coast, including Donges, St Nazaire, La Rochelle and Nantes. At the same time anti-shipping sorties continued. On one of these, on 23 September, Blenheim V5684 crashed in the North Sea with the loss of all its crew. The work continued unabated into October with the further loss of Blenheim V6171 being incurred on 10th/11th on a *Nomad* shipping sweep by three aircraft to the Dutch coast. Only the pilot survived, Flying Officer E. A. Webb, to become a prisoner-of-war.

An unusual incident occurred on the 16th when a Blenheim from the squadron lost its bearings on a reciprocal course due to the wrong setting of the gyro compass. Final landfall was made in Wexford in Eire, with no apparent harm resulting for the crew. Towards the end of the month anti-shipping operations resulted in two further losses: on the 25th of Blenheim V5538 and on the 31st of Blenheim V5537, in both cases the crews being posted missing. On the latter occasion a 10,000 ton merchant ship was reported destroyed but the price paid was by Squadron Leader F. C. Phipps and his crew.

October was a busy month for unit movements. No. 53 Squadron moved to St Eval on the 19th to continue its work in the Western Approaches, being replaced by a No. 59 Squadron detachment from Thorney Island. There were many occasions when postings of personnel could not keep up with the changes on the operational stations, as Mr H. Schofield found out late in 1941:

'I was posted to No. 53 Squadron as a wireless operator but late in 1941 I went home on leave and then received a telegram to report to Bircham Newton. What a place

---

[9] Boiten, Theo: *Blenheim Strike* pp 274, 275.
[10] Ibid. p277.

'Shouldn't have joined.' (drawn by S.J. 'Robby' Robilliard, No. 206 Sqn Bircham Newton 1940)

to get to - down from Lancashire to London - then to King's Lynn and the transport to Bircham. I arrived on a black winter's night and was picked up and taken to the station. A sergeant found me a bed in an upstairs barrack room and the next morning I reported to the orderly room and told them I was rejoining No. 53 Squadron. "They are not here", I was told. "Where are they?", I asked. "How the hell should I know? There's a bloody war on!", was the reply. So I stayed in the barrack room all day. Next day I was sent back on leave and left Bircham Newton after two whole days! I never did find the squadron. Finally I was sent to Iraq - yes - Iraq 1941 and not 1991 - and finished in a wireless unit on the oil pipeline.'[11]

On 25 October No. 1401 (Met.) Flight moved in from Mildenhall with its Gladiators to join No. 1403 Flight. Soon the unit would be operating a variety of aircraft including Hurricanes and in 1942 some Spitfires, Blenheims and Mosquitoes. At the start of November tragedy again struck when Blenheim Z6163 of No. 500 Squadron crashed on take-off[12], reportedly due to bombs falling off the aircraft and exploding. John Stitt recalled just such an incident:

'With the better weather fading away, we began to realise that it was not all sunshine in Norfolk. The weather cost many lives. I well remember one very cold, dark and icy evening being in the NAAFI about to enjoy sausages and chips when the Tannoy called 'B' Flight to the dispersal. On our arrival the aircrew were in the Nissen

---

[11] Schofield, H: letter to author 16/7/91.
[12] or Z7449 according to *Norfolk Crash Diary* (Merv Hambling).

Gloster Gladiator of No. 1401 (Met.) Flight (later No. 521 Sqn) at Bircham Newton 1941-1942. (Eastern Daily Press)

hut on the phone to Operations. They were drawing attention to the icing conditions but Operations suggested they flew to the coast and if things were bad to return to Bircham Newton. We started them up and they taxied to the far side of the airfield, turned and started their take-off. All we could see were the two glowing exhaust rings. Suddenly there was a blinding white flash under the Blenheim and it climbed vertically into the night. As soon as it lost its momentum it fell to the ground and burnt. Inspection of the airfield the following morning revealed a large shallow crater where a bomb had dropped off the aircraft during the take-off run. Later on, all operations at night were flown from Docking and this entailed flying aircraft and ground crews over there during the afternoon.'[13]

The problem of rescue services for downed aircrews was beginning to concentrate minds at the highest level in this the third year of the war. Prior to World War Two no single organisation existed for this purpose and everything depended on a number of groups acting more or less independently; the Navy, the Royal National Lifeboat Institution (RNLI), RAF high speed launches (HSLs) at various coastal locations and vessels in and around the coasts. Thus, a new Directorate of Sea Rescue Services was established in January 1941 at the Air Ministry and executive control of ASR more than 20 miles from the coast came under the control of the AOC Coastal Command. Additional squadrons were redesignated from Fighter Command for the work and two squadrons, Nos 279 and 280, were to operate within Coastal Command equipped with Hudsons.

From the beginning of the war ASR had been a vital task as the air war grew in intensity. New methods had been devised to maximise the chances of survival for downed aircrew. The first of these was pioneered at RAF Thornaby in 1940, the *Thornaby Bag*,

[13] Stitt, John.

which consisted of a piece of parachute fabric strengthened by tapes and buoyed by floats made from Kapok pads taken from Mae West lifejackets. The bags contained tins of food, water, cigarettes and a first aid kit. Their use was so successful that the equipment was ordered to be held at every RAF station. Bircham Newton followed this up by developing the *Bircham Barrel*, a supply dropping container carried in the bomb rack of an aircraft and then dropped to ditched survivors. This was a cylindrical container, normally the tail container of a 250 lb bomb, with a reinforced frame and an inner canvas bag, the whole being made watertight. It contained distress signals, water, food and a first aid kit. By July 1941 Blenheim aircraft from Bircham Newton were successfully dropping the *Bircham Barrel* and in August improvements were designed to make it more visible to downed aircrew, consisting of a float connected to the barrel by a buoyant cord which ensured that on dropping, the rope spread out across the sea so that it could be seen and caught. By September 1941 arrangements were in hand to enable a wide range of aircraft at other stations to operate the *Bircham Barrel* in ASR work.[14]

In November 1941 No. 16 (GR) Group formed one of the new squadrons at Bircham Newton, No. 279 equipped with Hudsons for ASR duties with the motto 'To See and Be Seen'. No. 280 Squadron was established with Ansons, initially at Thorney Island. The general improvements in ASR co-ordination had led to a rise in the rate of recovery of downed aircrew to around thirty-five per cent by the middle of 1941 but there was clearly much room for improvement. No. 279 Squadron Hudsons were the first to be equipped with the so-called *Lindholme Gear*, five floating containers which included a large M-type dinghy, plus rations and survival equipment. This equipment combined with the ASV (Air-to-Surface Vessel) radar on the aircraft to plot location, was a great step forward in this life-saving work. However, the shortage of Hudsons in early 1942 and the need for training meant that the squadron did not become fully operational for a number of months. During 1942 the dinghy was developed into the Mk I Airborne Lifeboat, designed for use with the Hudson.[15] Hugh Wilkins, a bomb armourer with No. 279 Squadron, recalled some of these events:

'.......Our main job as armourers was loading the Lindholme dinghies onto the bomb carriers. These dinghies were inflated after being dropped into the sea when a soluble plug activated an air bottle. On several occasions, doubtless by reason of a faulty plug, the dinghy became inflated whilst loading so that one or two armourers were trapped in the bomb-bay - quite a humourous situation. Later on, the squadron became more aggressive and we loaded anti-sub bombs.'[16] Another 279 Squadron armourer, Corporal Geoffrey Cardew, remembered squadron routine at the time:

'I was posted to No. 279 Squadron from the station armoury, Felixstowe, shortly after Easter 1942 as a fitter armourer/gun.......the armoury was in the hangar so it was no

[14] For this information I am indebted to Donald N. Thurston and Huby Fairhead of the Norfolk and Suffolk Aviation Museum.
[15] Ashworth, Chris: *RAF Coastal Command 1936-69* pp170-4.
[16] Wilkins, Hugh C.: letter to author 10/9/91.

distance to go when an aircraft had a major service, but it was a bit of a drag to the dispersal.....There must have been about half a dozen armourers, two corporals and a sergeant. Our job was to service the guns and Very pistols and to load and check the Lindholme dinghies. These latter consisted of four containers, each about four feet long, made of cardboard and painted yellow, one with an inflatable dinghy and the others with an assortment of rations, flares and fluorescent dye etc. They were linked together with ropes and had a drogue that kept them in line, making it easier for them to be grabbed in the water. There used to be set of them in the War Museum just after the war but I don't know if there are any at Hendon RAF Museum......At night the aircraft used to be flown to the satellite aerodrome at nearby Docking.'[17]

Inevitably, there were times when things went wrong, either through carelessness or inexperience, as Syd Roberts of No. 279 Squadron explained:

'Every aircraft had its own (Form) '700', that is a daily record of its Daily Inspection (DI). There are two of these, one in the Squadron Office and a 'travelling' 700 which remains on the aircraft in case it should be grounded on an away airfield and would still be required to undergo an inspection. This form had to be signed by each tradesman after his inspection. One evening whilst doing my checks I opened the bomb-doors to find that there was no equipment loaded. After I had loaded the equipment I sought out the bloke who had signed the form the previous day in order to tick him off. One of my mates on hearing me in action, so to speak, remarked that the aircraft had been on an operation but had been unable to find any sign of an aircraft or crew in the North Sea. Imagine if there had been and the bomb-aimer had pressed the button and nothing would have happened!'[18] Hugh Wilkins, then a bomb armourer with No. 279 Squadron, recalled other incidents:

'Gun armourers were always in trouble, usually after accidentally firing guns without unloading them when testing. On one occasion when the guns on a Hudson were being harmonised in the hangars a burst was fired through the squadron offices which had windows looking onto the hangar. It was reported that had the adjutant not been stooping at that moment to retrieve some papers from the floor he would have had it. In fact it was a fairly regular sight to see gun armourers reporting to the Guardroom with full pack.'[19] Equally serious was an incident related by Syd Roberts:

'In addition to checking that all the equipment and electrics were in working order, we also had to "break" the Very Pistol to ensure that it wasn't loaded and that the strikes were in order. On one occasion an armourer whilst doing the DI, instead of breaking the pistol pressed the trigger with the result that the Hudson went up in flames, thus losing £30,000 in a few moments (that is what a Hudson cost in those days).'[20]

At long last No. 500 Squadron were replacing their old Blenheims for the more powerful Lockheed Hudson and there was a brief lull in operational flying while training

---

[17] Cardew, Geoffrey: letter to author 30/7/91.
[18] Roberts, Syd: letter to author (undated).
[19] Wilkins, Hugh.
[20] Roberts, Syd.

took place. John Stitt recalled 'that our clapped-out Blenheims were collected by the ATA and you can imagine our shock when an Anson arrived and disgorged a number of ladies. We started up the engines for them and away they went. Great people!'[21]

By the end of November 1941 deteriorating weather proved yet another obstacle to business as usual. The first fatalities with the new aircraft came in a tragic accident on 1 December when Hudson AM718 crashed near the Docking-Choseley road on a night test flight with the loss of all six of the crew.[22]

By the end of the month two units had departed, No. 608 Squadron detachment for Thornaby and No. 59 Squadron detachment for Thorney Island. As Christmas 1941 approached there were many triumphs and disasters of the past year to reflect on. The six months of the anti-shipping campaign since July had proved costly. The combined campaign of No. 2 Group Bomber Command and No. 16 Group Coastal Command, of which Bircham Newton units were a part, had succeeded in bombing 499 ships for the loss of 55 bombers, 23 aircraft of Coastal Command, and four fighters. On other fronts, the axis powers seemed to be carrying all before them in the Middle East, the Russian Front and now the Far East where Japan was on the march having just crippled the US Pacific Fleet at Pearl Harbor. The main direct threat to Britain was to our supply routes in the Atlantic and so far the U-Boats seemed to be operating almost unchallenged. The

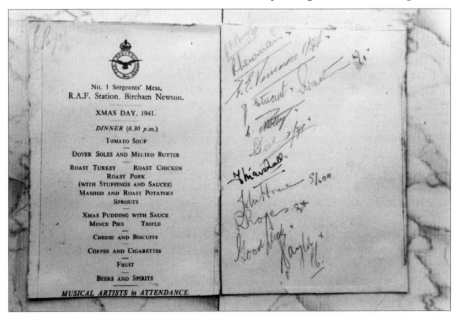

Christmas 1941, Sergeants' Mess. (Bob Collis / Norfolk & Suffolk Aviation Museum)

---

[21] Stitt, John.
[22] P/O A.F.N. Ladefoged (pilot) †, AC1 Richard Chadwick †, AC1 Hilton †, A. Lonergan RAAF †, and WOp/AG Sgt F.L. Morgan †. (Sixth crew member not known).

English Channel and the North Sea were vital sea lanes not only for the coastal convoys but also for the German capital ships as they attempted to force passage into the Atlantic, to cause further havoc wherever possible. Altogether, there must have been more than a few sombre thoughts in the short respite brought by the customary Christmas celebrations, RAF-style, at Bircham Newton.

There was no let-up in the activity of a large RAF station like Bircham Newton in the early days of January, as recalled by Hugh Wilkins of No. 279 Squadron:

'On 2 January a large draft of armourers and other trades arrived to report at the guardroom in bleak weather. Of course as usual we were unexpected and we were left standing outside the guardroom for some hours. Eventually we were detailed to collect beds and bedding and to find room where we could. I and others found that the camp was already bursting at the seams and our beds had to be erected in spaces between beds already in use, so that we could only enter our beds over the foot of somebody else's. This was in 'Mons' block. After a day or two conditions improved.....'[23]

Flight Lieutenant Don Rogers, formerly of No. 500 Squadron, returned to Bircham Newton on 14 January as Station Navigation Officer. Amongst other things he was in charge of the Watch Office to monitor all aircraft movements, with a direct link to the Operations Room. Unusually he was also President of the Mess Committee (PMC), Sergeants' Mess, mainly to check the daily takings before they were locked away and transported weekly to the bank in King's Lynn. Another duty was to look after the dummy airfields, the 'Q' sites, and this involved a weekly site inspection to ensure that the correct lighting procedure was followed to (hopefully) attract enemy aircraft away from Bircham Newton. He goes on: 'I offered them (the corporals on site) a bottle of whisky if they attracted any bombs on their sites, but am sorry to say that in the six months I was at Bircham Newton, I only had to buy one bottle of whisky!'[24]

At regular intervals Don Rogers had to liaise with the so-called 'map queen', a WAAF Corporal whose duty it was to keep all the maps at the station up to date, so that the navigators had the most accurate versions available. There was at times some conflict between Don and the Station Intelligence Officer as to who had the major responsibility for this, but the situation was complicated by a growing attachment between Don and the 'map queen' and the maps at the Station were probably unusually accurate during that period! The WAAF in question was the only daughter of a wealthy farmer in the direction of Cromer and one weekend the farmer illegally killed a pig so that a large pig's fry-up was enjoyed at the farm. However, a more serious relationship was out of the question with all the uncertainties of wartime: 'I did not want to upset her as I still wanted her to keep the maps up to date.'[25]

On the operational side, the New Year 1942 seemed to bring with it another adversary to cope with, 'General Winter', which was particularly severe. This might well have contributed to the loss of Hudson V9097 of No. 500 Squadron which crashed in a

[23] Wilkins, Hugh.
[24] Rogers, Don: *Wartime Recollections*.
[25] Ibid.

Memorial to crew of No. 500 Sqn Hudson who perished at Lowlands Farm, Bacton on 16 January 1942. (author)

field during a snow storm at Lowlands Farm, Bacton, on 16 January. The crew of four were killed, Pilot Officer J. Macgillivray (pilot), Sergeant J. Brownsell (WOp/AG), Sergeant R. B. Wark (WOp/AG) and Sergeant W. A. Sanger (AG)†. A memorial to the crew was erected by relatives close to the spot and is looked after by members of the Royal Air Forces Association. Each year, on the Sunday closest to 16 January, a poppy wreath is laid and a short service held.

It was on the night of 29/30 January that a young New Zealander recently arrived at No. 500 Squadron, Pilot Officer Mick Ensor, set out on his 11th operation, a *Nomad* to patrol Heligoland and then along the Danish and Norwegian coastline, in the most dreadful weather conditions.[26] Because conditions were so bad, Mick and his crew were the only airmen flying from the squadron that night. Near Heligoland, they spotted three supply ships and proceeded on a bombing run but while taking evasive action from flak the aircraft hit the sea and, damaged, the starboard engine cut out and the instruments ceased to function. Finding themselves off course and over Holland, still facing intense flak from ground batteries, Mick finally was able to set a course for home and after two and a half hours reached landfall only to face a blinding snow storm. With all the dangers of icing to contend with and over unknown territory they struggled through the storm eventually to do a forced landing at Winterton-on-Sea, just 45 miles from Bircham Newton. It was a lucky escape thanks to the skill of the crew and the sturdiness of the Hudson's construction. The only injuries suffered were a black eye

---

[26] Orange, Vincent: *Ensor's Endeavour* pp 35-50.

and broken tooth of the navigator, Sergeant Bert Paige. In the cold light of day Mick and his crew discovered that they had only just missed high tension cables and tall poles erected in the area to discourage German parachutists! As the crew enjoyed mugs of hot tea in the farmhouse kitchen it was fascinating for Mick to discover that they had landed just under five miles from Rollesby, the village his grandfather had left many years previously when he had emigrated to New Zealand.

The result of this episode was that Mick Ensor was awarded the Distinguished Flying Cross and Bert Paige the Distinguished Flying Medal.

The late January weather conditions were so appalling that a Beaufighter reported that the sea had frozen solid in a particular area on the 28th. A No. 279 Squadron Hudson had a lucky escape during an ASR sortie when the aircraft lost height due to the weight of ice in nil visibility, the instruments failed, and both pilot and navigator struggled to control the machine as it hit the water twice, losing the escape hatch. After three minutes the aircraft managed to fly out of the storm as the crew regained control, the instruments started to work except for the R/T and a successful landfall was made.

The ASR role at Bircham Newton was becoming more prominent as more fighters and bombers were ditching in the North Sea on return from operations, and the freezing cold at this time of year meant that ditched aircrew without a life-raft could not hope to survive for more than ten minutes in the open sea, hence the importance of speed in locating downed pilots. It was not only the aircrews which endured the conditions, but life for the ground crews was hard in that grim start to 1942, as Donald Samson, corporal-fitter recalled:

'I was detached from No. 30 Maintenance Unit at Sealand in North Wales for what was supposed to be five to seven days at Bircham Newton for a hush-hush job. "Take your small kitbag and a change of underwear in your side-pack". We travelled by service lorry - all day - to RAF Grantham where we bedded down for the night, reaching Bircham Newton the next afternoon. It transpired that some Vickers Wellingtons had been recalled from Iceland to have their engines changed and prepared for dispatch to the Middle East. These aircraft were in white camouflage of course. We had trouble!!!........Temperature in January 1942 was a good deal below zero centigrade and restricted the use of spanners etc to around five minutes after which fingers and tools "merged". We were working outside of course. Being from another unit we were not on the strength of Bircham Newton so we had to make the best of off-duty hours - which we did in a Nissen hut full of tables and forms, all of which we burned in the single stove to raise the sleeping temperature to zero. We slept fully dressed and froze stiff. My boots wore out in the third week (five to seven days - what a joke!!!!) and I had to go on sick leave to replace these: they gave me a pair of service PT plimsoles - big deal! We left - with no regrets - and returned courtesy of LNER to London and LMS to Chester.....I reckon that after service with a fighter squadron at Kenley, Prestwick and Northolt, Norfolk in winter was definitely no place to be!'[27] Hugh Wilkins of No. 279 Squadron also recalled the grim winter weather of early 1942:

---

[27] Samson, Donald R.: letter to author 24/10/91.

'The airfield was snowed up for long periods and with only grass runways it was difficult to keep the aircraft flying. Early one morning with a blizzard blowing and with no chance of aircraft taking off, a duty gun armourer and I set off to a dispersal point on the other side of the perimeter. Spotting a wind-sock in the driving snow we thought we had reached our destination, only to find that we had completed a circuit of the 'drome and had arrived back at the main hangar.'[28]

There was little improvement in the weather during early February and operations did not resume until around the 7th. On the 8th a Beaufighter of No. 248 Squadron failed to return from a patrol to recce enemy shipping. On the same day four Hudsons of No. 500 Squadron set out on an anti-shipping strike. One aircraft returned early owing to an oil leak but a convoy was sighted and one 4,000 ton vessel hit amidships. Two aircraft returned only to crash-land at Docking, one of them Hudson AM845 with the loss of all the crew.[29]

The New Year brought yet another challenge for Coastal Command. Hitler had become convinced that Britain intended to invade Norway and therefore ordered major naval units to move into that sector of the North Sea, including the battle cruisers *Scharnhorst* and *Gneisenau*, then sheltering at Brest. Aerial photographs revealed increased naval activity in the area and British Intelligence drew the conclusion that a break out of these naval units through the Channel and into the North Sea was imminent. Thus Bomber and Coastal Command units were placed on high alert and the main hope for offensive attacks lay with the torpedo-bomber Beauforts, centred on North Coates, and the Royal Navy Swordfish torpedo-bombers which were not expected to inflict more than damage to the enemy ships. However, the reconnaissance role during this period was vital and this is where Nos 248 and 500 Squadrons came in.

Matters came to a head on 12 February when a large enemy convoy was sighted and the panic was on to locate and mount attacks on the shipping. Unfortunately the day turned out to be an anti-climax due to a lack of co-ordination and preparation combined with bad weather, much of which lies outside the scope of this story. Four Hudsons of No. 500 Squadron took off at 1335 hrs ready to attack the ships but the expected rendezvous with fighters and other aircraft over Manston did not materialise and the aircraft returned to base. Later in the afternoon a Beaufighter of No. 248 Squadron sighted the enemy convoy near the Dutch coast in visibility of only half a mile, and flew inside the destroyer screen to within 100 yards of the *Scharnhorst*, having to take violent evasive action because of the flak. The wireless failed and the aircraft was unable to report the position, finally making a landing at Lakenheath. Beauforts from Thorney Island were unable to locate the convoy and landed at Docking after a sea search. A number of unsuccessful attacks were made on the ships by Beauforts, and an Avro Manchester from No. 83 Squadron landed at Bircham after one such bombing sortie, having been damaged by flak. A Wellington from No. 103 Squadron arrived at Langham after trying and failing to locate and bomb the enemy cruisers. After all these

---

[28] Wilkins, Hugh.
[29] Pilot: P/O W. Hollingsworth †.

efforts, the ships safely reached the ports of Wilhelmshaven and Kiel, a lucky escape for the German navy! Flight Lieutenant Don Rogers, Station Navigation Officer, commented on these events:

'......The German High Command had taken advantage of the weather forecast which was extremely accurate and neither the Swordfish from the Fleet Air Arm in Kent nor the Beaufort strikes managed to do any damage to the German fleet which, in the awful weather conditions, got through. There was a great public outcry and most of the aircrew in Coastal Command, particularly the strike squadrons, felt it deeply.'[30]

Meanwhile a sea search on the 13th by Hudsons resulted in what was possibly No. 279 Squadron's first loss when an aircraft failed to return. The following day seven Beaufighters from No. 248 Squadron set out on a recce to the Dutch coast and one aircraft failed to return. On the 17th Hudson AE647 of No. 500 Squadron crashed on Brancaster beach shortly after take-off on a *Nomad* operation with the loss of the crew[31].

During February No. 502 Squadron arrived for a brief spell from Limavady in Northern Ireland, equipped with Whitley VIIs, before moving on to St Eval for anti-submarine patrols in the Bay of Biscay. Bircham Newton continued to be a maintenance base for the squadron after its departure.

The Beaufighters of No. 248 Squadron left for Dyce on the 17th while No. 500 Squadron remained at Bircham Newton for a few more weeks, losing another aircraft on the 21st after a sweep by four Hudsons. No. 279 Squadron were out on a sea search for a downed Wellington on the 26th which had been reported off the Norfolk coast. A raft was sighted, one aircraft wheel and an unoccupied dinghy but there was no sign of the missing crew.

With the coming of March there were sea mists to contend with, adding to the difficulties of recce patrols and ASR work. A Blenheim of No. 1401 (Met.) Flight had an unconfirmed sighting of a submarine on the surface on the 18th. The visibility was so poor that the sighting took place from a height of 50 feet. In the course of the month a No. 217 Squadron detachment of Beauforts came from Leuchars for a brief stay and on the 31st No. 407 Squadron, Royal Canadian Air Force arrived with Hudsons. In early April No. 500 Squadron departed for the much colder surroundings of Stornoway in the Hebrides, after many epic months of operations. Springtime had at last arrived and a very busy time lay ahead for the squadrons at Bircham Newton.

---

[30] Rogers, Don.
[31] Pilot: F/Sgt A.B. Giles †.

CHAPTER 10

THE CANADIAN DEMONS AND THE DUTCH
April 1942 to March 1943

'....The Dutch naval airmen were great ones for having parties and always seemed to
have an excuse for one.....'
'Most of the Canadians had only just got used to flying over the sea at about 1,000 feet
as they had never seen the sea before, having learned to fly over the plains of Canada...'
(Flight Lieutenant Don Rogers on the Dutch of No. 320 Squadron and the Canadians of
No. 407 (Demon) Squadron RCAF)

The offensive work in this theatre of air operations consisted mostly of anti-shipping
operations but this was at a very high cost to Coastal Command. In the last four months
of 1941 anti-shipping strikes had resulted in the sinking of about 15 enemy vessels, but
with the loss of 46 aircraft of the Command. If anything, there were more disappointments
to come, because from January to April 1942 six ships were sunk, at a cost of 55 aircraft.[1]

At the start of April 1942 the Order of Battle at Bircham Newton comprised Nos
279 (ASR) Squadron, 407 (Demon) Squadron RCAF, both equipped with Hudsons and
No. 1401 Meteorological Flight with a variety of aircraft on its strength including the
Hudson, Blenheim, Gladiator and later the Spitfire and Mosquito. In February No. 1403
Flight had been absorbed by No. 1401.

No. 407 Squadron was one of seven RCAF units to serve with Coastal Command,
nicknamed 'The Demons' for its reputation as a strike unit. Commanded by Wing
Commander A. C. Brown DFC from January to September 1942, the squadron had arrived
at Bircham Newton with its more experienced ranks depleted by heavy casualties suffered
in the early part of 1942. Nearly all the aircrew were Canadian with over half the ground
crew becoming RCAF. During the six months it was in Norfolk the aircraft operated
mainly from Docking in the region of the Dutch, north German and Danish coasts.

An early loss for the squadron was on 6 April when one aircraft out of four failed
to return from a morning anti-shipping patrol. The crew were posted missing, Pilot
Officers Foley and Lowry, and Sergeants McCann and Leckie. A Hudson from No. 279
Squadron (V8996) crash-landed three miles west of Docking on the 13th but on the 18th
No. 407 Squadron lost another aircraft on a strike patrol.

A new squadron arrived from Leuchars on the 20 April, No. 320 (Netherlands)
Squadron, equipped with Hudsons, to join No. 407 in anti-shipping work. The Dutch
motto was 'Animo libero dirigimur' ('We are guided by the mind of liberty'). When the
unit was formed in 1940 it was composed of members of the Royal Netherlands Naval
Air Service who had escaped after the German occupation. Commanded by Lieutenant-
Commander W. van Lier it would remain at Bircham Newton for nearly twelve months.

---

[1] Terraine, John: *The Right of the Line* p421.

Flight Lieutenant Don Rogers, the Station Navigation Officer, recalled the Dutch airmen:

'The Dutch naval airmen were great ones for having parties and always seemed to have an excuse for one. I remember a party for Queen Wilhelmina's birthday and another for Orange Day, and on one occasion Prince Bernhardt came up to see them and we had another gigantic party......and I was told to get a glass and join them. I found that they had just had delivered from South America several cases of Bols Gin, courtesy of the Free Dutch Government (*sic*). I had never tasted Bols Gin in my life but was soon drinking it merrily from my tooth mug. By about 7 o' clock we were all as tight as ticks and I cannot really remember how we got down to dinner. The other thing I recall about this squadron was their string band which was composed of gentlemen from the Dutch East Indies, playing their string instruments in the most rhythmic fashion.'[2]

Towards the end of the month, on the 28th, a Hudson of No. 407 Squadron failed to return from a *Nomad* patrol of two aircraft. Altogether it had been a depressing period for the squadron, with little to show for its losses. There was a distinct improvement in May, although losses continued to be high. No. 407 Squadron carried out seven strikes in the month during which 27 enemy ships were attacked totalling 83,000 tons. One early example was on 5 May when an enemy convoy was sighted off Terschelling. In spite of intense flak one ship was damaged and all the aircraft returned to base safely, although one of the pilots was wounded.

At dusk on the 7th, the squadron's first anniversary, a reconnaissance aircraft reported a convoy of 12 vessels off Terschelling, and Wing Commander Brown led 12 Hudsons in a low level attack which damaged several ships. The following day saw No. 320 Squadron's first loss since arriving at Bircham Newton, as a result of a patrol, with aircrew Sergeants Jansen and Vos, LAC Koehl and Corporal van Klaveren.

Anti-shipping operations off the Dutch coast on the 15th consisted of a strike in two waves, the first of nine aircraft from No. 407 Squadron led by Flight Lieutenant R. M. Christie, and the second wave of two aircraft from No. 407 Squadron and eight aircraft from No. 320 Squadron, this formation being led by Pilot Officer F. A. Kay DFC (of No. 407). Just as twilight was fading the convoy was located and the aircraft attacked through intense flak from destroyers and escort ships A total of four Hudsons were shot down in the course of the battle. Pilot Officer Kay was wounded in the hands and legs by a shell that exploded just below the cockpit, but he completed his bombing run and managed to get his badly damaged aircraft back to a crash landing at Docking. The navigator, Pilot Officer Angus L. Kippen RCAF, was killed† and the Hudson wrecked. Pilot Officer James W. Creeden's aircraft made it back to the English coast but crashed at Digby, all the crew being killed†. Flight Lieutenant Christie nursed his aircraft back to Docking and crash-landed with his wounded observer (Johnson) aboard. Of No. 320 Squadron, one aircraft crash-landed at Docking, a second (AE525 coded NO-H) was shot down by a night fighter and crashed into the North Sea just off Terschelling with the loss of all its crew. At least six enemy vessels had been hit (over 20,000 tons) but seven No. 407 Squadron Hudsons out of eleven were missing or destroyed. In the

---

[2] Rogers, Don: *Wartime Recollections.*

course of the battle 21 men from No. 407 Squadron had been killed, one was taken prisoner and four were injured[3], making it one of the blackest days in the station's history.

A Blenheim of No. 1401 Flight failed to return from a *Rhombus*[4] on 27 May. The following two days saw successive strikes by aircraft of Nos 320 and 407 Squadrons, with five aircraft from No. 320 and eight from No. 407 attacking shipping off the Dutch coast on the 28th. Several ships were claimed as damaged and one sunk. Many of these operations were known as *Rovers*, armed searches for shipping at low level without a designated target in mind. Such an episode took place off the Dutch coast on the 29th, resulting in the loss of two of No. 320's aircraft and another from No. 407 Squadron. One of the Dutch Hudsons, AM939, was hit by flak and ditched in the North Sea off the island of Terschelling. Squadron Leader H.

No. 407 Sqn crew inspecting damage to a Hudson after returning from a sortie during 1942. CO W/Cdr A.C. Brown 2nd from right. (Winifred Gunter)

Schaper and his crew were picked up by a flakship and became prisoners-of-war. A second Hudson from the squadron, V9122, was said to have collided with a barrage balloon cable and also ditched off Terschelling. The crew were posted missing. The third aircraft, AM650 from No. 407 Squadron, failed to return, its crew also being posted missing.

It was clear that these low level, mast-high attacks were proving unacceptably costly both in terms of crews and aircraft for the results obtained. One one occasion a bomb door was left impaled on the mast of the target! German defences were becoming increasingly deadly so that in the two months of April and May 1942 No. 407 Squadron had lost half of its crew strength, with 41 dead, two prisoners and five injured. It was estimated that in the previous three months one in four of all attacking aircraft had been lost. Apart from this it was commonplace after every operation to have two or three aircraft returning to base so badly damaged as to be useless in the future. An additional factor was the posting of some of the most experienced crews to the Middle East theatre. Overall, such had been the mauling endured that there was a comparative lull in operations while fresh crews were introduced and trained. Within a short time the AOC, Sir Philip Joubert, banned low level attacks to reduce the losses and medium level bombing became the order of the day. This of course led to a reduction in the sinkings

---

[3] Hitchins, W/Cdr F.H.: *No. 407 (Demon) Squadron.*
[4] Pre-planned met. sortie over the North Sea.

of enemy ships and, without an efficient bombsight being available as yet, medium level attacks did not always produce the desired results. At the same time the suitability of the Hudson for this type of work was open to question although the aircraft itself was rugged and reliable. Beaufighters of the type employed by No. 235 Squadron at Docking would be more effective in the tasks ahead. By the end of the year planning was well advanced for Beaufighter Strike Wings to take over eventually from the Hudsons and Hampdens. The first of these was established at North Coates, Lincolnshire, in November 1942 and a second in 1943 at Wick in the north of Scotland.[5]

In the meantime the work of No. 279 (ASR) Squadron continued unabated during June. On the 2nd, a Hudson was attacked by an enemy fighter during a sea search and some of the crew were wounded. The aircraft landed safely at Eastchurch. Another Hudson managed to evade an attacker and return to base. Some aspects of life with the squadron at around this time were recounted by Geoffrey Cardew, posted to Bircham Newton as a fitter armourer/gun shortly after Easter 1942:

'It was the first time I had been on an operational unit and I looked forward eagerly to the experience. After booking in at the guardroom I was given a billet in Mons block, dumped my kit there and went for a stroll to get some idea of the surroundings. As I went down the road towards what I thought would be the village I heard an aircraft taking off; I stopped and saw a white Hudson roaring down the grass runway; the next minute there was a crunch, a sudden silence and then aircrew running away from the crashed kite. No one was hurt and I carried on with my stroll thinking that that was not exactly an auspicious start to life on an RAF aerodrome.'[6]

The Met. Flight was active, with typical sorties being *THUM* ascents[7] usually by a Gladiator and *PRATA*[8] sorties by a Spitfire. *PAMPA*[9] flights were undertaken also by Spitfires, later Mosquitoes. Such flights were unarmed and crew skill had to be of the highest order to fly deep into enemy territory and return safely. Another Met. patrol was the *Rhombus* flown on a pre-set course at just under 2,000 feet using a Hudson or Blenheim. There was a setback on 4 June when Hudson V9102 of No. 1401 Flight crash-landed on the airfield probably after such a sortie.

An anti-shipping strike on 20 June of five Hudsons from No. 407 Squadron led to the loss of one aircraft, with the crew posted missing. On the 23rd a sea search by a Hudson of No. 279 Squadron resulted in the sighting of a Wellington circling a dinghy with five men. In due course a Supermarine Walrus landed and rescued the dinghy crew and the Hudson returned to Bircham Newton after successfully co-ordinating the rescue, only to have its own undercarriage collapse on landing.

An unexpected chance to practise higher level bombing tactics came with Operation *Millennium II* on the night of 25/26 June, Bomber Command's third 1,000-

[5] See Nesbit, Roy Conyers: *The Strike Wings*, HMSO 1995.
[6] Cardew, Geoffrey: letter to author 30/7/91.
[7] *T*emperature / *Hum*idity ascent.
[8] A very high level met. sortie usually flown by a Spitfire (up to 40,000 feet).
[9] A flight deep into enemy territory, usually flown by Spitfires, later Mosquitoes.

bomber raid, this time on Bremen. All the Commands and Training Units had been combed to provide additional aircraft and No. 407 Squadron contributed 11 Hudsons, No. 320 Squadron six aircraft and No. 304 Squadron based at Docking provided seven Wellingtons. Flight Lieutenant Don Rogers, Station Navigation Officer, recalled the occasion:

Ops Room, Bircham Newton.   *Crew Room, Bircham Newton.*

'All serviceable Hudsons from Bircham Newton were involved and I went to the briefing in the Ops Room, and you can imagine the look on the crew faces when they were told that they were going to fly on a bombing mission at night across the North Sea and drop their bombs on Bremen at 15,000 feet. Most of the Canadians had only just got used to flying over the sea at about 1,000 feet as they had never seen the sea before, having learned to fly over the plains of Canada. They certainly hadn't done much night flying. Fortunately the weather was quite reasonable on the night of 25 June and I decided that my place was on the airfield to see them all go safely and I also waited up to see them come back. One Canadian pilot put "red on blue" and I gather dropped his bombs somewhere near Liverpool, fortunately without doing a great deal of damage. From the west coast of the UK he then flew east quite happily unaware of what he had done! In the early hours of the morning just as it was getting daylight aircraft started to appear and land. Quite a few Hudsons, some Wellingtons and then I saw a damn great Stirling coming in. I was quite sure the airfield was not big enough to land a Stirling and told the airfield crew to send up a red flare. However, the Stirling took no notice and the pilot dropped it just over the hedge and stopped the aircraft about 100 yards short of the perimeter, and taxied slowly to join the ranks of the other aircraft lined up outside the Watch Office. I went over to have a word with the pilot and saw the seven crew leave the aircraft. I can still remember my amazement. The young men looked as though they had just left school. The captain could not have been more than 19 years of age, and it made me feel very old at 23.'[10]   One No. 320 Squadron Hudson failed to return from the Bremen raid, along with one Wellington from No. 304. On this occasion No. 407 Squadron survived unscathed.

High level bombing training continued, but a less typical incident took place one night in July when six aircraft from No. 407 Squadron took off for the bombing range at Donna Nook in Lincolnshire. At the same time some Luftwaffe raiders were setting out to bomb targets along the Humber. One of the raiders was attracted by the flares and lights at the bombing range, joined the circuit and released its load of incendiaries and high explosives, much to the surprise of the ground personnel!

The ASR work of No. 279 Squadron was being reinforced by the Ansons of No. 280 Squadron based at Langham, but often flying from Bircham Newton or Docking. Needless to say both squadrons had a busy operational schedule with ever-increasing numbers of downed aircrews to rescue in the North Sea as the bomber offensive over Germany took its toll. Heavy bombers from other squadrons were regularly coming into Docking short of fuel or damaged and the aircrews were no doubt relieved to see the Norfolk airfield. Not so fortunate was a Mosquito of No. 1401 Flight (DK289) which failed to return from a Met. sortie on 26 July. It was during this period that the ASR work of the squadrons came under closer scrutiny, as related by Don Rogers, Station Navigation Officer:

'.....A signal had arrived from Coastal Command addressed to all station navigation officers, stating that all navigators' logs should be examined and analysed following any operation.....I have already mentioned that these searches for dinghies had not been at all successful. When the first navigators' logs came into my office, it was evident as to why. First of all the logs themselves were pretty ropey but it was fairly clear to see that some Hudsons had been nowhere near where they were supposed to have been because of their landfall when they were returning to Bircham Newton. If pilots making for Cromer finished up somewhere near Lowestoft or conversely near the mouth of the Humber, it was quite clear they had been miles off track. The searches carried out for these dinghies usually took the form of parallel track searches depending on the direction and speed of the wind and tidal currents, and if a dinghy had been sighted properly, it was easy to work out where perhaps six hours later it should be. A Hudson would fly out and cover the area where the dinghy might be by flying a series of parallel courses each, say, ten miles long making 180 degree turns and flying on a reciprocal course supposedly parallel to the track it had just covered, and so on.

'Perhaps a dozen tracks of ten miles would cover a large area and if the dinghy was there it should have been seen. When the Hudsons left Bircham Newton or Docking they would start off using the wind direction that had been given to them in the Ops Room by the Met. Officer. When they crossed the coast and went out to sea, the wind frequently freshened or altered direction by ten or twenty degrees. Unless the navigator spotted this, the aircraft would not arrive in the right place.......It was terribly difficult for

---

[10] Rogers, Don.

a navigator lying on his stomach in the nose of an aircraft flying at about 1,000 feet above the sea to measure the drift accurately. Some navigators produced good logs and by working backwards from their landfall it was quite easy to work out where they had been and an awful lot of them had not covered the area they were supposed to search........I had been working on these logs for some time and, as requested, had sent off to Coastal Command a resumé of my findings which, to be honest, made dismal reading as I had to say that seventy-five per cent of the aircraft had never covered the right search area. The navigators themselves were getting a little worried about this when I was able to plot on the maps starting from their landfall where they must have been. Gradually the exercise came to the attention of the flight commanders who also came to see me to find out what the hell was going on.

'......The Station Commander called me in one day and said: "You have got a visitation from two boffins who are coming from Coastal Command to see you." The following day two civilians arrived and were shown to my room and questioned me at length as to why I had reached the conclusions I had. I pulled out one or two navigators' logs where there were particularly bad landfalls and with the compass courses the aircraft had flown, was able to prove that they were so far out at the end of two to three hours' flying that the wind speed and direction must have been quite different to the wind speed and direction which was being logged in the aircraft. By using the adjusted wind speed direction and backtracking, it was quite possible to plot where the aircraft had been and sure enough, two out of three logs analysed showed that the Hudson had never been near where the dinghy had been sighted.' From then on a weekly report was sent to Coastal Command after every navigator's log had been analysed but the inevitable happened: 'By now, the squadron commanders had received a rocket from Coastal Command about the poor navigation in the squadrons and I was right up to my neck in it from everybody - not the most popular person on the station.' Within a short time, however, Flight Lieutenant Rogers had been posted to the Royal Naval Air Station at Crail, in Fife.[11]

As July 1942 progressed No. 407 Squadron were trying out a new type of operation where one aircraft acted as a 'Rooster' to locate and shadow a convoy while homing the strike aircraft to the scene, then dropping flares or flame-floats to illuminate the target. Such an operation was carried out by six Hudsons on 26 July. On 30 July a Met. Spitfire reported a large enemy convoy and 11 Hudsons of No. 407 took off on a 'Rooster' shadow strike. The results were disappointing, one Hudson (AM860) running out of fuel and crash-landing at Ringstead, and the other aircraft returning to various airfields including Wittering, Manston, Bradwell and North Coates. On other occasions the squadron worked with the Hampden torpedo-bombers of No. 415 Squadron, then based at North Coates.

At the end of July No. 1401 Met. Flight was disbanded and re-formed as No. 521 Met. Squadron under the command of Squadron Leader D. A. Braithwaite. Aircraft included Gladiators Mks I and II, Spitfire V, Blenheim IV and Hudson III.

---

[11] Rogers, Don.

Swordfish II DK698 'B' of No. 819 Sqn FAA, 1942. (Ray C. Sturtivant)

Two Fleet Air Arm squadrons arrived on 6 August, No. 811 from Machrihanish and a sister unit No. 819 from Langham, both with Swordfish. Only three days later six aircraft from No. 819 and five from No. 811 set out on a 'gardening' (mine-laying) operation, from which two Swordfish of the latter squadron failed to return. An ASR search in

Swordfish of No. 819 Sqn FAA forming up. (Ray C. Sturtivant)

conjunction with Walruses proved unsuccessful and the crews must be assumed to have been posted missing. On 20 August ten Hudsons of No. 407 Squadron and three of No. 320 took off on a 'shadow' strike and attacked an enemy convoy off the Dutch coast, all the aircraft returning safely at 2019 hrs. A similar operation was mounted on 4 September, this time with eight aircraft from No. 407 Squadron, five from No. 320 and four Swordfish of No. 819 Squadron, the latter taking off from Docking. On the 6th nine aircraft from No. 407 and eight of No. 320 set out armed with bombs, accompanied by five Swordfish of No. 819 Squadron with torpedoes, to attack targets off Dunkirk, Cap Gris-Nez and the Frisian Islands. One No. 407 Squadron Hudson failed to return.

September was a busy month for the Bircham squadrons. On the 8th a No. 521 Squadron Mosquito failed to return from a *Pampa* patrol. The next day Nos 407 and 320 Squadrons were on a 'Rooster' operation against an enemy convoy, during which 48 flame-floats were dropped to illuminate the convoy. These burned for 15 minutes, in spite of German attempts to destroy them with flak and this technique of target-marking proved its worth. On the 10th five aircraft from No. 320 Squadron and four from No. 407 were on a strike operation. One aircraft returned with engine trouble and another sustained damage but was able to crash-land at Docking, with the crew uninjured. Once again on the 11th flame-floats were used by aircraft of No. 320 Squadron and although the target marking was successful the number of aircraft tasked was not sufficient to make much of an impact. On the 16th a Hudson of No. 407 Squadron acted as a 'Rooster' for ten No. 320 Squadron aircraft which succeeded in locating and attacking some enemy vessels. A similar operation was mounted on the 23rd, with a No. 407 Squadron Hudson acting as 'Rooster' for No. 320 Squadron, totalling 11 aircraft, in an attack off

Swordfish of No 819 Sqn FAA ready for take-off, 1942. (Ray C. Sturtivant)

Texel. Flame-floats and flares were used and some hits claimed. The same day the Swordfish of No. 819 FAA Squadron left for Thorney Island after a busy operational period.

Five Hudsons from No. 320 Squadron set out on the 26th accompanied by five Swordfish from No. 811 FAA Squadron and five from No. 812 FAA Squadron based at Docking to attack enemy shipping off the Frisian Islands. One aircraft was damaged. On the 29th a *Pampa* Mosquito encountered heavy flak over Hanover at 29,000 feet but was able to return safely with useful intelligence about shipping movements.

By the end of the month No. 407 Squadron was preparing to move out to St Eval. The new medium level tactics and night-bombing of ships from 4,000 feet had not been an outstanding success, but losses had been considerably reduced although night fighters still represented a serious threat. One problem had been a shortage of aircraft, with older Hudsons being the only machines available. Indeed, aircraft shortage was a chronic problem during 1942 in Coastal Command, the bulk of available resources being diverted to the Bomber offensive. No. 407 Squadron's commanding officer Wing Commander Brown had completed his tour and received the DSO and the squadron set off for its new base on 1 October under its new CO, Wing Commander C. F. King, who was shortly to be killed in an accident during bombing practice. By November the squadron had returned to Docking to resume its anti-shipping operations. At the end of the year the 'Demon' Squadron began conversion training to Wellingtons, but in 17 months of anti-shipping operations at Thorney Island and Bircham Newton the squadron had won three DSOs, seven DFCs, six DFMs and 25 Mentions in Despatches. 180 attacks had been made on enemy vessels and a total of 24 Hudsons had been lost, from whose total of 99 aircrew only eight became prisoners-of-war. Other casualties on operations brought the total to 102 killed or missing, and in training or ground accidents 28 members of the squadron died.[12]

There was another tragedy involving No. 521 Met. Squadron on 4 October, when Hudson FH379 coded TE-W crashed shortly after take-off on a *Rhombus* patrol after a collision in thick fog with the mast of a MF/DF station. The crew were killed.[13]

On 9 October another FAA unit No. 812 Squadron arrived with its Swordfish from Docking, only to move on to Hatston on 3 November. At the end of October No. 811 FAA Squadron left for Thorney Island. There was also a considerable movement of personnel to overseas postings during the month. Hugh Wilkins, a bomb-armourer with No. 279 Squadron, takes up the story:

'During the year most of us had been posted on Preliminary Warning Overseas Draft. The method of selection was placing all names in a hat under the supervision of one of our senior NCOs and the required number drawn out - after which those drawn went on ten days' leave and returned to the squadron for duty - this seemed as fair a method as any other I came across. Significantly the one bod who never fell for a draft was one named Davis who played the piano in the Sergeants' Mess. In fact I met Davis

---

[12] Hitchins.
[13] Pilot: F/O R.C. Porter. †

144

at RAF Waterbeach just prior to VE-Day and he was still serving in the UK....Thus it was no surprise when early in October '42 most of us were posted to the Med and flown out from Mount Batten, Plymouth in support of Operation *Torch*[14] - to see somewhat more action than we had done at Bircham Newton.'[15]

Yet another Hudson (FH466) from No. 521 Squadron was destroyed on 1 November after catching fire on take-off for a *Rhombus*. The crew were lucky to survive, more or less unscathed. The following day No. 280 (ASR) Squadron Ansons flew in from Langham to work alongside No. 279 Squadron. In the meantime No. 320 Squadron were still fully operational, often working with No. 407 Squadron, as on 9 November when two of No. 320's aircraft took off from Thorney Island with one of No. 407 Squadron to strike at shipping off Ijmuiden. One No. 320 Squadron Hudson failed to return, with crew Flight Lieutenants van Loon and de Boer.

The following day there was an abortive strike against the 7-8,000 ton raider *Neumark*. One No. 407 aircraft and three from No. 320 took off from Manston to seek out the vessel which was expected to pass through the Straits on a north-easterly course. Various ships were sighted but not the intended quarry and the aircraft made an uneventful return to base.

On 20 November 11 Hudsons from No. 320 Squadron took off to attack an enemy convoy off the Hook of Holland, an operation from which all the aircraft returned safely. Two days later the crew of Hudson VI (EW903) of No. 320 Squadron were not so lucky as they became victim to a night fighter during a *Nomad* patrol off the Dutch coast, and crashed in the North Sea. The crew were posted missing, Sergeant C. L. G. Van Heugten (pilot), and Sergeants L. A. Hoogteiling, J. de Ligt, and J. A. Den Ouden. On the 25th 11 Hudsons of No. 320 Squadron joined No. 407 Squadron on a 'Rooster' to attack enemy shipping which had been reported off Ijmuiden. Some damage was claimed to have been inflicted and the aircraft returned safely. On the same day, 25 November, No. 415 Squadron RCAF arrived at Bircham Newton with its Hampdens for three days, before setting off again for Thorney Island. It would only be a matter of months before they were back in Norfolk, this time on detachment to Docking.

No. 279 (ASR) Squadron had its share of setbacks as on 27 November when Hudson T9407 crashed on take-off and on the 30th a Hudson had a lucky escape in an attack by an enemy fighter while on patrol, which left the air gunner and wireless operator wounded. At around this time the squadron was evaluating an Armstrong Whitworth Albemarle for possible long-range sea search work, but the aircraft was judged to be unsuitable for that role.

At the end of November Nos 1611 and 1612 Anti-Aircraft Co-operation Flights arrived from Langham, with Henleys, Tiger Moths, a Hurricane and an Oxford Mk I. These had originally been part of No. 1 AACU which had been based at Bircham Newton earlier in the war, and had subsequently worked with No. 5 Heavy Anti-Aircraft Practice Camp at Weybourne and No. 11 Light Anti-Aircraft Practice Camp at Stiffkey.

---

[14] The Anglo-American landings in French NW Africa in November 1942.
[15] Wilkins, Hugh: letter to author 10/9/91.

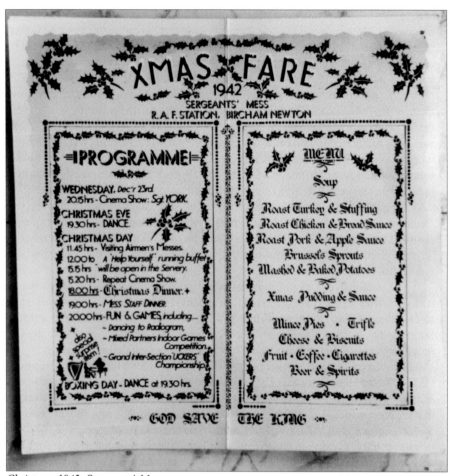

Christmas 1942, Sergeants' Mess.

At the start of December the Flights were disbanded and re-formed as No. 695 Squadron.

Anti-shipping strikes by No. 320 Squadron continued into December. An attack against shipping by a Hudson off the Frisian Islands on the 7th ended in failure owing to the inexperience of the bomb-aimer in handling the bomb-release mechanism. The squadron was often acting in conjunction with No. 407 Squadron based at Docking, as on 23 December, when one No. 407 aircraft acted as the 'Rooster' for eight No. 320 aircraft in pursuit of an enemy convoy north of Ijmuiden. Unfortunately, the single 'Rooster' aircraft failed to return from the operation.

In early February 1943 No. 415 Squadron RCAF was on detachment at Docking, its official base being at Thorney Island. 'The Four Hundred and Fightin' Fifteenth', as they became known, were equipped with the obsolete Hampden, a type which had been withdrawn from Bomber Command owing to its inadequacy in the daylight bombing role and vulnerability to enemy fighters. The conversion of the Hampden to a torpedo-bomber for Coastal Command did nothing to improve its performance and it lived up to its nickname of 'Hambone' or the 'Flying Suitcase'. In January the squadron had been presented with its official badge by the AOC No. 16 Group, which depicted a swordfish striking at its prey, with the motto 'Ad Metam' ('To the Mark').[16]

On 4 February a Hampden had overshot and ground-looped at Docking. Another Hampden (AE435) crashed on take-off on the 18th from Docking on its way to an anti-shipping strike, with the loss of the crew[17]. However, five aircraft did carry out the patrol, located a convoy and attacked a 4,000-ton merchant vessel. Flying Officer A. Brenner and his crew, Flight Sergeant Rowe, and Sergeants Vautier and Glass launched a torpedo in the face of heavy anti-aircraft fire and the vessel was later reported to be on fire. The Hampden was seriously damaged with compass and W/T useless and the port engine on fire, but the crew were uninjured. Eventually the aircraft ditched and sank but the crew got into a dinghy. They were in the water for forty hours until spotted by a Walrus amphibian, which picked them up. Flying Officer Brenner and his crew later returned to the squadron.[18]

Towards the end of the month No. 320 Squadron were flying *Rovers*, armed low level shipping searches with no specific target, but often encountering enemy E-Boats with mixed success. A No. 521 Squadron Mosquito DZ475 went missing after a patrol on 25 February, and on 5 March Mosquito DZ362 crashed into the sea as a result of enemy action on a *Pampa* patrol. The pilot, Pilot Officer Hatton, was rescued but Flight Sergeant Bartolotti was posted missing, presumed killed.

By the middle of March 1943 No. 320 Squadron was preparing to move out to Methwold and re-assignment to No. 2 Group Bomber Command. Within a few days Whitley VIIs of No. 53 Squadron moved in from Docking for just over four weeks before leaving for Thorney Island. At the end of the month No. 521 Squadron was once again split into Flights, with No. 1401 remaining at Bircham Newton and Docking and No. 1409 Flight moving to Oakington to join Bomber Command. The ever-deepening penetration raids of Bomber Command by early 1943 required accurate met. forecasting. On 1 September No. 521 Squadron re-formed at Docking.

An important phase in the operational history of Bircham Newton had ended with the departure of No. 320 Squadron. As mentioned before the Beaufighter Wings were going to bear the brunt of anti-shipping work from other airfields, but the ever-expanding and vital tasks of ASR and Met. patrols would continue for some time to come.

---

[16] *Swordfish: the Story of 415 Squadron* p11.
[17] WOII P.B. Campbell (pilot), WOII Z.M. Niblock (WOp/AG), WOII R.E. Vokey (WOp/AG), F/O K.R. Maffre (Obs.) †.
[18] *Swordfish*, p12.

CHAPTER 11

'ONE OF OUR AIRCRAFT IS MISSING...'
March to December 1943

'To See and Be Seen'
(Motto of No. 279 (ASR) Squadron)

'We detrained at Docking Station, a small deserted branch line place, in a steady drizzle which didn't do much for our spirits, and were taken by three-tonner to an apparently deserted dispersal on the north side of the airfield where we were ensconced in Nissen huts.....'
(Air Cadet I. R. Dick on arrival at cadet camp at Bircham Newton, summer 1943)

No. 407 'Demon' Squadron had finally left Norfolk for Skitten, Caithness, in February 1943 and in the meantime No. 53 Squadron was using the opportunity at Bircham Newton for training, having recently re-equipped with the Armstrong Whitworth Whitley VII. Formerly stationed in Trinidad, the squadron had finally retired its Hudsons, one of the last ones being delivered to Eastleigh on 15 March. There is still some debate about the squadron identification code carried by the Whitleys. Jock Manson, No. 53 Squadron historian, takes up the story:

'At the beginning of 1943, Coastal Command ordered their squadrons to remove their codes for security reasons (the Germans had 'sussed' the system). Our Hudsons were still making their way back to the UK from detachment in Trinidad and still operating the 'PZ' code. The Squadron Operations Record Book for the Whitley period is pretty sparse and the aircraft are referred to in the Form 540 as "Whitley 'B'" etc. All of this would seem to suggest that the Whitleys carried single-letter codes.......53's next proper code ('FH') was not applied to its Liberators until around June, 1944.'[1]

Bircham Newton was considered too short an airfield for Whitleys to operate successfully so there were doubts about the move from Docking in early March, which unfortunately seemed justified by events, since on 17 March Whitley BD425, with Sergeant Milligan as the pilot, overshot the landing in a cross wind while ferrying the aircraft, the undercarriage collapsed and the fuselage broke in two. On the 26th, the squadron had its only fatal accident at Bircham when Whitley EB331/U captained by Sergeant Kirby failed to return from a navigational exercise. The following day a rescue launch picked up the body of one of the crew members, Sergeant Matthews, and a medical examination revealed the cause of death due to splinters, so the loss was presumed to have been the result of enemy action.[2]

---

[1] Manson, J.M.C.: letter to author 15/8/92.
[2] Ibid.

There was another mishap on 15 April when Flight Lieutenant Sutton overshot on landing his Whitley after returning from a navigational exercise. The undercarriage collapsed but luckily there were no injuries on this occasion. On the 28th the squadron finally moved to Thorney Island.

On 17 April an ASR search by a No. 280 Squadron Anson resulted in the aircraft making a forced landing four miles south of Wells, once again with no resulting injuries. ASR work was becoming increasingly vital with the massive build-up in the Allied bombing campaign, both of Bomber Command and the US Eighth Air Force. Inevitably there were more ditchings in the sea, and therefore training became essential both for the rescuers and for the aircrews who might have to be rescued. Thus one officer from each station was selected to undergo training at the School of Air Sea Rescue and there was some evidence that the training had been worthwhile in the saving of more lives, for example in the rescue of a Halifax crew on 5 May which had ditched 50 miles east of Spurn Head. A No. 279 Squadron aircraft successfully dropped the lifeboat and the survivors were able to board it.[3]

Such work was not without considerable risk as the ASR Hudsons could often be easy targets for marauding enemy fighters, as events of 15 May demonstrated. A No. 279 Squadron Hudson was attacked by a Dornier during a sea search and in the encounter the rear gunner, Flight Sergeant Rusby, was killed by a round entering the rear of the turret. However, the aircraft was able to return to base. Now that No. 279 Squadron had become fully operational a ceremony was held at the station in April in which the Squadron Crest was presented by the AOC No. 16 Group, 'To See and Be Seen'.

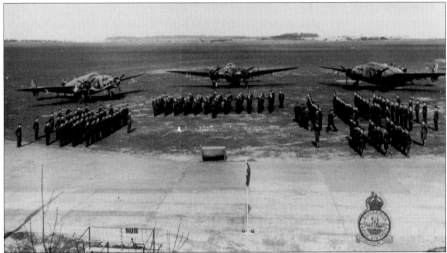

Presentation of No. 279 Sqn crest by AOC No. 16 Group Coastal Command, April 1943. Motto 'To See and Be Seen'. Photo taken from top of No. 2 hangar with Hudsons in background. (S.H. Daly)

---

[3] Ashworth, Chris: *RAF Coastal Command 1936-69* pp174-5.

Hampdens of No. 415 Squadron were in Norfolk on detachment from their home base at Thorney Island, operating mainly from Docking. On 24 May they were working with No. 1401 Met. Flight on *Rhombus* patrols. During the last week in May a succession of bombing raids by Allied aircraft on German targets led to one of the busiest periods yet experienced by No. 279 Squadron, in which the unit contributed to the rescue of no less than 156 aircrew. Aircraft from the squadron, which was commanded by Wing Commander B. G. Corry DFC, were able to pinpoint downed United States Army Air Force B-17 Flying Fortresses and drop *Lindholmes*, with the rescues being completed with the help of the Walrus amphibian or nearby friendly vessels.

A sea search on 1 June was for a missing British Overseas Airways Corporation (BOAC) Liberator which had been shot down by a Ju88 while on a flight from Lisbon. One of the passengers was the film star Leslie Howard but sadly no trace of the aircraft was ever found.

It has already been mentioned (see Ch. 10) that Coastal Command was looking for more suitable aircraft for ASR work and that the Armstrong Whitworth Albemarle had been evaluated but without success. The Anson was judged clearly inadequate for long-range search work, and Hudsons were in short supply. The Vickers Wellington was considered but in the end its heavier contemporary the Vickers Warwick was selected, and that aircraft was converted for ASR duties in early 1943 designed to carry two *Lindholmes*. Thus the Warwick Training Unit was formed at Docking on 28 June to train aircrews.

A successful ASR was co-ordinated by a Hudson of No. 279 Squadron for a Hampden of No. 1401 Met. Flight on 18 July. The aircraft was reported to have ditched after a *Rhombus* and sent out an SOS which had been picked up at Bircham Newton. In the sea search that followed an oil patch was sighted along with K-type dinghies tied together with four aircrew who appeared unharmed. The Hudson dropped smoke floats at intervals and eventually a high-speed launch (HSL) headed towards the spot and the rescue was completed just after midday. It was around this time that a young cadet in the Air Training Corps, I. R. Dick (later Squadron Leader), was present at Bircham Newton during a cadet camp:

'I went to Bircham Newton with a group from No. 1992 Squadron (Camberwell) ATC. We detrained at Docking Station, a small deserted branch line place, in a steady drizzle which didn't do much for our spirits, and were taken by three-tonner to an apparently deserted dispersal on the north side of the airfield where we were ensconced in Nissen huts. It was a long walk round the edge to the NAAFI for a 'char and wad' - if you had the money for these delights! The airfield was all grass and came under Coastal Command, being equipped with Warwicks (with their row of aerials on the roof), Beaufighters, Hudsons and Mosquitoes - one at least being the Tsetse version with its six-pounder cannon. I got a flight in a Hudson on an air-test and was rather worried by the flapping tail-plane! The interior of the aircraft was entirely bare......One day the cry went up: "Stranger in the circuit" as a Stirling circled the field. Aircraft were hurriedly cleared from the perimeter to allow for an obstruction-free approach. The Stirling made a perfect three-point landing, rolling to a stop in the middle of the field and all the off-duty aircrew gathered on the tarmac to see who the expert pilot was. The door opened and down the ladder stepped a pin-up style young blonde. Thinking she was but a passenger, one of the assembled crowd asked where the pilot was. The "mirage" assured the group that she was the pilot and there was no one else on board! She was just delivering some equipment and was soon away, her take-off being as perfect as her landing.........'[4]

A dramatic rescue took place on 26 July when two Hudsons of No. 279 Squadron sighted a downed American B-17 Flying Fortress with two dinghies containing ten men. A lifeboat was dropped and the men climbed aboard, a 'fix' was obtained and an HSL contacted. The lifeboat was taken in tow and the rescue completed.

The Warwick Training Unit had a minor setback on 13 August when one of its aircraft, BV276, caught fire at Docking. There were no reports of casualties. The unit was engaged in trials in the dropping of the Mark I Lifeboat and the aircraft were later to be equipped with the Mark IA or Mark II Lifeboat, ASV radar and better fuel capacity. No. 280 Squadron began replacing its old Ansons for Warwicks during August at Langham, before leaving for Thorney Island on 25 September. The Warwick Training unit was redesignated the Air-Sea Rescue Training Unit (ASRTU) on 13 October and moved to Thornaby on the 20th.

An indication of the dangers faced by these ASR aircraft from enemy action, let alone the difficulties and hazards of the flying conditions, is illustrated by the events of 24 August. Two No. 279 Squadron Hudsons were out on a sea search and located a dinghy for which a lifeboat was dropped. Two Stirlings had joined the circuit as well, circling the dinghy, but the friendly aircraft were joined by two Me110s. One Hudson, 'R', was attacked and shot down, its crew being posted missing (Flight Sergeant Neil and Flying Officer Whapham). Before long, the ASR Hudsons were accompanied by Mustang or Spitfire fighters to provide some protection from patrolling enemy aircraft.

A sea search for a ditched Lancaster resulted in a successful rescue on 4 September when a dinghy with five occupants was sighted. A *Lindholme* was dropped and the crew saved. One of the best days for the rescue squadrons was on 6 September when a total of 131 aircrew were saved, mostly from downed American B-17 Flying Fortresses which had run out of fuel on return from a raid on Stuttgart.

A Gladiator of No. 521 Squadron made a forced landing near King's Lynn on 12 September after a *THUM* sortie. The pilot was reported to be unhurt.

The squadron had another loss on 10 October when a Hampden (L4204 coded TE-L) crashed on take-off from Docking in poor visibility on a *Rhombus* patrol. The aircraft apparently hit a gun post. There was no mention of any casualties. The following month on 8 November a Gladiator from the same squadron (N2309) crashed in a forced landing at Magdalen Road, King's Lynn.

The work of No. 279 Squadron continued throughout the rest of 1943. It had been proposed that the squadron re-equip with Warwicks in place of its Hudsons but

---

[4] Dick, S/Ldr (Ret'd) I.R.: letter to author 9/8/91.

the plan was abandoned in favour of forming a new squadron of Warwicks, No. 281, at Thornaby. It was essential to improve the capacity and effectiveness of the ASR squadrons as the Allied bombing campaign was reaching a new climax with the Battle of Berlin which lasted from November 1943 until March 1944. This inevitably resulted in more aircraft ditching in the sea after being crippled by flak or night fighters, and the ASR squadrons certainly rose to the challenge, even as the weather deteriorated in December with fog and gales to contend with. During that month No. 279 Squadron flew 168 hours by day and ten by night. It was estimated at the end of 1943 that the ASR squadrons together had saved 1,684 aircrew out of 5,466 presumed to have ditched in the sea, and the achievement attracted the special commendation of Lieutenant General I. C. Eaker, commanding the US Eighth Air Force, in a letter of 24 December addressed to the AOC Coastal Command.[5]

Meanwhile in the middle of November No. 415 Squadron RCAF had arrived from Thorney Island with its Wellington XIIIs and Fairey Albacore I biplanes and on 1 December Nos 1611 and 1612 Anti-Aircraft Co-operation Flights were disbanded to form No. 695 Squadron. This new squadron would operate at Bircham Newton for the remainder of the war on anti-aircraft co-operation and target-tug duties in the Norfolk area, equipped with a total of 24 aircraft including Westland Lysanders, Hawker Henley IIIs, Hurricane IICs, Miles Martinet Mk Is, a Tiger Moth and later various Marks of the Spitfire and the Vultee Vengeance IV. The squadron liaised with various Royal Artillery units between Lowestoft and Weybourne and with the RAF Regiment defence unit at Langham.

ASR patrols, training, and meteorological work would play an ever-greater part in the life of Bircham Newton as 1943 ended but the new year would witness probably the final offensive chapter in the history of the station, with the arrival of No. 415 Squadron for a prolonged stay. There was much vital work to be done but the grass airfield was no longer suitable for the operational use of the larger, heavier aircraft coming into service. However the units at the airfield were about to play a part in the preparations for what would become the decisive campaign of the European war during 1944, Operation *Overlord*.

---

[5] Ashworth p176.

CHAPTER 12

HITTING THE SHIPS, CADET CAMP AND MET. FLIGHTS
January to July 1944

'.....The chances of hitting the enemy personally are nil, and the chances of getting the greatly desired "Gong" are just about the same.....'
(Wing Commander C. G. Ruttan, CO of No. 415 Squadron (RCAF))

The arrival of No. 415 Squadron RCAF opened another chapter in the offensive strike capability present at the east coast airfield. The anti-shipping campaign of 1942 and 1943 in which squadrons from the station had played such a gallant part, in the face of appalling losses, had begun to yield positive results by the end of 1943. The war against the U-Boat was gradually being won in 1943 in the Battle of the Atlantic thus ensuring Britain's survival, but there was still the need to guarantee Allied supremacy in the Channel and the North Sea if there was to be any chance of launching the invasion as planned in 1944. Apart from protecting our own coastal shipping trade, every means had to be found to bear down upon German shipping which was so crucial to the enemy war effort. Firstly, the passages through the Channel and North Sea were vital sea routes for U-Boats and naval units seeking access to the Atlantic and then returning for replenishment to home ports. Secondly, the use of the French, Dutch and Scandinavian ports enabled the Germans to maintain the flow of essential raw materials for her war effort and civilian population. A successful Allied campaign in this theatre would effectively mean a blockade in which Germany would be land-locked.

There was some evidence that the anti-shipping campaigns were paying off. The Germans had lost over a quarter of their available merchant tonnage, and the flow of trade from the ports of the occupied countries was being disrupted. It was only in the Baltic that the Germans had more freedom to operate their merchant shipping. One example of the problems was the reduction in the iron ore trade from Sweden to the Dutch ports, which forced the Germans to import their raw materials from Spain via the infinitely more difficult and dangerous route through the Bay of Biscay. Nor were the enemy obtaining any respite at all from RAF Coastal Command, the newly-established Beaufighter Strike Wings at North Coates in 1942 and Wick in 1943 were seeing to that, delivering devastating fire power to any German convoys they could find.

A new threat had emerged in the Channel and North Sea in the shape of the E-Boats, fast flotillas of torpedo boats that could operate flexibly and under cover of darkness if necessary, a considerable danger to our convoys. This was a challenge taken up by No. 415 Squadron in Operation *Deadly* towards the end of 1943 and early 1944, first at Thorney Island and continuing at Bircham Newton. The squadron had ceased to operate Hampdens in September but as Beaufighters would not be available until early 1944, Fairey Albacores and modified former Bomber Command Vickers

Vickers Wellington GR XIII MF639, with ASV aerials, No. 415 (RCAF) Sqn early 1944. (Ray C. Sturtivant)

Wellingtons were delivered. The Wellington Mark XIIIs and one Mark Ic were equipped with ASV Mark II[1], GEE (a navigational aid), and VHF R/T. Firstly, enemy forces would be located by radar, and a GEE position transmitted to Chatham HQ and relayed to our own vessels, then the Wellington would continue to shadow the enemy and assist our own intercepting ships by means of VHF R/T. The Albacores had ASV Mark II and VHF R/T and were also armed with six 250-lb bombs. They would receive radar information about the location of enemy vessels and when in the air be directed towards their target by VHF R/T. Although the Albacore was slow it could make its attack approach by shallow glide, and hopefully surprise the enemy.[2]

The first Operation *Deadly* sorties were flown on 5 November 1943 from Thorney Island. Then, on the 15th, the squadron moved its Wellington Flight to Bircham Newton, the Servicing Echelon to Docking and the Albacore Flight to Manston. This rather complicated arrangement was justified on the grounds that these various units were operating different roles but the dispersal of the parts caused a considerable headache to squadron command and administration. Under the command of Wing Commander C. G. Ruttan, Operation *Deadly* patrols were flown by Wellingtons from Bircham Newton on the 15th, 19th, and 27th November, continuing into December. These early operations achieved little success. Few targets were sighted and there were failures of the ASV and VHF radios. Patrols were abandoned on several occasions, although during December the squadron flew a total of 405 hours by night. There was clearly a lot of work to be done as the New Year 1944 dawned.

---

[1] Air-to-Surface Vessel (radar).
[2] *Swordfish: The Story of 415 Squadron* pp18-19.

The ASR work continued into January 1944. Four Hudsons of No. 279 Squadron were dispatched to a location where a Bomber Command aircraft had been reported ditching in the sea in flames, after a raid on Berlin on the night of 1/2 January. One aircraft was equipped with an airborne lifeboat. Because of severe cross-winds only half the search area was covered, and the aircraft returned to Docking with no success reported.

On the 5th and 14th there were Operation *Deadly* patrols by Wellingtons of No. 415 Squadron but little was achieved except radar contacts on the 14th. On neither occasion were the No. 415 Wellingtons able to divert British MTBs (Motor Torpedo Boats) or Beaufighters to the targets which presented themselves on radar. Wing Commander Ruttan expressed his frustration to RCAF Overseas HQ about the problems of his command, two different aircraft types operating from five different bases, Albacores from Manston and Thorney Island and Wellingtons from Bircham Newton, Docking and Sculthorpe. In addition there was a poor standard of training, insufficient and inadequate aircraft, with the Wellingtons at this stage carrying no offensive weaponry. Morale in the squadron was also a problem owing partly to pressure from No. 16 Group to discipline crews which had made errors often due to lack of training or experience, for example when aircraft were forced to abandon a sortie owing to equipment or other failure. Wing Commander Ruttan continued:

'All crews, ground and air, now feel that a system of "Gestapo" work is being carried out and that it is only for them to make one small error and 16 Group, or any others under it, have them on parade. The chances of hitting the enemy personally are nil, and chances of getting the greatly desired "Gong" are just about the same. In other words, they feel that they are not getting sufficient credit for the great amount of work that they are doing.'[3]

A major setback to the squadron was suffered on 20 January when the Albacore of Squadron Leader E. W. Cowan, based at Manston, was lost on an anti-shipping sortie. This was a severe blow to the squadron as Squadron Leader Cowan commanded 'A' Flight.

On the 15th Hudsons of No. 279 Squadron joined Warwicks of No. 280 Squadron and other aircraft on a sea search following the Bomber Command raid on Brunswick which had resulted in 38 aircraft being lost. Nothing was found. Further sea searches followed on the 23rd owing to heavy bomber losses the previous night. Again, nothing was found by the four No. 279 Squadron Hudsons dispatched. On the 26th there was another abortive sea search, this time for a downed Beaufighter of No. 236 Squadron from North Coates. Three Hudsons failed to make any contacts on the 29th on a search after bombers had been heavily mauled on the the night of the 28th. The results of the bomber offensive was often in evidence at Docking, for example, after the Berlin raid on 30/31 January when a No. 626 Squadron Lancaster crash-landed at the airfield already severely damaged. The wireless operator was killed but the rest of the crew survived badly shaken.

---

[3] DG Hist: National Defence HQ, Ottawa, Canada. Also referred to in *Swordfish* p20.

On a lighter note No. 415 Squadron held a social evening on 4 February when the OC of 'B' Flight and aircrew captains entertained the ground servicing personnel. Two kegs of beer were provided and the 'smokes' supplied by the Auxiliary Services. The location was the Airmen's Auxiliary Services Hut at Docking. February proved a more successful month for the squadron. *Deadly* patrols continued but there were also *Gilbey* sorties, which involved using ASV to direct torpedo or bomb-carrying Beaufighters to enemy targets off the Dutch coast. Sadly two Wellingtons were lost on operations, Flight Lieutenant J. F. Acer and his crew of seven on the 7th and Squadron Leader M. W. Gibson, commander of 'B' Flight, and his crew of six on the 8th. Distress signals were received but the crews were never found. An additional factor that must have given pause for thought were the German V1 flying bombs that were reported heading through patrol areas at approximately the same altitude as the Wellingtons.

On 21 February the Hudsons of No. 48 Squadron flew in from Gibraltar for three days, preparatory to moving to their new base at Down Ampney in Wiltshire to convert to Dakotas and a new transport role.

A sea search on the 22nd proved fruitful resulting in the rescue of ten US Army Air Force aircrew from two dinghies lashed together, thanks to the dropping of a *Lindholme*. The activity during February is illustrated by the operational flying hours of the month, No. 279 Squadron's total being 467 hours by day, 10 by night; for No. 415 Squadron the total (including those for detachments) was 315 hours; and No. 521 Squadron based at Docking flew 206 hours by day, nil by night.

On 1 March No. 233 Squadron flew in from Gosport in Hampshire with Hudsons for a few days before converting to the Dakota at their new base, Blakehill Farm in Wiltshire.

For No. 415 Squadron, March proved to be an active and successful month. Whilst on detachment at North Coates with the Wellingtons on 1 March, Pilot Officer K. T. Ashfield attacked a merchant vessel on a *Deadly* patrol which had already been hit by Beaufighters and the vessel was set alight. On the 5th Flying Officer R. H. Watt and crew lead three 'Torbeaus'[4] of No. 254 Squadron (based at North Coates) in a *Gilbey* patrol to a convoy of a merchant vessel and three 'M' Class minesweepers north of Schiermonnikoog. The ships were illuminated with flares, torpedo attacks made and the merchant vessel was left burning. On the 10th the same crew were leading Torbeaus of No. 236 Squadron, also based at North Coates, on another *Gilbey* and two merchant vessels were attacked north of Borkum Island. One of the vessels was damaged. Other operations included armed reconnaissance flights which were flown by the Wellingtons from Docking in the direction of the Dutch coast but these mostly proved uneventful, apart from occasional flak directed at the aircraft from E- and R-Boats[5].

---

[4] Torpedo-carrying Beaufighters.

[5] E-Boats: small, fast craft capable of speeds up to 40 knots, armed with torpedoes and light guns, and frequently used in mine-laying operations. R-Boats: slower than E-Boats and used for mine-laying.

The squadron was visited on the 11th by the AOC Coastal Command, Air Chief Marshal Sir W. Sholto Douglas, who took the opportunity to address aircrew personnel and discuss policy matters with Wing Commander Ruttan.

The ASR work continued with varying degrees of success. There was a successful rescue on 6 March in which three survivors were picked up by a Walrus. On the 19th four Hudsons of No. 279 Squadron, one carrying an airborne lifeboat, went in search of a downed Pathfinder Mosquito but nothing was seen. A tragic incident followed on the 23rd when a high speed launch from Lowestoft had been reported on fire and the rescued aircrew had taken to a rubber lifeboat which had then been shot up by marauding fighters. A *Lindholme* was dropped but the container failed to open. A second drop was made by a Liberator but the container opened 100 yards downwind and the survivors failed to reach it. A few days later, on the 26th, a Hudson of No. 279 Squadron (AM554 'E') crashed shortly after take-off on its way to investigate the report of a crashed aircraft of No. 100 Group. The aircraft was destroyed by fire but the crew were lucky to escape. The following day another Hudson was dispatched to a position where there had been a reported aircraft ditching on the night of 26/27 March. A marine marker was dropped and wreckage and bodies were found. A *Lindholme* was dropped but there was no sign of life and eventually an HSL salvaged the lifeboat and picked up the bodies.

April 1944 was a successful month for the Wellington Flight of No. 415 Squadron, with a total of 39 Operation *Deadly* patrols, four *Gilbey* and 22 armed reconnaissance patrols completed, the latter along enemy convoy routes close to the Dutch coast between the Hook of Holland and Den Helder. However, during the month enemy ships were sighted on only one of the *Deadly* patrols, which tended to be flown over open water and enemy shipping, very sensibly, usually clung to the coastline. The *Gilbey* patrols were more eventful, mostly flown from North Coates, as on 1 April when Pilot Officer G. C. Krahn took off to direct 'Torbeaus' to a convoy of 22 enemy ships north of Langeoog Island. The outcome was that one ship was torpedoed.

Armed reconnaissance patrols often produced results as shipping was more plentiful in 'protected' waters and on ten occasions during the month vessels were attacked or sighted. A typical sortie was on 8 April when Flying Officer D. M. Brotherhood took off from Docking and encountered enemy shipping north of Terschelling Island. Braving heavy flak the Wellington crew were unable to pinpoint a suitable target in the thick haze and deteriorating weather, and eventually the bombs were jettisoned and the aircraft returned to Docking. There was better luck for Pilot Officer K. T. Ashfield on the 19th when he attacked enemy shipping near Zandvoort. Two vessels were hit by bombs and damage was claimed. Pilot Officer Krahn continued the run of good fortune on the 23rd when he intercepted a convoy of 11 ships north-east of Ameland. A direct hit was claimed on one 'medium motor vessel'. Further success was claimed on the 27th when Flying Officer R. H. Watt DFC attacked a convoy of ten enemy R-Boats near Den Helder. Five enemy aircraft appeared and the attack was broken off but two ships were claimed as damaged.

By the end of the month *Deadly* patrols were being replaced by 'cross-over' patrols which covered the open water of the English Channel between Brighton and the Isle of Wight. In the meantime, No. 415 Squadron's proposed transfer to Bomber Command was delayed because of the need to concentrate all available air power in the Channel area to defeat the German E-Boat menace, particularly in the run-up to D-Day. The only other development was that the Albacore detachment at Manston was now to transfer to Thorney Island.

AIR TRAINING CORPS' CAMP 1944

A fascinating snapshot of Bircham Newton life in Spring 1944 was supplied by Charles Hall, the aviation cartoonist 'Holly', from a diary he compiled at the station at ATC Camp from 8 to 29 April. This includes not only facts about daily routine but also lists of aircraft and units present, with diagrams, in the sort of detail only to be expected from a 16 year-old air cadet obsessed with everything to do with aircraft and flying. He counted 108 aircraft present of 33 different types ranging from Gladiators to Fortresses. The Hudsons of No. 279 ASR Squadron were 'mostly coloured all-white apart from camouflaged top surfaces' and there were several RAF Coastal Command Fortress IIAs being serviced, having arrived direct from the Azores (from 206 Squadron). 'We homed in on one B-17E FL451, coded 1-A, which was nicknamed *Lucy 'lastic'*, with nose art depicting a young lady with red knickers at half-mast!'[6]

Beaufighters were inspected, presumably awaiting delivery to one of the Strike Wings, fitted with rocket rails, torpedo crutches and four 20 mm cannon. Four Gloster Gladiators were encountered from the Met. squadron, K7972, K8043, N5621 and N5902. The 0800 hrs daily take-off by a Gladiator was noted, on its way to a met. patrol. The 'Black Beauties of Bircham', or Albacores of No. 415 Squadron with squadron code NH were a spectacle with their matt black finish for night operations. These aircraft were at the station for servicing, their main base being Thorney Island. Also noticed were some target-towing aircraft of No. 695 Squadron, Hurricane IIDs, Martinets and 18 Henleys. There was a solitary Vickers Warwick Mark I (BV316) which was being checked for possible defects in tyres and wheels as a result of heavy landings. Much information was unofficially gathered from various unsuspecting ground crews, no doubt with the aid of some boyhood guile and a mixture of hero-worship and flattery.

Two old aircraft were found in a corner of a dusty hangar, a Piper Cub Sports Model in RAF camouflage but with a civil registration G-AFIZ. The other was less familiar and there was no way a keen young ATC cadet was going to be persuaded that the aircraft was an old Tiger Moth, when he knew it was not. A shilling was wagered that it was a Tiger Moth, some research was rapidly carried out and the machine's true identity discovered, an Avro Avian G-ABEE which had not been flown for at least two years! The wager was won by the cadets and 12 pint glasses of still lemonade were bought from the NAAFI!

---

[6] This aircraft belonged to 206 Sqn (previously at Bircham Newton), and had been flown from Lagens in the Azores to Bircham Newton, prior to the re-equipment of the squadron with Liberators at St Eval.

Diary extracts on pages 159-62 from the late Charles Hall (the cartoonist 'Holly'), Air Training Corps' cadet summer camp, Bircham Newton, 1944. (Reproduced by kind permission of his widow Mrs Victoria Hall).

BIRCHAM NEWTON

APRIL 8th - 29th '44

See
Ap.¹⁶13 '84

Base for 279 AIR-SEA-RESCUE Squadron using Lockheed Hudsons.

Hudsons are Mk. III, V & VI.

III — no cooling gills. no spinners.

V — Has " " Spinners.

VI — Has " " No spinners.

Nearly all fitted with Radar (A.S.V.-2) and a few are fitted to carry lifeboats. These airborne lifeboats, carried only under the Mk III Hudon are 22 ft. long & six feet wide.

Camouflage of Hudsons.

Mostly all - white (dirty) except for

— J (Black un/s) EW 514

159

extreme top decking of fuselage,
which is green & grey.
A few are camouflaged on
fuselage sides and all top-surfaces,
with pale green undersides.
One has black undersides.

168

HUDSON REGISTRATION.

415 Sqn. ALBACORES.

These came to Bircham Newton, from another station for servicing. All had Radar, and wing-racks besides torpedo or mine crutches. They had flame-trap exhausts and were painted matt-black all over.

ALBACORE I — REGISTRATION.

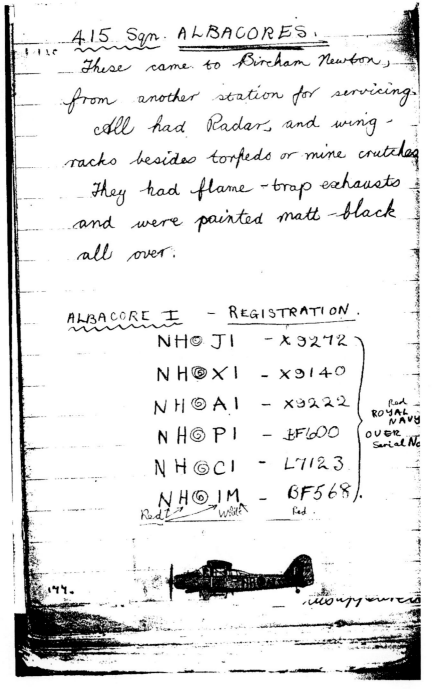

NH⊙J1	— X9272	
NH⊙X1	— X9140	
NH⊙A1	— X9222	Red ROYAL NAVY OVER Serial No
NH⊙P1	— BF600	
NH⊙C1	— L7123	
NH⊙1M	— BF568	

Red ← → White   Red.

144.

some Wellingtons was supposed to house a camera for torpedo-bombing:.

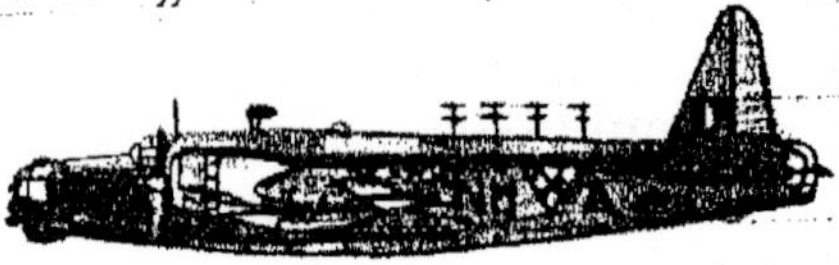

415 Squadron (Canadian) of Coastal Command Wellingtons from Docking.

WELLINGTON Before ~~XIII~~ – REGISTRATION.

NH ⑥ A	JA 635	Bulge under nose.
NH ⑥ B	HZ 649	
NH ⑥ D	MF 213	Bulge.
NH ⑥ G	HZ756	
NH ⑥ H	HZ 659	
NH ⑥ J	HZ721	
NH ⑥ L	HZ653	
NH ⑥ M	HZ650 (Mk 8)	
NH ⑥ O	HZ644	

NH in pale blue – individual letter

187. in red. All had RADAR (ASV.3.)

181. [illegible] in [illegible] perspex

The highlight of the camp was a flight to Coltishall in Hudson Mk VI FK450. 'For take-off we were asked to go forward and sit on the main spar, but for landing, we were sent to the rear end..... "otherwise the b..... tail will never stay on the ground."' There was a visit to Docking to inspect the Wellington Mk XIIIs of No. 415 RCAF Squadron, bristling with aerials. A reminder if ever one was needed of the daily operational routine came with a Tannoy broadcast one morning which stated: 'As a result of a successful strike by two Wellingtons from this station, a direct hit was obtained on a large enemy vessel.' The Wellingtons were visited again 'to stand in awe and look for non-existent flak damage'.[7]

Another cadet present at the camp was Edwin A. Shackleton, of No. 786 Squadron, Ipswich Northgate School. He recalled the Hudson flight described but also flights in Hudson MkV AM848 and in Ventura MkV FP571. He also remembered the episode of the Piper Cub and Avro Avian.[8]

MET. FLIGHTS

Lockheed Venturas of No. 521 Squadron based at Docking were flying *Rhombus* sorties over the North Sea in co-operation with No. 519 Squadron based at Skitten in Caithness. Flying Officer (later Flight Lieutenant) D. L. Turner of No. 519 Squadron described how the system worked:

'This route was codenamed *Rhombus*. There were two sorties per day, one sortie being flown by each squadron. The route was from Bircham Newton or Docking or Langham to a point off the north Danish coast and thence to Wick or its satellite Skitten, or vice-versa. It was a "shuttle" run, taking a crew two days. For example, a No. 519 Squadron aircraft would fly from Skitten to Docking one day, then back to Skitten (on the reverse route) the next. On the same two days (at a different time), a No. 521 aircraft would fly from Docking to Skitten, returning the second day. This shuttle arrangement started on 5 March 1944 when my crew flew the run to Docking (from Skitten) in a Ventura GR.V (FN961). We returned the next day (6 March). As far as I know, this arrangement continued until the end of the war in Europe.......We (my crew) did not fly many *Rhombus* sorties, since we were, in general, assigned to the *Recipe* route, up the Norwegian Sea from Wick/Skitten.'[9] Flying Officer Turner's captain was R. G. 'Bob' MacNeil who recalled their first *Rhombus* sortie of 5 March from his diary:

'Tuesday, 29 February: briefed at Wick for first *Rhombus*. March 1, March 2, March 3, March 4 - snow, snow and more snow. On the 4th all hands turned out to shovel the mess. We cleared the top end of a short runway, to where it joined our main runway, thus creating a dog-leg......

---

[7] Hall, Charles: letters to author July/Aug. 1991 and extracts from diary. Also article in *Aviation News* 15-28 April 1988.
[8] Shackleton, Edwin A.: letter to author 22/11/91.
[9] Turner, D.L.: letter to author 7/5/92.

'Sunday March 5, awakened at 3.30 a.m. (briefed at Wick last night), to start things off. After breakfast got off deck at 4.55. A bit shaky take-off (crooked runway - see snow clearing). Weather nice near Norway and sunrise beautiful from top of climb. Landed at Docking around 9.00 a.m. (Norm's old squadron is here....He was KIA a couple of weeks ago-Wellington[10]). Looked around the station...weather beautiful down here. Had good quarters tonight. Bathed and shaved before turning in...Tired.

Monday March 6: On the job at 2.30 a.m. Briefed at Bircham Newton. Breakfast. "Ropey" take-off (grass 'drome). At top of climb another beautiful sunrise. Had a fairish glimpse of Norway. Nearly hit Scapa on return. Rec'd eight letters today, more photos from home. Slept five hours after lunch. Had two eggs for supper. Played some poker.....'[11]

Bob MacNeil and his crew flew similar operations on 29/30 June, 8/9, 22/23, and 28/29 September, 8/9 October and 19/20 November. According to his logbook a Hudson was often used for these flights.

Another No. 519 Squadron pilot at the time was Flight Lieutenant Donald MacNeil (no relation of the former) who flew similar sorties from Skitten/Wick from June 1944:

'When we landed at Docking we would get the WAAF MT driver to stop at a pub on the way to Bircham Newton and have a "noggin" or two! We had a 4 a.m. take-off from Wick, landing at Docking around 8.30 - then the day off. We usually went to King's Lynn in the evening, then return next day - take-off from Docking 10 a.m. and back at Wick 12.30.'[12]

COUNTDOWN TO D-DAY

The ASR Squadron, No. 279, was fully engaged in sea searches during May 1944, flying a total of 366 hours by day and night. On 6 May a Hudson had trouble with its port engine on a sea search and was recalled to base, crash landing near West Rudham. The crew were shaken but unhurt.

The Wellington Flight of No. 415 Squadron concentrated on armed reconnaissance patrols and cross-over patrols during May, the latter over the open waters of the English Channel with the intention of preventing E-Boats reconnoitering English coastal areas. On 7 May an armed recce in the area of the Hook of Holland by Pilot Officer K. T. Ashfield was prematurely aborted because the starboard engine failed. As the aircraft lost height to 700 feet Ashfield nursed the machine back to Norfolk, eventually reaching Langham when the port engine failed on the final turn, the aircraft now at 300 feet. There was a forced landing in a ploughed field just after 1 a.m., and the crew were uninjured. The next morning they were shocked to discover that the field where the aircraft landed had 15-foot tree trunks scattered all over it as a precaution against landing by enemy gliders, all of which they had somehow missed!

---

[10] Reference to WO N.C.E. West RCAF of 415 Squadron, with whom Bob had crewed earlier, missing when Wellington of F/Lt Acer went down 7 February (see p156).
[11] MacNeil, R.G. (ex-WOI 519 Sqn): letter to author 5/2/92.
[12] MacNeil, Donald S.: letter to author 10/12/92.

A number of vessels were claimed as damaged as a result of these armed recces, for example on 8 May (two vessels claimed damaged), 9 May (one probably damaged), and 10 May (one probably damaged). The cross-over patrols were largely uneventful because they covered areas mostly avoided by enemy shipping. Patrol 'L' covered a section of the English Channel half way between the Cherbourg Peninsula and the Isle of Wight, extending some 40 miles east and west and about 20 miles wide. Patrol 'M' covered a similar rectangle of about 800 square miles immediately to the east of this area. The two patrols covered the approaches to the English Channel from Swanage almost as far as Beachy Head.

A major problem to contend with during May was the appalling weather which hampered operations and often resulted in early returns to base. Even at Bircham Newton office and ground staffs were shivering in their overcoats and heating was restored to the offices on 16 May! Towards the end of the month better weather returned. Some luck was encountered by Pilot Officers W. M. Cole and G. Mathon, but not of the operational variety, when they bagged half a dozen pheasants one day on an excursion in the countryside. Pheasants have been called 'Norfolk sparrows' for very sound reasons! In the event the two airmen skilfully avoided the attentions of a local police constable and an especially sumptuous dinner was served in the mess the following night, thanks to the King's Sandringham estate! But there were continuing problems for No. 415 Squadron owing to its dispersed parts between Devon and Norfolk, with the Wellington Flights under the control of Coastal Command and the Albacore Flights under Fighter Command. In the meantime preparations continued for the eventual transfer of the squadron to Bomber Command. Among awards for the squadron during that month was a DSO for Wing Commander Ruttan.

June 1944, the invasion month, was the busiest time for all the Coastal Command squadrons, and certainly not least for No. 415, its last full month in Coastal Command and at Bircham Newton. The Germans had anticipated an Allied invasion at some point along the Channel coastline and had assembled a large number of small armed vessels to harass the invasion forces, and then to disrupt the flow of supplies and reinforcements. There was no doubt that this represented a considerable threat to the successful outcome of D-Day on 6 June. The main threat came from E-Boats, R-Boats, modified Tank Landing Craft (TLCs), armed trawlers and other small auxiliary vessels, most of which operated at night. It was the cross-over patrols of the Wellingtons of No. 415 Squadron which yielded most results until the 16th of the month, and no less than five enemy ships sunk were claimed.

On 6/7 June Flying Officer H. L. Parker took off from Docking at 2215 hrs and sighted some three E-Boats off Ventnor in the Isle of Wight. He attacked the group from 1,500 feet and one E-Boat capsized, later claimed as sunk or damaged. The following night three Wellingtons led by Wing Commander Ruttan attacked a group of five E-Boats. One was later claimed to have been sunk. Operations continued on successive nights and on 12/13 June Pilot Officer G. C. Krahn sighted 17 E-Boats in the Ostend area and was ordered to illuminate the target for Beaufighters. There was heavy flak and

Krahn's Wellington was seen to go down with both engines on fire, the sole loss of the month. The same night Flying Officer F. J. Paterson picked up a probable submerged submarine contact off Barfleur. The contact was lost but on a course for base accurate flak was encountered two miles west of Tilbury Docks but luckily no damage was caused. On the 16th the crews of two Wellingtons sighted a Halifax ditching 23 miles off the Dutch coast. One of the pilots, Flying Officer Sheen, switched his IFF[13] to Distress and two Warwicks and two Typhoons were homed to the area, and the Halifax crew were eventually rescued.

From 16 June the squadron concentrated on armed recce patrols as by now the Normandy beachhead was secure. A total of 15 operations of this kind were flown in which a merchant vessel was claimed to have been hit and two E/R-Boats sunk and two more probably damaged. On the 16th and 17th Wellington crews reported seeing individual jet aircraft on cross-over patrols, and flying bombs were sighted on the 18th. A Ju88 attacked a Wellington during an armed recce on the 23rd, a rare event now but fortunately evasive action was taken and no damage sustained.

The transfer of squadron personnel to Bomber Command had now begun, with a quarter of the ground crew leaving the squadron on 9 June. RAF crews of No. 524 Squadron gradually took over the aircraft at Docking before continuing the work of No. 415 at Bircham Newton from 25 July. But the latter unit continued armed recce and cross-over patrols until 12/13 July, six merchant vessels being damaged and two E-Boats probably sunk. Sadly, on the final day of operations Flying Officer R. J. Sheen and his crew failed to return from an armed recce, the day after a Wellington from No. 524 Squadron suffered the same fate.

---

[13] Identification Friend or Foe.

CHAPTER 13

THE FINAL EFFORT
July 1944 to September 1945

'All ranks must realise that for Coastal Command the war goes on as before. We started first we finish last. I call upon all squadrons for a great final effort against our old enemy.....'
(Air Chief Marshal Sir W. Sholto Douglas, AOC-in-C Coastal Command, 5 May 1945: quoted in *Sholto Douglas: Years of Command* by Robert Wright[1])

Throughout the anti-shipping campaigns of 1944 the work of No. 279 (ASR) Squadron and No. 521 (Met.) Squadron continued in roles which were somewhat less dramatic but no less essential for the war effort. Ken Border recalled the period he spent with No. 279 Squadron at Bircham Newton:

'I was posted to No. 279 Squadron at Bircham Newton in the summer of 1944 after completing a Flight Mechanic (Airframe) course at Halton. On this course the section on rigging had been greatly shortened to allow more time on other aspects as it was considered very unlikely that we would ever encounter biplanes unless we were unlucky enough to be posted to an EFTS[2] with Tiger Moths......I travelled by rail to Docking and was picked up by the truck which ran a shuttle between Bircham and Docking satellite airfield, calling at the railway station. As the truck drew near to Bircham the first aircraft that I saw on the dispersals were Gladiators. By this time it was too late to begin the process of booking in, so I was sent to a reception hut on a site on the opposite side of the road for the night. The next morning I started doing the rounds and nobody could (or would) tell me what aircraft the squadron flew and it wasn't until I actually went to the flight office that I found to my relief that it wasn't the Gladiators, which belonged to No. 521 Squadron.

'......279 Squadron was equipped with Hudsons, mostly Mark IIIs, some of which carried lifeboats and they were kept busy in the summer of 1944. I recall life at Bircham being very hectic with little or no leave and that depending on the work load. In one of the 'C' hangars new Mosquitoes and Beaufighters were being modified for the Strike Wings, and several times I organised a lift in a Beaufighter being delivered to North Coates (which was fairly near my home) and each time the 36- or 48-hour pass was cancelled at the last minute.

'....I always understood that concrete runways were not laid at Bircham Newton because of the unstable sub-soil. While I was there the BRC[3] netting track was closed at dusk. Night operations were not permitted except in the most extreme emergency and

---

[1] Quoted by permission of HarperCollins Publishers Ltd.
[2] Elementary Flying Training School.
[3] Presumably 'British Reinforced Concrete Ltd' (author).

the field was inspected each morning by AMWD[4] before any flying could start. No. 279 Squadron maintained night stand-by from Docking and every day just before dusk a Hudson flew there with a rigger and a fitter as well as the aircrew, returning to base the following morning. The squadron had a Blister hangar and Nissen hut on the far side of Docking airfield near the railway line and the crew took rations with them, usually cooking supper in the hut with the rations supplemented by eggs bought from a farmer just across the railway line.'[5]

The routine work of No. 521 (Met.) Squadron continued, with Venturas on *Rhombus* sorties and Gladiators on *Thum* patrols, flying a total of 265 hours during July. One Ventura (FP566) was damaged in a belly-landing near Stanhoe Church on 16 July after its engine cut on landing approach. No. 524 Squadron Wellingtons had taken up the challenge of the anti-shipping offensive, clocking up 425 hours' flying during the month.

In August No. 524 Squadron were flying cross-over patrols, armed reconnaissance and *Gilbey* sorties, an example of the latter being on the 15th when there was an operation with the Beaufighter squadron based at North Coates, No. 254. E-Boats were still very active and high on the target list. A No. 279 Squadron Hudson spun into the sea during a sea search by four aircraft of the squadron on the 19th, a busy month in which the squadron flew a total of 802 hours by day, 13 by night.

By the late summer of 1944 the Allied armies were advancing on the continent and the German threat by sea and air was diminishing, so many of the more routine and social aspects of life on a station like Bircham Newton were becoming more prominent. Early in August, 30 Italian 'Co-operators' arrived for duty from RAF Hednesford. A new extension to the station church was consecrated by the Bishop of Norwich on the 13th and on the 15th leave commenced for all personnel. For entertainment there were two visits by ENSA to put on shows and the usual cinema performances and dances. A WAAF handicraft exhibition was held in Station HQ.

Air Training Corps' camps were held each week during August, being inspected by a succession of VIPs including Air Chief Marshal Sir Arthur Longmore, former AOC Coastal Command, and Air Marshal Sir Patrick Playfair. The numerical strength of personnel at the Station at the end of August was 76 RAF officers and just under 400 other ranks, with WAAF officers totalling eight with eight senior NCOs and 329 other ranks. At the satellite Docking there were 12 RAF officers and just under 100 other ranks. The WAAF complement there was one officer and just under 70 other ranks.

On 1 September there was a sea search for a missing Mustang pilot by a No. 279 Squadron Hudson, the result of which was unreported. The same day a Wellington of No. 524 Squadron (MF234) flew into the sea off Hunstanton after an engine cut but the fate of the crew was not reported. During the month a new unit was formed, the Coastal Command Preparation Pool (CCPP), to evaluate coastal aircraft and armament. The unit's

---

[4] Air Ministry Works Department.
[5] Border, Ken: letter to author 18/1/94.

strength included Beaufighters, Mosquitoes, Wellingtons, Albacores, Fortresses and Halifaxes and it remained at the station until August 1945.

Another unit flew in on the 7th, No. 855 FAA Squadron, with its Avenger IIs from Lee-on-Solent in Hampshire. The squadron flew a number of *Rover* patrols before moving on to Docking on the 14th and Machrihanish on 13 October.

A Gladiator of No. 521 Squadron (N5594) came to grief after hitting a mast in fog after take-off from Docking on 14 September, most probably on its way to a *Thum* patrol. The pattern for September at Bircham Newton seemed to be 'Buoy' patrols, *Rhombus* and *Thum* sorties, ASR searches, armed reconnaissance patrols by Wellingtons of No. 524 Squadron and a succession of *Gilbeys* at the end of the month by the latter unit, in co-operation with Beaufighters from the North Coates Strike Wing.

During the month some 70 additional Italian Co-operators arrived for duty from RAF Hednesford. There was a special Battle of Britain Commemorative parade held at the Parade Ground on the 17th, followed by the march past and salute by the station commander. Notification was received on the 23rd that the station had won the RAF Units Gardens Competition for 1944! Among the many comings and goings of personnel were a number who had previously served at the station, for example, Wing Commander B. G. Corry DFC, formerly CO of No. 279 Squadron, posted at the end of August from HQ No. 16 Group as Wing Commander Flying at Bircham Newton. At the end of September Squadron Leader the Hon. George Bellew MVO returned as station intelligence officer, a post he had held in 1942.

The CCPP at the end of September recorded 24 Beaufighters in, 37 out; six Mosquitoes in, one out; two Wellingtons in, six out; nil Albacores in and four out. By August 1945 the unit had repaired or modified 168 Mosquitoes, 305 Beaufighters, 16 Albacores and ten Swordfish. Station personnel strength at the end of September for Bircham Newton and Docking totalled 2,906 which included 431 RAF and RN officers; nine WAAF officers; 203 senior NCOs RAF and RN (aircrew); nine WAAF senior NCOs; 254 senior NCOs RAF and RN (ground); 1,575 other ranks RAF and RN and 425 other ranks WAAF. Also at the station were 100 Italian Co-operators.

On 1 October another FAA Squadron arrived, this time with Swordfish Mark II from Swingfield in Kent, No. 819. The unit undertook a number of detachments to Belgium until returning to Bircham Newton in early 1945 for disbandment. On 2 October a No. 524 Squadron Wellington failed to returned from an armed reconnaissance. This appears to have been the last loss from operations of a Bircham Newton-based aircraft during the war. The squadron had another setback on the 16th when one of its Wellingtons undershot the runway at Langham while the airfield was shrouded in fog. No report of casualties was recorded. Docking was temporarily out of use at the time as it was waterlogged and operations were diverted to Langham.

Tragedies involving aircraft from other stations still happened from time to time, one example being that of a No. 460 Squadron Lancaster (PB351) which crashed at Houghton Hall on 23 October. The aircraft caught fire and the station fire tender was called out. The deceased personnel were taken to the mortuary. On the 27th a Hudson of

No. 521 Squadron failed to return from a special Met. sortie, but it is not clear under what circumstances the loss occurred.

The end of October 1944 saw the departure of No. 279 Squadron for Thornaby after a prolonged period of service at Bircham Newton. In its time at the station the unit claimed to have rescued or assisted with the rescue of 359 aircrew and 41 seamen. Only a day or so later, on 1 November, No. 524 Squadron left for Langham. This was effectively the end of operational flying from Bircham Newton. There was still important work to be done by No. 521 (Met.) Squadron which had moved on to Langham in October, remaining there until November 1945. Flight Lieutenant D. L. Turner recalls the winding-down process:

'The last time my crew flew a *Rhombus* was on 19/20 November 1944 when we landed at Langham. We finished our tour of operations with that sortie.'[6]

As on other stations, educational and vocational training (EVT) began to play an important part in preparing servicemen and women for the return of peacetime, with the establishment of an EVT School at Bircham Newton on 15 November. A chief instructor and eight instructors arrived for duty. LAC (later Sergeant) John Floyd, formerly with No. 415 Squadron, was among the new instructors:

'.....I found that the other men and women on the course were accommodated in the married quarters but I rushed round to Barrack Block 5 and my erstwhile mates soon found me a bed. Each one of us on this course had to prepare and present a ten minute talk on "an original subject". I was then (and still am) a bit of a tram and bus buff, so I spoke on "How to Read Your Bus Ticket"! The officer in charge of the course (Flight Lieutenant Walter Faires) was so impressed he later sent me some tickets which had been issued to passengers riding on the mule tramway in the holy city of Mecca!'[7]

With the end of operational flying the strength of the station fell at the end of November to 2,051 personnel and to 1,561 at the end of December 1944. Activities like lectures on current affairs were on the programme for December, as on 11-14 December when a series of such lectures were delivered by Lord Stansgate. The usual traditional Christmas festivities were held, with other ranks being waited on by senior NCOs and officers, followed by a football match during Christmas Day between officers and senior NCOs. The other less congenial events taking place were occasional District Courts Martial, Bircham Newton being a centre for such work. Individuals were tried for such crimes as theft, absence without leave and desertion from HM Forces.

By the end of February 1945 station strength, along with the satellite, had declined to 1,472. The month of March saw the EVT courses continuing and the usual programme of educational lectures, the selection for the month including 'India', 'Seabirds and Seals' and 'The African Colonial Empire'.

There was still some flying and the occasional mishap, for example, on 8 February when a Lancaster (PD348) of No. 227 Squadron had an engine failure after take-off and belly-landed near the station. A Beaufighter of the CCPP crashed near Sculthorpe on a

---

[6] Turner, D.L.: letter to author 7/5/92.
[7] Floyd, John D.A.: letter to author 15/2/92.

Sergeants' Mess, early 1945. (Don Nelson)

training flight on 7 March and another Beaufighter of the same unit (RD431) belly-landed in a field also near Sculthorpe on the 14th. There were no reports about the fate of the crews.

On 12 March No. 598 Squadron arrived from Peterhead in Aberdeenshire with its various aircraft which included the Oxford I, Martinet I, Lysander IIIa, Hurricanes Marks IIc and IV and the Beaufighter I. The squadron had since 1943 been engaged in anti-aircraft co-operation duties in the north of Scotland but the time had now come to prepare for disbandment which happened on 30 April.

A steady stream of VIPs continued to visit the station, as on 2 May when Air Chief Marshal Sir Arthur Longmore inspected the burial plot at Great Bircham Churchyard.

VE-Day Parade at Bircham Newton, May 1945. (Don Nelson)

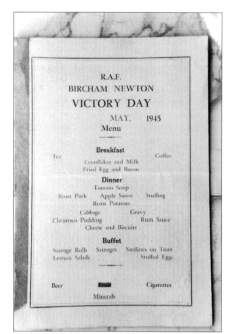

VE-Day Celebrations. (Bob Collis / Norfolk & Suffolk Aviation Museum)

VE-Day on 8 May followed the pattern seen on most RAF stations. There was a 'stand-easy' for the two-day period of celebrations. Victory all-ranks dances were held at Bircham Newton and the Docking satellite. The following day there was a Thanksgiving Drumhead Service on the parade ground at 1100 hrs and in the afternoon a Victory Sports Meeting with cinema shows in the evening. On the 12th revised peacetime working hours were introduced 'as far as the exigencies of the Service permitted' from 0830 to 1630 hrs daily.

Tragedy could still cloud the relief brought by a hard-won peace, since during the month there was a fatal accident involving Squadron Leader R. L. J. Fitch DFC of No. 2 Armament Practice Camp, in circumstances which are unclear. The other disaster was the crash of a Martinet (NR610) of No. 695 Squadron on 20 May, which dived into the ground south-east of Downham Market, killing the crew, WO Underwood and Flight Sergeant Adams. The next day a Mosquito (RF858) of the CCPP overshot and dropped out of control at Docking but there were no reports of injuries to the crew.

On 22 May No. 119 Squadron flew in with Swordfish III aircraft for disbandment on the 25th. The squadron had been re-formed from the Albacore Flight of 415 Squadron based at Manston in July 1944 before moving to various airfields in Belgium to fly anti-E-Boat and U-Boat sorties. A major part of the work was locating and destroying midget submarines during March, which had resulted in four being sunk.

EVT courses continued and on 24 May Air Vice-Marshal F. L. Hopps visited to deliver a lecture to all personnel on the subject of their responsibilities now that hostilities

No. 119 Sqn at Bircham Newton on its last day before disbandment, May 1945. Fairey Swordfish III in background. (John D.A. Floyd)

in Europe had ceased. June saw the beginning of the Service release of personnel. Bircham Newton was also accommodating RCAF officers and men in No. 18 Aircrew Holding Unit, awaiting their return to Canada. Numbers reached a peak of 1,500 personnel in July and by September its task was completed. Parliamentary elections in June for the Canadians involved the transport of personnel to RAF North Creake on 2 June and polling booths were set up for the British elections at the station from the 2 to 26 July.

No. 695 Squadron finally left for Horsham St Faith on 11 August to continue anti-aircraft co-operation duties. The CCPP was finally wound up during the month. VJ-Day celebrations on the 15th and 16th included a special dinner in the Airmen's Dining Hall, a sports meeting and evening film shows. On the 19th a Special Thanksgiving Drumhead Service and March Past at the parade ground rounded off the memorable programme. The station commander Group Captain J. Norwood took the salute.

On 10 September the satellite at Docking was placed on a Care and Maintenance basis and on the 15th Bircham Newton was opened to the public for a display of aircraft and equipment in commemoration of the Battle of Britain. Approximately 4,000 people attended the event and £68 was raised for the RAF Benevolent Fund.[8] The end of an era came on 21 September when Bircham Newton and Docking were transferred from Coastal to Flying Training Command, the station now being administered by HQ No. 54 Group.

A poignant close in the wartime chapter of Bircham Newton's history came on 14 July 1946 with the unveiling by His Majesty King George VI of the Cross of Sacrifice in the War Graves area of St Mary's Church, Great Bircham. This was the first such cross to be erected after the war. The total number of burials there is 78, comprising 37 airmen,

---

[8] See Appendix V.

Cross of Sacrifice, War Graves area, St Mary's Church, Great Bircham.

one soldier and one sailor from the forces of the United Kingdom, 17 airmen of the Royal Canadian Air Force, four airmen of the Royal Australian Air Force, six airmen of the Royal New Zealand Air Force, one airman of the South African Air Force and 11 Luftwaffe airmen. Many who linger at that spot might well reflect on the scale of sacrifice endured at Bircham Newton throughout the war years for there are many graves far beyond Bircham Newton and numerous unknown resting-places. During the war, a total of approximately 55 flying units served at the station, albeit some for brief stays. In that period the tally of airmen killed or posted missing amounted to at least 355, and at least eight became prisoners-of-war. An approximate total of 177 aircraft were destroyed in the course of duty, 138 as a result of operations, mostly anti-shipping sorties, and 39 in the course or training or accidents. Was it worth the cost? It is almost impossible to make an accurate assessment of the number of ships sunk or disabled as a result of the work of Bircham-based squadrons, as there is often some dispute about claims made, but there can be no calculation of the damage inflicted on the morale of German seamen, or the undoubted havoc and uncertainty which disrupted German shipping movements along the English Channel and in the North Sea. There was also the vital and often unsung work of the ASR squadrons, especially No. 279, and of course the essential contribution of the Meteorological units whose work was crucial in the planning of offensive operations, not least that of D-Day. The real achievement of the Coastal Command units like those based at Bircham Newton must lie in the enormous triumph it represented for human courage, skill and endurance, in the face of adverse weather, often inadequate and obsolete aircraft and equipment, flying for many hours over the cold, bleak North Sea towards a resourceful enemy, with little prospect of rescue in the event of having to ditch the aircraft. Such was the almost daily routine for most of the war years.

CHAPTER 14

INTO THE COLD WAR

'......Soon the memories will come flooding back and the faces will once more be alive....You will once more remember the life that you led for twenty months, the hours of bumpering and "bulling", the silent, hasty exits from the mess with packets of toast and hard-to-conceal tea......no one can say where they will be, but you will never forget the days you shared at Bircham Newton....the brief moments of glory and the few light-hearted moments that made it all so much worthwhile.'
(44th Entry Magazine, Administrative Apprentice Training School (AATS), Bircham Newton 1961-2)

After the transfer to Flying Training Command there was an interval of about 15 months before another flying unit arrived at the station during which nothing very significant happened at Bircham Newton, or at the Docking satellite. The service accommodation could still be brought into use for the large numbers of air and ground crew surplus to requirements and awaiting their turn to be demobilised. The famous actor the late Richard Burton was a trainee navigator who found himself at RAF Docking towards the end of 1945. By all accounts[1], Burton, along with fellow trainee and actor Robert Hardy, made their presence felt in the neighbourhood of Docking in pubs and with local girls by night, and in poaching game by day. Befitting his nickname 'The Squire of Docking', Burton preferred living in a large house in the village rather than the cold and damp Nissen huts at the camp and there did not seem much that the Royal Air Force could do about it. It must have been with immense relief to the Service that Burton was demobbed in 1947.

Sport was the saving grace in the lives of these bored, under-worked trainees and some post-war sportsmen owed much to the time then available for rugby and football in the RAF. One such was Danny Blanchflower, later captain of the Northern Ireland football team, who was at Docking at the same time as Burton.

No. 27 Aircrew Holding Unit was established at Bircham Newton over the winter of 1946/47, just before another major change in the station's status.

On 21 October 1946 the station came under the control of Transport Command. In November the first flying unit for some time arrived from Bramcote in Warwickshire, No. 1510 RAT (Radio Aids Training) Flight, renamed No. 1510 BABS (Beam Approach Beacon System) Flight in August 1947. This unit, nicknamed *Mike O'Brien's Flying Circus* after its CO, used Oxfords and Ansons to provide rapid training for crews in the use of the BABS system. The urgency was due to the jamming by the Soviets of the navigational and approach facilities and ground controlled equipment in the narrow corridor permitted to aircraft flying into the Western Sectors of Berlin. Another unit

---

[1] Junor, Penny: *Burton, The Man Behind the Myth* (Sidgwick & Jackson 1985) pp35-6.

associated with this was No. 1559 RAT Flight which flew in from Oakington with Oxfords in March 1947 along with No. 1555 RAT Flight in the same month from Bassingbourn. Both RAT Flights disbanded in August.

An insight into life in the BABS Flight at Bircham Newton in 1947 was provided by Mike D. Stimson who was posted to No. 1510 Flight on 1 May 1947. Mike was Welsh-born, an ex-miner who had served as an aircrew wireless operator from 1944-45, assisting in night supply drops to the French Resistance and day drops to Airborne troops during the Rhine crossing. Demobbed in February 1947, he rejoined the RAF and soon found himself in possession of a rail warrant valid from Brynannan, near Neath, to 'Bircham Newton'. On arrival in King's Lynn Mike was advised to 'change at Docking' for Bircham Newton, but there was no mention of getting off the train there, as he relates:

'.........So when Docking came along, I leapt out with all my kit, having had a weary journey and leaving home after eight weeks' indulgence of pub going, dances and having a good time, although the Air Force had just split up my first romance. So I got off at Docking and sat on a bench, waiting for a train to Bircham Newton - I didn't know where the devil it was! Eventually a porter came over to me and I wouldn't try to imitate his Norfolk dialect but he said:

"What be you waitin' for, then?"

"For the train to Bircham Newton", I replied.

"Y'll be waitin' a bloody long time for that, lad - they've not laid the railway line to there yet!"

"How far is it?", I asked.

"Look", he said, pointing in the direction of the airfield. "There! That's Bircham Newton."

"How do I get there?"

"You walks! Go down that road there to those crossroads", he pointed, "then you turn right and you goes up there!"

So eventually I got to the camp, reported to the guardroom and the sergeant pointed me in the direction of Station Headquarters, so I headed off with all my kit, footsore, tired, fed up, and cold as it was blowing at the time. I walked into the HQ, and was told I shouldn't have come in the front door - that was only for the Boss! So I went round to the back door, to a window where I pressed a button and when a WAAF appeared I announced: "Signaller 2B Stimson, and I have come to join 1510 BABS Flight".

"You're in the wrong building! Go to that building in front of that hangar there!" and she slammed the window down. So I rang again:

"Which hangar? There are two at least!"

She got a bit shorter and said, "The nearest one here", and bang went the window.

Well I'm glad to say that that lady subsequently became my wife!'

Mike Stimson got to the right place at last and met his CO, Squadron Leader Mike

O'Brien, a short and chunky ex-bomber aircrew, a Huddersfield Irishman. Mike goes on: '*Circus* was about the right word because I looked out and saw these ancient Ansons. About five or six came into land, and three or four fellows got out, and then some more fellows emerged to take the aircraft over. They only stopped long enough to change crews. As a wireless operator I became a radar instructor.' They had so few aircraft that those they had were in constant use in a conveyor-belt type system of training. Many of the crews were from the Commonwealth, Australia, and South Africa and most had already served in Bomber and Coastal Command in wartime:

'Bircham was very much as it is now - no runways, no landing lights, no nothing, just a caravan being towed around whichever end of the field the wind happened to be blowing from. The trees that are there now weren't there then. You could look straight across from Station HQ to the south-east to the WAAF Block and the Salvation Army canteen (two of the things that mattered most to me!).'[2]

In October 1947 the Transport Command Initial Conversion Unit (TICU) moved in from Bramcote to provide introductory training for Transport Command aircrews, but no aircraft were used. The other unit, the BABS Flight, did much of its flying from nearby Sculthorpe as Bircham Newton lacked paved runways, landing lights and modern airfield control facilities. The TICU crews moved on to flying instruction in Douglas Dakotas or Avro Yorks at Leicester East or Dishforth after their introductory course was completed. One of the officers who served in the unit at Bircham Newton in 1947/48 was Squadron Leader (later Group Captain) Leonard Trent VC, DFC. He had led a formation of 11 Venturas of No. 487 New Zealand Squadron on a raid to Amsterdam Power Station from Methwold on 3 May 1943, and had been shot down along with ten out of the 11 aircraft. He spent the rest of the war as a prisoner, but when released was awarded the VC when the story of that raid became known. Leonard Trent must have been 'the officer working in Air Traffic who wore the ribbon of the Victoria Cross' noticed by Bob A. Clayton in 1948, then a young raw recruit attached to Air Traffic Control working in the Watch Office.[3]

Mike Stimson was having a busy time in No. 1510 BABS Flight throughout 1947 and into 1948 as a Flying Radar Instructor. He and his pilot, Flying Officer Dave Zalla, were on one occasion given the unusual task of flying an Anson to RAF Wymeswold in Leicestershire to 'have the machine weighed'. It was always a relief to have a break from 'looking at radar screens'. On the flight home Mike was naturally curious to know why the machine had been weighed:

'What do you weigh an Anson for?', he asked Flying Officer Zalla.

'To see if it has got woodworm!', came the reply.

'You don't get woodworm in aircraft!'

'You get it in these aircraft', replied Zalla, 'They have wooden main spars......'

'Does this one have woodworm?' asked Mike.

---

[2] Stimson, Mike D.: audio tape to author 1991.
[3] Clayton, R.A.: letter to author 24/5/93.

'Yes, it's condemned!', said Zalla.

'Then what the hell are we flying it for?'

'Because we have to fly it back to where we got it from to destroy it!'

An incredulous Mike Stimson arrived back at Bircham Newton. The pilot asked 'Chiefy' to come out and the condemned aircraft was taxied to a corner of the field. The engines were cut, the crew emerged and the Very pistol was taken from the aircraft and when all was safe, a cartridge was fired and the aircraft burst into flames, destroying everything including the radar equipment, much to Mike's horror. Apparently the policy was that no part of an infected aircraft could be put into a hangar along with other machines.

Ansons Mk I, flight dispersal, July 1948. (R.A. Clayton)

No. 1510 BABS Flight at Bircham Newton in 1948, with Anson in background. F/O Dave Zalla standing second from right, and Mike Stimson (WOp) standing extreme right. (M.D. Stimson)

178

The knowledge that some of the aged aircraft they were flying in had woodworm was a sobering thought to the newly married Mike Stimson! The dangers faced by crews in the elderly Ansons were all-too obvious, endless near misses from jets from West Raynham, making present-day air traffic control seem a Sunday afternoon outing, the constant risk of mechanical failure in spite of the efforts of ground crews and the unpredictability of the local weather. The underpowered and slow Anson had great difficulty in gale-force winds. On one very stormy day Mike recalled watching an Anson almost stationary over the airfield for 20 minutes facing a 40-50 m.p.h. gale, a speed greater than the stalling speed of the aircraft! Then Mike and his crew took off in the direction of King's Lynn, into the wind as they doubted they could make Sculthorpe in these conditions. The aircraft struggled to get to Lynn, then the pilot realised that if they turned the machine around they would fly back so fast that they would never be able to loop round into Bircham. So the pilot put flaps down and throttled back and they flew *backwards* from King's Lynn to Bircham Newton with the engines just ticking over, the aircraft virtually gliding. Eventually, on reaching the airfield the pilot had almost to lay the machine down as they had no speed to manoeuvre, the wind was so violent. They finally got down safely and stopped in less than 100 yards!

In his time with the BABS Flight Mike Stimson survived one forced landing and one crash, fortunately without serious injury. He left for North Luffenham, Rutland, on 7 September 1948.[4] Both the Transport Command Initial Conversion Unit (TICU) and the BABS Flight were disbanded in September 1948.

On 1 October 1948 Bircham Newton was transferred to Technical Training Command. The Officers' Advanced Training School moved in from Hornchurch on 25 October, the Equipment Officers' School and the Secretarial Branch Training Establishment arriving from Digby, Lincolnshire, in March 1949. From June 1951 the entire establishment became known as the RAF School of Administration, training many thousands of students from foreign and Commonwealth countries as well as from the Royal Air Force.

Squadron Leader R. G. Woodman DSO, DFC was senior officer on an Officers' Advanced Training School course in the spring of 1952. During the latter part of the war he had served at Great Massingham with No. 169 Squadron and so was no stranger to Norfolk. He recalled a visit by Queen Mary to the station, in which he was assigned the duty of looking after her and her retinue. They got on extremely well although at one point the squadron leader was soaked in the pouring rain as he ran between the Mess and the hangar where he was due to lead the march-past. Later, Queen Mary related how she always gave lifts in her Daimler to hitch-hiking airmen and also had special medallions made to give them and this story is confirmed by Squadron Leader Woodman who has met a number of airmen so honoured![5]

Life as a national serviceman was recalled by Ron Ross, then Leading Aircraftman, who was stationed at Bircham Newton from January 1951 to November 1952 and billeted in Atlantic Block:

---

4   Stimson, Mike D.
5   Woodman, S/Ldr R.G.: letter to author 18/7/91.

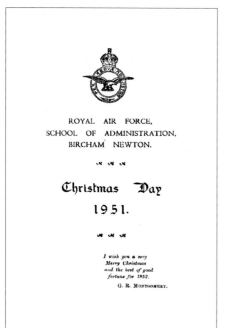

ROYAL AIR FORCE,
SCHOOL OF ADMINISTRATION,
BIRCHAM NEWTON.

Christmas Day
1951.

I wish you a very
Merry Christmas
and the best of good
fortune for 1952.

G. R. MONTGOMERY.

Autographs

"Astra Press" R.A.F. Henlow.

RAF School of Administration, Christmas Day 1951, menu. (Ron Ross)

'While life there was to say the least very strict, it was a time in my life that I enjoyed very much - being so far from the town you had to make your own enjoyment on the camp - the highlight of our week was our Saturday visit to Lynn, and most of our crowd were keen on football, so we supported King's Lynn playing in the old Eastern Counties League.' Ron played football as reserve goalkeeper for his unit throughout 1951-2, and he had a few scrapes with authority. On one occasion he and a few pals were sitting in the Salvation Army canteen but not wearing collars and ties when they were spotted by an RAF policeman. Ron was unable to make a rapid enough exit and found himself on a charge. However the charge was admonished. Later on, and only a few weeks before the end of his service, he was on a ground defence exercise and lost his identity card, a chargeable offence. The officer in charge took sympathy on him and he was let off![6]

Although flying units were no longer present, the airfield continued to be used as a Relief Landing Ground for the Harvards and Provosts of No. 3 Flying Training School at Feltwell, until that unit closed in 1958. HRH The Duke of Edinburgh made several flights to Bircham Newton from White Waltham and Smith's Lawn (Windsor Great Park) in the course of flying training in 1952 and 1953 in Chipmunks WP861 and WP912, accompanied by his instructor Flight Lieutenant C. R. Gordon. The Duke recalled the extent of the damage by the great storm and floods of 1953 which he witnessed from

---

[6] Ross, Ron: letter to author 25/7/91.

his Chipmunk trainer, when the sea wall was breached in several places along the coast and about 1,000 acres of the Sandringham estate remained under water for several days.[7] The Duke was to visit the station on many occasions later on, for example in a Whirlwind helicopter during January 1958, maintaining the long-standing Royal links with Bircham Newton.

In 1957 Hunstanton Urban District Council formally adopted the station and personnel often participated in civic functions. Her Majesty the Queen attended a Mess Party on 1 April 1958 to celebrate the fortieth anniversary of the station and of the

There will be a mess party at the R.A.F. Station, Bircham Newton, today to mark the anniversary, and television sets will be tuned in to the function being attended by the Queen.

Bircham Has Important Role But Boasts One Plane — A Chipmunk

BIRCHAM NEWTON, just south of Docking, has been known to airmen for as long as there has been a Royal Air Force. Since being taken over by the Service on its formation 40 years ago, it has had an almost continuous history in a variety of roles.

Today, perhaps befitting a station which has seen the complete growth of the R.A.F. and is as steeped as any in the tradition of four decades, it is the Royal Air Force School of Administration, responsible for office advanced training and the specialist training of equipment, account-tant and administrative officers.

Each year hundreds of officers, not only from this country and the Commonwealth but from many foreign countries, pass through the school.

Little Glamour

Its present-day role is thus an important one, although the work, by its nature, may escape the glamour attached to the stations with bombers or fighters.

Bircham Newton today has, in fact, but one plane of its own—a Chipmunk. It enables the officers to keep in touch during their stay there, to allow them to keep up their flying hours.

But it has not always been so; there have been more stirring roles. During the last war Bircham Newton was a Coastal Command station, with a satellite airfield at Docking. Its operations included the protection of East Coast shipping, air-sea rescue and meteorological flights. Aircraft from the station took part in the Thousand Bomber raid on Bremen in June, 1942.

First V-Bomber

In the closing months of the first World War, the station saw the development of Britain's first "V-Bomber" — the V.1500 Super Handley Page. This aircraft brought Berlin within bombing range of Britain for the first time.

The V.1500 was an outstanding aircraft for its time. It had four engines and could carry 30 250lb. bombs and a crew of six. It weighed about 14 tons and had a wingspan of 126 feet. It was the first aircraft to have a tail gun position, a feature not repeated for nearly 20 years.

The first "V-Bomber," however, never went to Berlin. It was all ready to go when the Armistice was signed.

1918—The first "V" bomber—the Super Handley Page V.1500. Picture taken at Bircham Newton.

VEHICLE PARK IS ORIGINAL HANGAR

Since 1948 Bircham has been part of the Technical Training Command and its hangars now house equipment and sectional parts of aircraft; instruction rooms; model stores and offices.

Bordering the Sandringham Estate, the station has always held the interest of the Royal Family. Many of them have visited it at one time or another, and King George VI conferred decorations on many of the fliers there during the last war.

Prince Philip learnt to fly there and is still a fairly frequent visitor. Only recently he was flying at Bircham with his helicopter.

The station buildings, which cover an extensive area, are a mixture of old and new. The original hangar, built over 40 years ago, is still in use—as a vehicle park. Some of the quarters bear the names "Zeebrugge" and "Mons"— indicative of the time when they were built.

But there are also modern quarters, messes and offices. Many of the permanent staff are civilians, and thus the station is a considerable employer of local labour.

Press Report to mark 40th Anniversary of the opening of the RAF station, 1 April 1958.
(Eastern Daily Press)

---

[7] HRH Duke of Edinburgh: notes sent to author 12/3/97.

founding of the Royal Air Force, an event at which television cameras were present. By this time the only aircraft at the station was a solitary Chipmunk retained to enable officers to maintain their flying hours.

The Officers' Advanced Training School became the Junior Command and Staff School in 1958, and in the following year the Administrative Apprentice Training School became the last RAF unit to be established at Bircham Newton. J. D. Upton recalled arriving at the station in 1961 as a seventeen year-old apprentice. A poem from the *44th Entry Magazine* sums up some of the more irreverent thoughts of apprentices at the time:

> A haven set midst green fair lands,
> This camp of ours, Bircham Newton, stands,
> A monument to Britain's might,
> Where AAs train and play and fight,
> To passers-by it thus appears,
> To us inside - Two b......... years![8]

300 WILL SEE LAST CEREMONY AT BIRCHAM NEWTON

A CEREMONY on December 18th will mark the closing down of R.A.F. Bircham Newton, after a distinguished career through two world wars and 46 years of R.A.F. history.

About 300 people have been invited to watch the last ceremonies which include the final graduation parade of 43 administrative apprentices, which will be reviewed by a top ranking R.A.F. officer. He will be accompanied by the Station Commander, Group Capt. A. D. Panton.

The present arrangements are for the visitors to witness Beating Retreat and the lowering of the ensign as Last Post is sounded.

PEERS

The invited guests include local officials and past station and squadron commanders who have served at Bircham Newton among them Lord Portal (1927) and Lord Tedder (1920-22).

Built in 1916 the station was used for training on the formation of the R.A.F. in 1918 and throughout the second world war Bircham Newton was a Coastal Command station with a satellite at Docking.

At the time of Dunkirk every available aircraft from Bircham was thrown into the protection of our troops withdrawing from the Continent. The station has been visited on occasions by the Royal family.

The amount of shipping destroyed by aircraft from Bircham Newton is difficult to estimate, but by the middle of 1943 over 100 ships had been sunk or badly damaged. Towards the end of the war air-sea rescue became one of the station's main tasks. In all 1152 sorties were flown and 359 aircrew and 41 seamen were rescued.

At the end of the war the station was transferred to Fighter Command and was later taken over for technical and advanced training. The present schools on the station are being transferred elsewhere.

During June, 1944, at the time of the Normandy invasion, the station's three squadrons flew an aggregate of 1330 hours.

Press Report 6 December 1962, on the forthcoming closing ceremony of the Station. (Evening News)

---

[8] Upton, J.D.: letter to author 9/7/91.

CEREMONY OF BEATING RETREAT

TO MARK THE CLOSING OF

ROYAL AIR FORCE, BIRCHAM NEWTON

18TH DECEMBER, 1962

Reviewing Officer : AIR MARSHAL SIR ALFRED EARLE, K.B.E., C.B.

AIR OFFICER COMMANDING-IN-CHIEF TECHNICAL TRAINING COMMAND

Beating Retreat by the Central Band of the Royal Air Force under the Direction of Flight Lieutenant R. A. Ponsford, l.r.a.m., a.c.r.m., Director of Music Royal Air Force.

Ceremonial by the Queen's Colour Squadron under the command of Squadron Leader R. Hardy, Royal Air Force Regiment.

ORDER OF PARADE

1. The Colour Squadron and Central Band march on
   Quick March "Eagle Squadron" ... ... *K. Alford*

2. Arrival of Reviewing Officer accompanied by Air Vice-Marshal A. A. Case, c.b.e., Air Officer Commanding, No. 22 Group, and Group Captain A. D. Panton, o.b.e., d.f.c., Officer Commanding, Royal Air Force Bircham Newton.

3. General Salute ... ... *Sims*

4. Colour Squadron March Past by Flights
   Slow March "Queen's Colour" ... ... *J. L. Wallace*

5. Colour Squadron March Past in close column of Flights.
   Quick March "R.A.F. March" ... ... *Walford Davies*

6. "The Retreat" by Trumpeters of Royal Air Force Central Band

7. Programme of music by Royal Air Force Central Band
   "Cavalcade of Martial Songs" ... ... *Traditional*
   "Lords of the Air" ... ... *M. North*
   "The Dambusters" ... ... *E. Coates*

8. Colour Squadron forms line of flights on Receiving Base
   "Steadfast and True" ... ... *C. Teike*

9. Prayers by Assistant Chaplain-in-Chief, Rev. L. J. Ashton

10. Colour Squadron advances in Review Order

11. General Salute ... ... *Sims*

12. Lowering of Royal Air Force Ensign
    "Last Post"

13. National Anthem

14. Colour Squadron and Central Band March Off in slow time
    "Auld Lang Syne" (*Traditional*)

Notes : (a) Guests are requested to stand and salute or uncover during the sounding of the Last Post and playing of the National Anthem and to stand during the two General Salutes.

(b) Guests are requested to remain in their places until the Reviewing Officer has left the parade hangar.

183

Ensign lowered for last time

Trumpeters sound Last Post, the Royal Air Force ensign is slowly lowered and 46 years of R.A.F. history at Bircham Newton come to an end.

Lord Tedder at close of Bircham Newton

THE CEREMONY of beating Retreat in one of the three main hangars where some of Britain's earliest V-bomber force was serviced marked the closing down of the Royal Air Force station, Bircham Newton, last night.

About 300 people, some of them with nostalgic memories of their own service at the station, watched the ceremony. Among them, wearing a bowler hat and civilian clothes, was Marshal of the Royal Air Force Lord Tedder, Deputy Supreme Commander of the Allied Forces from 1943 to 1945, who, in the early twenties, was C.O. of 207 Squadron when it was stationed there.

SUBDUED LIGHT

After the general salute came the sounding of Last Post. In the subdued light of the vast hangar, a single spotlight shone on the R.A.F. Ensign as it was lowered.

The National Anthem followed and with the Colour Squadron and Central Band of the R.A.F. marching off in slow time to the traditional "Auld Lang Syne," the reviewing officer and his party turned and left the hangar. It was the end of 46 years of R.A.F. history at Bircham Newton.

Earlier in the day there had been the last of the apprentice graduation parades at the station. Some 43 administrative apprentices, who had finished the course, took part, as well as two other entries who will be moving to Hereford.

Lord Tedder, who commanded 207 Squadron at Bircham Newton from 1920 to 1922, on his way to becoming one of the great names of the Royal Air Force, watched the closing down ceremony.

*Press report
19 December 1962,
on the Ceremony
at Bircham Newton.
(Eastern Daily Press)*

184

With the end of National Service and the steady reduction and rationalisation of RAF units, the station was nearing the end of its service life. The final official act was the ceremony to mark the station's closure on 18 December 1962, coinciding with the graduation parade of 43 apprentices. Three hundred people attended, among them Marshals of the RAF Lord Portal, who had been at the station in 1927, and Lord Tedder, present from 1920 to 1922. The Reviewing Officer was Air Marshal Sir Alfred Earle KBE, CB, the AOC-in-C Technical Training Command, accompanied by the station commander Group Captain A. D. Panton. The Central Band of the RAF and the Queen's Colour Squadron beat the retreat and the Last Post was sounded as the Ensign was lowered for the last time.

The remaining units moved away, the Junior Command and Staff School to Ternhill in Shropshire and the Apprentices School to Hereford. From June 1963 into the following year the airfield was used as a storage facility for the United States Air Force, but on 27 November 1964 the site was offered for sale by public auction, in lots, at the Duke's Head Hotel, King's Lynn.

There was a brief return to the airfield's former role during 1965, when the Tripartite Evaluation Squadron of the Central Fighter Establishment at West Raynham used the airfield as a dispersal site for the trials of the Hawker Siddeley Kestrel VTOL[9] aircraft, the forerunner of the famous and long-serving Harrier. Thus Bircham Newton has witnessed developments in military aviation which spanned most of the twentieth century. The Kestrel trials did not last long and the final disposal of the airfield for civilian use was imminent.

R.A.F. Bircham Newton for auction this year

THE R.A.F. airfield at Bircham Newton, near King's Lynn, one of the first R.A.F. stations in the country, which was opened in 1918, is to be sold by public auction.

Preparations for the sale have been going on for some time between the Secretary of State for Defence and the auctioneers, Messrs. Charles Hawkins & Sons, of King's Lynn and Downham Market.

THREE HANGARS

The date of the sale, to be announced shortly, is likely to be in November, at Lynn.

The station, which had a long and distinguished history before closing down on December 18th, 1962, covers 54½ acres and the floor area of the buildings covers over 384,000 square feet. It will be sold in several lots.

They include the technical site with three hangars, station headquarters, nine barrack blocks, sick quarters, messes, stores, garages and bulk fuel installations. The fine building previously used as the officers' mess will also be sold.

A spokesman for the auctioneers said it was impossible at present to estimate any price the station might fetch.

'UNIQUE'

It was a unique property and was likely to attract light industrial and manufacturing firms, he said, and would be ideal for assembly work.

One building alone had 45,000 square feet of uninterrupted floor space under one roof and with associated office blocks. All buildings were well maintained.

Part of the site could be developed as a hotel. There is one building with 54 bedrooms, and recreational facilities include hard tennis courts.

HANDLEY PAGES

The spokesman said the property was being sold as it was now surplus to the requirements of the Ministry of Defence. Airfield land had been offered back to the original owners.

When in operation the station was steeped in flying tradition, and in the closing months of the first world war it housed the V1500 Super Handley Pages.

During the second world war it was a Coastal Command station, with a satellite airfield at Docking, and its operations included the protection of East Coast shipping, air-sea rescue and meteorological flights. Aircraft from the station took part in the thousand bomber raid on Bremen in June, 1942.

CHIPMUNK

In its last years it was a Royal Air Force School of Administration, responsible for officers' advanced training and specialist training. Despite this important role it had only one aircraft—a Chipmunk.

Bordering the Royal Sandringham Estate, the station had always attracted the interest of the Royal Family, and Prince Philip learned to fly there.

Press report 4 August 1964, on forthcoming auction of RAF station. (Eastern Daily Press)

---

9 Vertical Take-Off and Landing.

By Direction of The Secretary of State for Defence

E R

THE FORMER R.A.F. STATION

BIRCHAM NEWTON

Near KING'S LYNN, NORFOLK.

King's Lynn 16 miles; Norwich 42 miles; Cambridge 61 miles

COMPRISING:

THE TECHNICAL SITE

THREE HANGARS (Total Area over 77,750 sq. feet)

NUMEROUS SUBSTANTIAL BRICK BUILDINGS
including
9 Barrack Blocks, Station Headquarters,
Sickquarters, Messes, Stores and Garages
with total floor area of
over 265,193 square feet

THE EXCELLENT MODERN and IMPOSING
OFFICERS' MESS

together with

SUBSTANTIAL PERMANENT BUILDINGS
with total floor area of
over 42,287 square feet
Ideally suited to a wide variety of purposes

THE PROPERTY EXTENDS IN ALL TO

ABOUT 53 ACRES

FREEHOLD — VACANT POSSESSION

CHARLES HAWKINS & SONS

will offer the above for Sale by Auction, in Lots,

at **THE DUKE'S HEAD HOTEL, KING'S LYNN, on**

Friday, 27th November, 1964

AT 3 P.M.

Auctioneers' Offices: Bank Chambers, King's Lynn. (Tel.: 2370 & 2473);
and Downham Market, Norfolk. (Tel.: Downham 2112/3).

Sale Notice for RAF Bircham Newton 1964.

In September 1966 the Construction Industry Training Board (CITB) opened a training centre at Bircham Newton, now the National Construction College, an establishment which has since become the largest of its type in the world. While the old grass airfield provides ample space for training personnel, the buildings and hangars are in constant use as workshops, offices and canteens and the former Officers' Mess and barrack blocks have been adapted for civilian accommodation. At the same time, the outward appearance of the site has been remarkably preserved as one of the most important examples of a surviving pre-war expansion airfield, with many buildings still dating from the 1920s. Veterans from many continents still come to relive former days, and to visit the War Graves at Great Bircham Cemetery.

As with many old airfields, stories circulate about ghostly happenings, many of which have been described elsewhere[10], and spread by word of mouth. One story from around 1948 was related by a pilot who shared a twin room in the Officers' Mess. One night he was transfixed by a 'black mass' on his bed, an incident witnessed by his room-mate. Some enquiries were made in Station Administration and it was apparent that during wartime a pilot who had lost his nerve had shot himself there. The upshot was that both beds were removed, the room was locked and subsequently used as a store.

Other accounts tell of sightings of a ghostly airman in the vicinity of the old squash court, which incidentally is one of the oldest surviving buildings at Bircham Newton. This is alleged to have been connected with a fatal crash close to the local

Squash Courts, probably oldest building still in existence on the site, 1991. (Bldg No. 153 - 2078/ 18). (author)

---

[10] *Ghost Stations*, by Bruce Barrymore Halpenny (Merlin Books Ltd 1986) pp104-11.

church. The story received some publicity in the early 1970s, notably on the late Jack de Manio's *Today* programme on BBC Radio, after reports of sightings by members of a BBC film crew who were making a training film. In 1973 an exorcism was conducted at the squash courts, possibly as a result of these events. There was a brief mention of another 'ghost', 'Docking Lil' of Hangar 1, but no details of this have emerged so far.[11]

Bircham Newton has also been chosen as a setting for wartime aviation films. In January 1992, a BBC TV drama about the Gulf War called *Friday On My Mind* had a filmset in one of the 'C'-type hangars where the mock-up of a Tornado bomber was constructed. Most recently, in February 2000, a film crew from the Japanese Fuji TV arrived to investigate the ghost stories which have received publicity over the years.

Bircham Newton remains today one of the best-preserved airfields in the country and it is gratifying to think that what airfield builders thought appropriate in the 1920s and 1930s, in a very different world, is still contributing to the nation's life.

---

[11] Upton, J.D.: letter to author 9/7/91.

APPENDIX I

SOURCES AND BIBLIOGRAPHY

UNPUBLISHED SOURCES

PUBLIC RECORD OFFICE, KEW
1. STATION OPERATIONS RECORD BOOKS
   BIRCHAM NEWTON inc. Appendices:
   AIR 28/70-77, 990.

2. OPERATIONS RECORD BOOKS (Form 540): No. 206 (GR) Squadron
   AIR 27/1221-1223: June 1936 to May 1941.

DG Hist Permanent Reference Files: 415 Squadron RCAF, National Defence HQ, Ottawa, Canada.

LOGBOOK (ARMY BOOK 425) of 2/Lt J. Gordon Webster RAF (RAF Museum Library, Hendon).

LOGBOOK of Air Vice-Marshal Sir Edward Fielden GCVO, CB, DFC, AFC (Courtesy of the Queen's Flight (now No. 32 (The Royal) Squadron)).

No. 206 (GR) Squadron: Squadron Standing Orders (issued 1st September 1936). (No. 206 Squadron, RAF Kinloss).

For personal accounts included in the narrative *see* Acknowledgements.

PUBLISHED WORKS

BOOKS

ASHWORTH, CHRIS, *RAF COASTAL COMMAND 1936-1969*, Patrick Stephens Limited 1992.

BOITEN, THEO, *BLENHEIM STRIKE*, Air Research Publications 1995.

BOWYER, CHAZ, *HANDLEY PAGE BOMBERS OF THE FIRST WORLD WAR*, Aston Publications 1992.

BOWYER, CHAZ, *MEN OF COASTAL COMMAND (1939-45)*, William Kimber 1985.

BOWYER, M. J. F., *ACTION STATIONS REVISITED: No. 1 Eastern England*, Crécy Publishing Limited 2000.

BOWYER, M. J. F., *AIR RAID! The enemy air offensive against East Anglia 1939-45*, Patrick Stephens Limited 1986.

BROOKES, ANDREW, *BOMBER SQUADRON AT WAR*, Ian Allan Ltd 1983.

BROOKS, ROBIN J., *KENT'S OWN - THE HISTORY OF 500 (COUNTY OF KENT) SQUADRON ROYAL* AUX AF, Meresborough Publications 1982.

BROWN, DAVID, *CARRIER AIR GROUPS: HMS EAGLE*, Hylton Lacy Publishers Limited 1972.

BROWN, DOUGLAS, *EAST ANGLIA AT WAR*. (Series).

BROWN, RON, *ALL ROUND THE COMPASS*, Janus Publishing Company 1993.

COOKSLEY, PETER G., *FLIGHT ROYAL*, Patrick Stephens Limited 1981.

DANIELS, S. B., *RESCUE FROM THE SKIES*, London HMSO 1993.

DYMOND, DAVID, *THE NORFOLK LANDSCAPE*, Hodder & Stoughton 1985.

FAIRHEAD, HUBY & TUFFEN, ROY, *AIRFIELDS OF NORFOLK & SUFFOLK*, Norfolk & Suffolk Aviation Museum 1990.
Part I includes Docking, Part II Coxford, Part IV Bircham Newton & Sedgeford, and Part V Langham.

FAIRHEAD, HUBY, *COLONEL TURNER'S DEPARTMENT* 1997.

FAIRHEAD, HUBY, *DECOY SITES* 1996.

FRANCIS, PAUL, *BRITISH MILITARY AIRFIELD ARCHITECTURE*, Patrick Stephens Limited 1996.

GRAY, GROUP CAPTAIN COLIN, *SPITFIRE PATROL*, Hutchinson 1990.

GUNN, PETER B., AIRFIELD FOCUS 5: *BIRCHAM NEWTON*, GMS Enterprises 1992.

HALLEY, JAMES J., *FAMOUS MARITIME SQUADRONS OF THE RAF* Vol I, Hylton Lacy Publishers Limited 1973.

HALPENNY, B. B., *GHOST STATIONS*, Merlin Books Ltd 1986.

HENDRIE, ANDREW, *LOCKHEED HUDSON IN WORLD WAR II*, Airlife Publishing Ltd 1999.

JAMES, JOHN, *THE PALADINS*, Futura 1990.

JEFFORD, WING COMMANDER C. G., *RAF SQUADRONS*, Airlife Publishing Ltd 1988.

JOHNSON, DEREK E., *EAST ANGLIA AT WAR 1939-45*, Jarrold Colour Publications 1978.

KENNETT, DAVID H., *NORFOLK VILLAGES*, Robert Hale, London 1980.

KENT, GROUP CAPTAIN J. A., *ONE OF THE FEW*, Corgi 1975.

JUNOR, PENNY, *BURTON: THE MAN BEHIND THE MYTH*, Sidgwick & Jackson, London, 1985.

LAMB, CHARLES, *WAR IN A STRINGBAG*, Cassell Military Paperback 2001.

LONGMATE, NORMAN, *THE BOMBERS*, Arrow Books 1988.

NESBIT, ROY CONYERS, *THE STRIKE WINGS*, HMSO 1995.

O'BRIEN, TERENCE, *CHASING AFTER DANGER*, Collins 1990.

ORANGE, VINCENT, *ENSOR'S ENDEAVOUR, biography of Wing Commander Mike Ensor DSO, DFC, AFC, RNZAF & RAF*, Grub Street, London 1994.

PARRY, SIMON, *INTRUDERS OVER BRITAIN*, Air Research Publications.

RAWLINGS, JOHN D. R., *COASTAL, SUPPORT AND SPECIAL SQUADRONS OF THE RAF*, Jane's 1982.

RAWLINGS, JOHN D. R., *FIGHTER SQUADRONS OF THE RAF AND THEIR AIRCRAFT*, Crécy Books 1993.

SANDERS, JAMES, *VENTURER COURAGEOUS*, Hutchinson 1983. (Biography of Group Captain L. Trent VC).

SMITH, DAVID J., *BRITAIN'S MILITARY AIRFIELDS 1939-45*, Patrick Stephens Limited 1989.

SPOONER, TONY, *COASTAL ACE*, William Kimber 1986. (Biography of Squadron Leader T. Bulloch).

SPOONER, TONY, *IN FULL FLIGHT*, Wingham Press, Canterbury 1991.

STURTIVANT, RAY, *ANSON FILE*, Air-Britain 1988.

STURTIVANT, RAY, *THE SQUADRONS OF THE FLEET AIR ARM*, Air-Britain 1984.

STURTIVANT, RAY, with JOHN HAMLIN and JAMES J. HALLEY, *ROYAL AIR FORCE FLYING TRAINING AND SUPPORT UNITS*, Air-Britain 1997.

TAVENDER, I. T., *THE DISTINGUISHED FLYING MEDAL: A Record of Courage 1918-1982*, J. B. Hayward & Son 1990.

TERRAINE, JOHN, *THE RIGHT OF THE LINE*, Hodder and Stoughton Limited.

THETFORD, OWEN, *AIRCRAFT OF THE ROYAL AIR FORCE SINCE 1918*, Putnam 1988.

WADE-MARTINS, PETER, *AN HISTORICAL ATLAS OF NORFOLK*, Norfolk Museums Service 1993.

WILSON, the late RAY, *RED ALERT - LYNN*, Panda Books 1985.

WRIGHT, ROBERT, *YEARS OF COMMAND: SHOLTO DOUGLAS, Marshal of the RAF*, HarperCollins Publishers.

YAXLEY, DAVID, *PORTRAIT OF NORFOLK*, Robert Hale, London 1977.

PRIVATELY PUBLISHED BOOKS

415 RCAF SQUADRON HISTORY, *SWORDFISH* (415 Sqn RCAF).

BIRKS, FLIGHT LIEUTENANT, *206 SQUADRON 1916-1986* (compiled for Squadron's 75th Anniversary).

HAMBLING, MERV, *NORFOLK CRASH DIARY* series from 1939-50.

HILLMAN, BRIAN & BEYNON, JOHN, *BRITISH, COMMONWEALTH & GERMAN WAR GRAVES IN ST MARY'S CHURCHYARD, GREAT BIRCHAM, NORFOLK*.
Copies available in St Mary's Church, Great Bircham or by application to Brian Hillman, 3 Grantly Court, King's Lynn PE30 4TN (email: bsh@lineone.net).

HITCHINS, WING COMMANDER F. H., *NO. 407 (DEMON) SQUADRON* (407 Sqn Reference File).

PERRY-KEENE, ALLAN, *REFLECTED GLORY*, An Autobiography, 1978.

VICKERS, WING COMMANDER T. R., *A HISTORY OF 221 SQUADRON*.

NEWSPAPERS

EASTERN DAILY PRESS

EVENING NEWS

LYNN NEWS AND ADVERTISER

ARTICLES

JOURNAL OF THE NORFOLK INDUSTRIAL ARCHAEOLOGY SOCIETY Vol 4 No. 5 1990:
'North West Norfolk Coastal Defences', by Erik Iosson.

FLYPAST March 1984: 'Between the Wars Bombers: Handley Page O/400, V/1500' by Ken Wixey.

FLYPAST April 1988: 'Airmen's Married Quarters' by Paddy Porter.

AVIATION NEWS 15-28 April 1988, article by Charles Hall ('Holly'). Journal now out of print.

APPENDIX II

RAF BIRCHAM NEWTON COMMANDING OFFICERS

WING COMMANDER THE HON.		
L. J. E. TWISTLETON-WYKEHAM-FIENNES	1924	- 21/2/27
WING COMMANDER T. O'B. HUBBARD MC, AFC	2/4/27	- 13/9/29
WING COMMANDER R. LECKIE DSO, DSC, DFC	5/9/29	- 11/4/31
WING COMMANDER C. PULFORD OBE, AFC	11/4/31	- 15/10/32
WING COMMANDER R. COLLISHAW DSO, OBE, DSC, DFC	15/10/32	- 27/8/35
WING COMMANDER R. G. GARDNER DSC	27/8/35	- 4/6/36
WING COMMANDER H. M. K. BROWN	5/6/36	- 27/9/37
GROUP CAPTAIN J. W. WOODHOUSE DSO, MC	27/9/37	- 12/12/38
GROUP CAPTAIN C. L. SCOTT DSC	12/12/38	- 13/12/39
GROUP CAPTAIN W. H. PRIMROSE CBE, DFC	13/12/39	- 15/3/41
GROUP CAPTAIN J. B. GRAHAM MC, AFC	15/3/41	- 14/3/42
GROUP CAPTAIN J. M. MASON DSC, DFC	24/3/42	- 27/11/42
GROUP CAPTAIN T. H. CARR DFC, AFC	27/11/42	- 2/9/43
GROUP CAPTAIN C. W. BUSK MC, AFC	2/9/43	- 24/7/44
GROUP CAPTAIN R. W. K. STEVENS	24/7/44	- 16/4/45
GROUP CAPTAIN J. NORWOOD	16/4/45	- 1947
WING COMMANDER L. H. ANDERSON	1947	- 1948
AIR COMMODORE A. McKEE CBE, DSO, DFC, AFC	1948	- 1949
AIR COMMODORE R. N. WAITE CB, CBE	1949	- 1950
GROUP CAPTAIN G. R. MONTGOMERY CBE	1950	- 1952
GROUP CAPTAIN E. J. LAINE CBE, DFC	1952	- 1955
GROUP CAPTAIN A. J. MASON DFC	1955	- 1957
GROUP CAPTAIN G. B. WALFORD OBE	1957	- 1960
GROUP CAPTAIN M. WYATT DFC	1960	- 1961
GROUP CAPTAIN A. D. PANTON OBE, DFC	1961	- 1962

APPENDIX III

UNITS PRESENT 1918 - 1962

BOMBER STATION

UNIT	FROM	CO(s)	TO	AIRCRAFT
No. 3 Sch of Aerial Fighting & Gunnery (redes. No 3 F Sch)	Driffield 28/5/18		Sedgeford 10/18	DH4; DH9; Dolphin; SE5A; Snipe; Camel; Avro 504K
166 Sqn	formed 13/6/18	Maj. C. H. Darley	disbanded 31/5/19	FE2B; HP V/1500
167 Sqn	formed 18/11/18		disbanded 21/5/19	HP V/1500
274 Sqn	re-formed 15/6/19		disbanded 30/1/20	HP V/1500
56 Sqn	Narborough 30/12/19		disbanded 22/1/20	SE5A
60 Sqn	Narborough 30/12/19		disbanded 22/1/20	SE5A
207 Sqn	re-formed 1/2/20	S/Ldr A. W. Tedder	Turkey 29/9/22	DH9A
7 Sqn	re-formed 1/6/23	S/Ldr C. H. Hayward; S/Ldr E. B. Grenfell; S/Ldr J. S. T. Bradley; W/Cdr C. H. B. Blount; W/Cdr C. F. A. Portal	Worthy Down 7/4/27	Vimy; Virginia III; Virginia II; Virginia IV; Virginia V; Virginia VI; Avro 504
11 Sqn	Andover 16/9/23	S/Ldr E. A. B. Rice	Netheravon 31/5/24	DH9A; Fawn
99 Sqn	Netheravon 31/5/24	S/Ldr G. R. M. Reid DSO, MC; S/Ldr L. T. N. Gould MC; S/Ldr W. J. Ryan CBE; W/Cdr B. E. Smythies DFC	Upper Heyford 5/1/28	Vimy; Aldershot; HP Hyderabad
32 Sqn	Kenley 30/6/24		Kenley 5/8/24	Snipe
39 Sqn	Spittlegate (Grantham) 21/1/28	S/Ldr H. V. Champion-de-Crespigny	India 29/12/28	DH9A
101 Sqn	re-formed 21/3/28	S/Ldr J. C. P. Wood; S/Ldr R. S. Lucy	Andover 10/10/29	DH9A; BP Sidestrand
35 Sqn	re-formed 1/3/29	S/Ldr G. S. M. Insall VC, MC; S/Ldr B. E. Harrison; S/Ldr H. M. K. Brown; S/Ldr J. F. Gordon; S/Ldr Y Buxton; S/Ldr A. P. Ritchie; S/Ldr C. W. Hill	Sudan 4/10/35	DH9A; Fairey IIIF; Fairey Gordon

207 Sqn	Eastchurch 7/11/29	S/Ldr E. A. Beulah S/Ldr J. W. Woodhouse S/Ldr J. L. Vachell S/Ldr G. G. Dawson S/Ldr P. E. Maitland S/Ldr R. J. Rodwell	Ed Damer, Sudan 28/10/35	Fairey IIIF; Fairey Gordon
21 Sqn	re-formed 3/12/35	F/Lt A. K. Sarel	Abbotsinch 22/7/36	Hind
34 Sqn	re-formed 3/12/35	F/Lt P. W. M. Wright	Abbotsinch 30/7/36	Hind
18 Sqn	Upper Heyford 7/1/36	S/Ldr C. R. Steele	Old Sarum 14/8/36	Hart, Hind
49 Sqn	re-formed 10/2/36	F/Lt J. C. Cunningham S/Ldr W. E. Dipple	Worthy Down 8/8/36	Hind

NO. 16 GROUP COASTAL COMMAND

UNIT	CODE	FROM	CO(s)	TO	AIRCRAFT
AACU 'B' Flt detached 3/6/36 (redes No. 1 AACU 10/2/37)		Biggin Hill		Flimston Down 10/5/37; returned 9/37 & aircraft to storage at Hendon 21/9/37	Wallace I; Wallace II
1 AACU 'C' Flt		Farnborough 15/5/38		Farnborough 26/9/38; returned 14/4/39; to Weston Zoyland 6/9/39	Wallace I
1 AACU 'D' Flt		Farnborough 28/4/38		closed 26/9/38; re-opened Farnborough & returned 28/4/39; to Cleave 6/9/39	Henley & various
1 AACU 'K' Flt		Cleave 6/9/40		Langham 6/12/41	Henley & various
1 AACU 'M' Flt		formed 27/9/40		Langham 7/10/40	Henley & various
206 (GR) Sqn	VX (peacetime WD)	Manston 30/7/36	W/Cdr F. J. Vincent DFC; W/Cdr H. O. Long DSO; S/Ldr H. H. Martin; W/Cdr J. L. Findlay RNZAF; W/Cdr N. H. D'Aeth; W/Cdr C. D. Candy	St Eval 30/5/41	Anson I; Hudson
220 (GR) Sqn	NR (peacetime HU)	re-formed 17/8/36	S/Ldr W. M. M. Hurley; S/Ldr F. P. Smythies; W/Cdr A. H. Paull AFC	Thornaby 21/8/39	Anson I
269 Sqn		re-formed 7/12/36	F/Lt J. A. Dixon	Abbotsinch 30/12/36	Anson
42 Sqn	AW	Thorney Island 12/8/39	S/Ldr H. Waring	Thorney Island 27/4/40	Vildebeest III & IV; Beaufort I
233 Sqn	EY	Leuchars (detachment) 6/39		Leuchars 9/39	Anson I
254 Sqn	QY	Sutton Bridge 28/1/40	S/Ldr G. K. Fairclough	Hatston 23/4/40	Blenheim IF; Blenheim IVF

197

Squadron	Code	Formation	Commander	Location / Dates	Aircraft
48 Sqn	OY	Thorney Island (detachments) 8/39		Hooton Park 7/40	Anson I
612 Sqn	WL	Dyce (detachments) 9/39		Dyce 11/40	Anson I
600 Sqn	BQ	Hornchurch (detachment) 12/39		Manston	Blenheim IF; Blenheim IVF
235 Sqn	LA	North Coates 25/4/40	S/Ldr R. I. G. McDougall; S/Ldr R. Clarke; S/Ldr I. M. T. de K. Bocock; W/Cdr H. T. Garlick	Detling 26/5/40; returned 24/6/40; Dyce 4/6/41; Docking 2/6/42; Chivenor 16/7/42	Blenheim IF &IVF
No. 2 GRU		formed 3/40	S/Ldr Purvis	Manston (detachment 4/40); Egypt 5/40	Wellington DWI
826 Sqn FAA	4F	Ford 7/5/40	Lt/Cdr C. J. T. Stephens; Lt/Cdr W. H. G. Saunt DSC	Jersey 21/5/40; returned 29/5/40; St Merryn 7/10/40	Albacore I; Swordfish I
815 Sqn FAA	L4	Cardiff 8/4/40	Lt/Cdr S. Borrett; Lt/Cdr R. A. Kilroy DFC	Ford 16/5/40; returned 20/5/40; Ford 23/5/40; returned 6/6/40; HMS Illustrious 11/6/40	Swordfish I
812 Sqn FAA	G3	North Coates 28/5/40	Lt/Cdr N. G. R. Crawford	North Coates 29/5/40	Swordfish I
229 Sqn	RE	Wittering 6/40	S/Ldr H. J. Maguire	Northolt 9/40	Hurricane I
816 Sqn FAA		HMS Furious (detachment) 1/7/40	Lt/Cdr T. G. C. Jameson	HMS Furious 6/7/40	Swordfish I
221 Sqn	DF	re-formed 21/11/40	W/Cdr T. R. Vickers	Limavady 2/5/41; Docking 25/12/41 to 8/1/42	Wellington Ia; Wellington IC; Wellington VIII
252 Sqn	PN	re-formed 21/11/40	S/Ldr R. G. Yaxley MC	Chivenor 1/12/40	Blenheim IF; Blenheim IVF
403 Met. Flt/1403 Met. Flt		formed 11/40; renumbered 1403 Flt 3/41		disbanded 1/8/42 to form 521 Sqn	Blenheim IV; Hudson III; Hampden I; Hereford I; Gladiator II

Squadron	Code	Formation	Commanding Officers	Movements / Dates	Aircraft
1401 Met. Flt	TE	Mildenhall 25/10/41		absorbed 1403 Flt 7/2/42; disbanded 1/8/42 to form 521 Sqn	Hudson III; Spitfire IIa; IV & V. Gladiator; Blenheim IV; Hurricane
53 Sqn	PZ	Thorney Island 10/2/41	W/Cdr W. B. Murray DFC; W/Cdr G. W. P. Grant	St Eval 23/2/41; returned 2/7/41; St Eval 19/10/41; returned from Docking 18/3/43; Thorney Island 28/4/43	Blenheim IV; Hudson V; Whitley VII
200 Sqn	TF	re-formed 25/5/41 ex-206 Sqn	W/Cdr C. D. Candy	Bathurst, West Africa 12/6/41	Hudson IV
500 Sqn	MK	Detling 30/5/41	W/Cdr M. Q. Chandler; W/Cdr G. T. Gilbert; W/Cdr D. F. Spotswood DSO, DFC	Stornoway 2/4/42	Blenheim IV; Hudson III; Hudson V
248 Sqn	WR	Dyce 21/6/41	W/Cdr S. G. Wise DFC	Dyce 17/2/42	Blenheim IVF; Beaufighter IC
608 Sqn (det.)	UL	Thornaby 30/6/41	W/Cdr R. S. Derbyshire; W/Cdr P. D. R. Hutchings AFC	Thornaby 12/41	Hudson V
59 Sqn	PJ	det. from Manston 1/3/41	W/Cdr J. A. C. Stratton	Thorney Island 2/6/41; returned (det.) 20/10/41; Thorney Island 18/12/41	Blenheim IV; Hudson III; Hudson V; Hudson VI
279 Sqn	OS	formed 16/11/41	W/Cdr V. H. P. Lynham DSO; W/Cdr B. G. Corry DFC; W/Cdr K. W. C. Bindloss; S/Ldr H. F. Cox	Thornaby 31/10/44	Hudson III; Hudson V; Hudson VI

Unit	Code	Formed/Base	Commander	Movements/Notes	Aircraft
407 Sqn RCAF	RR	Thorney Island 31/3/42	W/Cdr A. C. Brown DFC; W/Cdr C. F. King; W/Cdr J. C. Archer	St Eval 1/10/42; returned to Docking 10/11/42; Skitten (Wick) 14/2/43	Hudson III; Hudson V
217 Sqn (det.)	MW	det. from Leuchars 3/42	W/Cdr S. M. Boal DFC	Leuchars 4/42	Beaufort II
320 (R. Neth.) Sqn	NO	Leuchars 20/4/42	Lt/Cdr W. van Lier	Methwold 15/3/43 (to 2 Gp)	Hudson I; Hudson II; Hudson III; Hudson VI
521 (Met.) Sqn	TE	formed ex-1401/1403 Flts 1/8/42	S/Ldr D. A. Braithwaite; S/Ldr W. M. Bispham; S/Ldr K. E. Williams	Disbanded 31/3/43 to Nos 1401 & 1409 Flts; 1409 Flt to Oakington 1/4/43; Sqn reformed Docking 1/9/43	Hudson III; Spitfire VA/VB; Mosquito IV; Gladiator
811 Sqn FAA		Machrihanish 16/8/42	Lt/Cdr H. S. Hayes DSC, RN	Thorney Island 31/10/42	Swordfish II
819 Sqn FAA		Langham 6/8/42	Lt H. S. McN. Davenport RN	Thorney Island 23/9/42; returned from Swingfield 1/10/44 & det. to Europe; Sqn disbanded 10/3/45	Swordfish I; Swordfish II
812 Sqn FAA		Docking 9/10/42	Lt/Cdr B. J. Prendergast	Hatston 3/11/42	Swordfish I; Swordfish II
280 Sqn	YF	Langham 2/11/42	W/Cdr H. P. Burwood	Thorney Island 25/9/43	Anson I
1611 AA Co-op Flt		Langham 9/11/42		disbanded 1/12/43 to form 695 Sqn	Martinet; Henley
1612 AA Co-op Flt		Langham 8/12/42		disbanded 1/12/43 to form 695 Sqn	Martinet; Henley
415 Sqn RCAF	GX (later NH)	Thorney Island 25/11/42	W/Cdr C. G. Ruttan DSO	Thorney Island 28/11/42; returned 15/11/43; East Moor 12/7/44	Hampden I; Wellington XIII; Albacore I
Warwick TU	FI	formed 28/6/43		redes. ASRTU 13/10/43	Warwick; Wellington IC
ASRTU		ex-Warwick TU 13/10/43		Thornaby 20/10/43	Wellington IC & X; Warwick; Sea Otter I; Anson I

					Lysander; Henley III; Hurricane IIC; Martinet; Spitfire (various); Vengeance IV; Oxford; Harvard; Beaufighter
695 Sqn	4M	formed ex-1611 & 1612 Flts 1/12/43		Horsham St Faith 11/8/45	
2 Armament Training Camp		Thorney Island 16/6/43		discontinued 6/44; disbanded 1/9/45	Lysander; Martinet
48 Sqn	OY	Gibraltar 21/2/44	W/Cdr T. F. U. Lang AFC	Down Ampney 24/2/44	Hudson VI
233 Sqn	ZS	Gosport 1/3/44	W/Cdr M. E. Morrison AFC	Blakehill Farm 5/3/44	Hudson II; III; V
524 Sqn	7R	Docking 25/7/44	W/Cdr R. G. Knott DFC	Langham 1/11/44	Wellington XIII
855 Sqn FAA		Lee-on-Solent 7/9/44	Lt/Cdr J. B. Harrowar	Docking 14/9/44; Machrihanish 13/10/44	Avenger II
CC Prep. Pool		formed 6/44 ex-3504 Servicing Unit		08/45	Beaufighter; Mosquito; Wellington XIII; Fortress II; Albacore
119 Sqn	NH	(formed ex-Albacore Flt of 415 Sqn at Manston); Swingfield 1/10/44	S/Ldr N. Williamson	dets to Belgium & Manston; disbanded 25/5/45	Albacore; Swordfish III
598 Sqn		Peterhead 12/3/45		disbanded Ipswich 30/4/45	Oxford; Martinet; Hurricane; Beaufighter

FLYING TRAINING COMMAND 21/9/45 to 21/10/46 - 4 GROUP TRANSPORT COMMAND 21/10/46 to 1/10/48

UNIT	CODE	FROM	COs	TO	AIRCRAFT
No. 27 Aircrew Holding Unit		10/45		06/46	
TRANSPORT COMMAND INITIAL CONVERSION UNIT		Bramcote 10/46		disbanded 16/9/48	
1510 BABS (RAT) Flt	RF	Bramcote 22/11/46		disbanded 15/9/48	Anson I; Oxford
1559 (RAT) Flt		Oakington 9/3/47		disbanded 9/8/47	Oxford
1555 (RAT) Flt	DR	Bassingbourn 19/3/47		merged with 1510 Flt 31/8/47	Oxford

TECHNICAL TRAINING COMMAND 1 OCTOBER 1948

OFFICERS' ADVANCED TRAINING SCHOOL

From Hornchurch 1/10/48 to 1958

Chief Instructors:

G/Capt. J. B. Wallis
W/Cdr J. S. Laird
W/Cdr D. F. Allen
W/Cdr G. R. Bowler
W/Cdr E. M. Sopwith
W/Cdr J. W. Grey
W/Cdr F. Murray

**EQUIPMENT OFFICERS' SCHOOL AND
SECRETARIAL BRANCH TRAINING ESTABLISHMENT**
From Digby 3/49

1/6/51 RAF Bircham Newton, including the Officers' Advanced Training School, the Equipment Officers' School and the Secretarial Branch Training School known as

THE RAF SCHOOL OF ADMINISTRATION

JUNIOR COMMAND AND STAFF SCHOOL from 1958-62
(renamed from Officers' Advanced Training School)

Chief Instructors:
W/Cdr J. R. Denny
W/Cdr E. V. Masters
W/Cdr R. E. R. Adams
W/Cdr E. Baldwin

To Ternhill 1962.

ADMINISTRATIVE APPRENTICE TRAINING SCHOOL from 1959-62
W/Cdr W. H. Bentley
W/Cdr H. Arden
W/Cdr D. S. Cartwright-Terry

To Hereford 1962.

Aircraft used by the above units included:
Chipmunk T10 - for flying experience & maintenance airframes
Hunter F5 (WP190/758M)
Halifax BVII (LW205/617M)
Spitfire VB (EP120/5377M)

HRH The Duke of Edinburgh flew to the station on several occasions during 1952 and 1953 in the course of his flying training (de Havilland Chipmunks WP861 & WP912). Later, in January 1958, he flew to Bircham Newton in a Westland Whirlwind helicopter.

Other visiting aircraft included those from No. 3 Flying Training School at Feltwell, arriving on a PPO (prior permission only) basis.

STATION CLOSED 8 DECEMBER 1962

From 18/6/63 to 1964 USAF storage.

1965 Tripartite Evaluation Squadron of Central Fighter Establishment at West Raynham used BN as landing ground while evaluating Hawker Siddeley Kestrel FGA1 V/STOL strike and reconnaissance aircraft. Aircraft used were XS692, XS694, XS695. Use of membrane, polyester, aluminium matting and grass landing pads to find out effects of jet engines on them.

APPENDIX IV

CRASHES/LOSSES

SOURCES FOR APPENDIX IV

Norfolk Crash Diary (5 vols 1939-1950) by Merv Hambling
Anson File by Ray Sturtivant (Air-Britain 1988)
Lockheed Hudson in World War Two by Andrew Hendrie (Airlife 1999)
Blenheim Strike by Theo Boiten (Air Research Publications 1995)
British, Commonwealth & German War Graves in St Mary's Churchyard, Great Bircham by Brian Hillman & John Beynon: War Graves at Great Bircham *see* Appendix I (sources)
Mike Seymour (database on 206 Sqn losses)

Note: these crashes/accidents were either losses of Bircham-based units or aircraft from other units which crashed in the vicinity of the airfield. The incident(s) described took place at Bircham Newton unless otherwise stated.

Note: the symbol † indicates that the airman was buried at St Mary's Churchyard, Great Bircham

10/06/20
Handley Page 0/400 J2254 (No. 2 School of Aerial Navigation and Bomb-Dropping, Andover)

16/10/23
Vimy F9187 (7 Sqn)
Overturned in heavy night landing and badly damaged.

20/02/24
Vimy F8641 (7 Sqn)
Hit wire fence.

13/03/24
Vimy J7239 (7 Sqn)
Stalled & crash-landed.

24/03/24
DH9A J7043 (11 Sqn)
Stalled on take-off and crashed into parked J7044.

15/04/24
Vimy F8637 (7 Sqn)
Collided with hangar doors.

03/05/24
DH9A H3550 (11 Sqn)
Bounced and overturned on landing.

29/06/24
Snipe E6839 (32 Sqn)
Overturned landing in gusty weather.

27/02/25
Avro 504 H3083 (99 Sqn)
Spun and crashed on take-off.
Aircraft crashed from height of 2000 ft. close to aerodrome. Pilot, P/O Cecil S. M. Woode of 99 Sqn killed, and mechanic 1st Class AC Ernest Forrester injured. P/O Woode buried in Fersfield Churchyard. (Report in EDP[1] 28/02/25). See p30.

25/02/26
Hyderabad J7744 (99 Sqn)
Overturned on night landing.

18/03/27
Hyderabad J7741 (99 Sqn)
Sideslipped into ground to avoid collision with taxying Virginia while landing after two hour practice flight - crew injured - P/O Greeves, AC Crocker, F/O Grace (pilot), AC Hinderland. (Report in EDP Monday 21 March 1927 'Bircham Newton Air Smash').

14/05/27
Hyderabad (99 Sqn)
From North Coates - 5 aircrew - crashed at Bulldog Sands, the Wash. Sgt Mitchell, Price and Cpl Poulter.

25/04/29
Sidestrand J9178 (101 Sqn)
Crashed on take-off.

20/08/29
Sidestrand J9181 (101 Sqn)
U/c collapsed on landing.

06/01/31
Fairey IIIF: crash over Heacham.
Wing broke off machine at 4000 ft. Both crew parachuted safely - Sgt. Hudson (pilot). Only casualty a rat, which run out of a chicken coop in terror and was crushed by the falling aeroplane (EDP).

28/08/34
Report in local newspaper - 28 August 1934.
Civil aircraft with P/O Peter H. P. Simonds as passenger, of 207 Sqn. Crash at Morston. Simonds killed.

05/05/36
Hart K2451 (18 Sqn)
Collided on take-off with Hart K2441.

09/11/36
Anson K6199/B (220 Sqn)
Stalled on take-off.

---

[1] *Eastern Daily Press.*

26/10/37
Anson K6205 (220 Sqn)
Crashed on approach.

01/11/38
Anson K8836 (206 Sqn)
Failed to return with crew from night navigation flight over North Sea. No trace ever found.

13/12/38
Anson K8759 (220 Sqn)
Undershot & hit trees.

16/12/38
Anson K8757 (206 Sqn)
Hit boundary fence on approach.

12/04/39
Henley L3281 (1 AACU)
Crashed on landing.

22/04/39
Anson K6185 (206 Sqn)
Hit trees on night approach.

09/05/39
Anson K6210 (220 Sqn)
Mid-air collision with K6225 & crashed. Anson K6225 did not crash.

05/09/39
Anson K6183 'B' (206 Sqn)
Posted missing with crew - shot down by Heinkel He115 float plane - P/O L. H. Edwards, Sgt Heslop (nav), LAC J. Quilter, AC1 G. Sheffield. Later P/O Edwards PoW.

09/09/39
Anson K6187 VX-E (206 Sqn)
Became lost on return to base in blackout and ditched by Dyck light vessel 4 miles from Calais. Crew saved - P/O R. T. Kean (pilot), P/O Barnitt, (nav).

15/09/39
Anson 'U' (206 Sqn)
Forced-landed at Catfoss with engine trouble.

03/12/39
Blenheim P6888 (21 Sqn)
Crashed on landing.

06/12/39
Anson K6189 (206 Sqn)
Failed to return from patrol.

10/01/40
Vildebeest IV K6411 (42 Sqn)
Crashed on landing: stalled. Written off but no casualties.

Date?
Vildebeest K8078 AW-N (42 Sqn)

26/01/40
Anson 'U' (206 Sqn)
Crashed in field at Morston on return journey from search for enemy sub. Bad weather - snow storms etc. No injuries.

23/02/40
Blenheim L8837 (254 Sqn)
Stalled on landing.

20/03/40
Blenheim (254 Sqn)
Crashed while landing at Lossiemouth. Slight damage - no injuries.

25/04/40
Hudson N7312 (206 Sqn)
Crashed on landing.

25/04/40
Hudson N7403 (206 Sqn)
Crashed and caught fire on landing. Crew escaped.

03/05/40
Hudson N7319 VX-C (206 Sqn)
Attacked by 3 Me109s but crash-landed - P/O Kean (pilot). Rear gunner killed - LAC Townend†.

08/05/40
Blenheim IVf P4844 (235 Sqn)
Crashed in circuit at 0010 hrs. Sgt E. O. F. Schmid (obs)†

09/05/40
Blenheim I K7134 (235 Sqn)
Crashed on take-off at 2310 hrs.

10/05/40
Blenheim IVf N6193 (235 Sqn)
Belly-landed.

12/05/40
Hudson N7353 (206 Sqn)
Failed to return from recce flight along Dutch and German coast. Pilot P/O Gray.

12/05/40
Blenheim IVf L9324 LA-P (235 Sqn)
Crashed in North Sea after attack by Bf109s. Crew killed - Sgt J. C. Robertson (obs), LAC T. J. Lowry (AG), P/O N. A. L. Smith (pilot).

12/05/40
Blenheim IVf L9189 LA-O (235 Sqn)
Crashed at Dutch coast after attack by Bf109s. One Me110 claimed shot down. Crew - Sgt H. R. Sunderland (obs) & LAC R. H. Tyler (WOp/AG) - both killed. Sgt N. A. Savill (pilot) PoW. (Wreckage salvaged by R. Neth. Air Force August 1967.)

18/05/40
Hudson N7329 (206 Sqn)
Lost after raid on Hamburg from Thornaby.

18/05/40
Hudson N7400 (206 Sqn)
Lost after raid on Hamburg from Thornaby.

19/05/40
Hudson I N7363 (206 Sqn)
Lost near Dutch coast on anti-shipping patrol. Crew missing - Sgt W. Jones, Sgt E. A. Judge, Cpl A. J. Metcalfe, AC1 H. C. Mewett.

22/05/40
Hudson N7402 (206 Sqn)
Failed to return from anti-shipping patrol. Crew missing - P/O J. A. Clark, P/O M. J. Giles, LAC L. J. Britton DFM, AC1 J. F. Peel.

24/05/40
Blenheim IVf L9259 (235 Sqn)
Lost in North Sea off island of Schiermonnikoog after attack by enemy fighter, on anti-shipping patrol. Crew killed - P/O M. E. Ryan (pilot) & Sgt W. Martin (obs). Missing LAC A. G. Smith (WOp/AG).

25/05/40
Blenheim IVf L9256 (235 Sqn)
Collided with Anson N9897 (206 Sqn).

26/05/40
Blenheim IVf P6956 (235 Sqn)
Detling-based? Aircraft spun in at Docking at 1745 hrs. P/O C. D. Warde (pilot) baled out. LAC E. P. Armstrong (AG) killed & P/O A. H. Murphy† killed.

20/06/40
Hudson I P5120 VX-C (206 Sqn)
Crashed on landing.

20/06/40
Albacore I 'P' (826 Sqn) FAA.
Failed to return from bombing raid to Texel.

20/06/40
Albacore I 'R' (826 Sqn) FAA.
Failed to return from bombing raid to Texel.

23/06/40
Albacore 4K/L7093 (826 Sqn) FAA.
Crash landing during bad weather. Damaged only.

27/06/40
Blenheim IVf P6958 LA-D (235 Sqn)
Shot down during recce by 6 a/c of Maas and Scheldt estuaries and south end of Zuider Zee, looking for invasion barges. Crew killed - P/O Hugh S. Pardoe-Williams (pilot), Sgt C. W. Thorley (obs), P/O Edward A. Saunders (WOp/AG).

27/06/40
Blenheim IVf N3543 LA-U (235 Sqn)
Shot down on above recce. Crew killed - P/O A. R. Wales (pilot), Sgt J. W. Needham (obs), Sgt T. C. Jordan (WOp/AG).

27/06/40
Blenheim IVf L9447 LA-Y (235 Sqn)
Shot down on above recce. P/O John R. Cronan (pilot) - killed, Sgt Philip L. Lloyd (WOp/AG) - killed, Sgt Aubrey O. Lancaster (obs): **latter sole survivor from 4 a/c lost that day**, PoW Stalag Luft 3 (Sagan).

27/06/40
Blenheim IVf P6957 LA-R (235 Sqn)
Shot down on above recce. Crew killed - P/O Peter Weil (pilot), Sgt Sidney K. Bartlett (obs), Sgt Alan Kempster (WOp/AG).

29/06/40
Hudson N7299 (206 Sqn)
Lost control when flarepath extinguished without warning.

04/07/40
Hudson N7368 (206 Sqn)
Failed to return from ASR for Hampdens off Texel.

04/07/40
Hudson P5162 (206 Sqn).
Failed to return from ASR as above.

22/07/40
Blenheim IVf P4835 (235 Sqn)
Forced-landed at Horsham St Faith with engine failure.

24/07/40
Whitley N1371 (77 Sqn)
Damaged by flak and forced-landed on one engine.

30/07/40
Whitley N1367 (77 Sqn)
Damaged while taxying.

03/08/40
Hudson T9282 (206 Sqn)
Failed to return.

04/08/40
Hudson VX-E (206 Sqn)
Missing with crew. P/O Gilbert, Sgt Gannon, and 2 others.

05/08/40
Hudson P5133 VX-D (206 Sqn)
Stalled and crashed in flames near Syderstone. Crew killed inc. P/O R. T. Kean (pilot) and P/O R. Rustom†.

06/08/40
Hudson P5153 (206 Sqn)
Crash-landed. Bombs exploded.

07/08/40
Hudson N7395 (206 Sqn)
Overshot on landing & bombs exploded.

07/08/40
Albacore 4L (826 Sqn) FAA
Collision with Hudson during night landing.

14/08/40
Hudson N7401 (206 Sqn)
Aircraft crashed in Docking circuit. P/O Herbert G. Ballantyne (pilot) killed†, P/O J. Stephenson
(pilot) killed†, Sgt Eddie Fitzgerald (WOp/AG) killed - buried in Norwich.

15/08/40
Hudson (206 Sqn)
Attacked by enemy seaplane north of Borkum. Crashed in flames in sea.

30/08/40
Blenheim IVf L9262 (235 Sqn)
Spun into ground near Bagthorpe. P/O J. S. Priestley† (pilot).

01/09/40
Hudson N7367 (206 Sqn)
Swung on take-off, caught fire and bombs exploded.

02/09/40
Albacore (826 Sqn) FAA
Shot down by flak on bombing raid of invasion barges.

03/09/40
Hudson N7351 (206 Sqn)
Hit trees on take-off & belly-landed at Docking.
(see letter on p 108)

07/09/40
Hudson T9276 (206 Sqn)
Stalled on landing avoiding a Hurricane.

11/09/40
Blenheim IVf Z5725 (235 Sqn)
Blenheim IVf L9396 (235 Sqn)
Both crews (above) missing on attack on enemy shipping at Calais - F/Lt F. W. Flood, P/O N. B.
Shorrocks, Sgt Sharpe, P/O Wickens-Smith, P/O A. Green, Sgt R. Watts.

11/09/40
Albacore I (826 Sqn) FAA
Same raid as above - a/c shot down - Lt Downes and Sub-Lt Mallex picked up. Stevens (AG)
missing.

13/09/40
Blenheim IVf L9393 (235 Sqn)
Crashed in forced landing nr Grimston.

23/09/40
Beaufort L9852 (22 Sqn)
Stalled on night landing at Docking.

27/09/40
Beaufort N1117 (22 Sqn)
Flew into ground at Docking on night approach after being damaged by flak.

29/09/40
Hampden P4395 (50 Sqn)
Crashed on take-off due to engine failure.

30/09/40
Albacore I 'P' (826 Sqn) FAA
Failed to return from raid to Vlaardingen.

01/10/40
Hampden P4411 'C' (50 Sqn)
Crashed at Docking at 0615 hrs after raid on Berlin. Machine destroyed but crew safe.

08/10/40
Whitley T4137 GE-K (58 Sqn)
Crashed near Docking on return from ops. Crew killed. P/O R. A. Hadley† (pilot).

10/10/40
Hudson T9357 (206 Sqn)
Hit hedge on landing at Docking.

14/10/40
Hudson N7362 VX-F (206 Sqn)
Failed to return from patrol. No result from ASR which continued until 16/10. P/O Lascelles (pilot).

16/10/40
Hudson T9303 (206 Sqn)
Failed to return.

21/10/40
Whitley (58 Sqn)

24/10/40
Blenheim P4858 'Z' (17 OTU) (based Upwood)
Attacked by He111 while on training flight over Docking. Crash-landed. Crew unhurt.

24/10/40
Beaufort.
Attacked and damaged over Docking. Landed safely.

28/10/40
Blenheim T2229 (105 Sqn)
Crashed near airfield 0036 hrs with flak damage.

16/11/40
Hudson T9382 VX-B (206 Sqn)
Forced-landing at Birchington - hit over target by shell. Tried to make Manston but ditched in sea off Birchington. F/Lt Dias and crew unhurt (AG sprained ankle) - all waded ashore safely.

17/11/40
Hampden X3008 (44 Sqn)
Overshot at airfield at 0935 hrs in bad weather on return from ops.

19/11/40
Hudson N7300 VX-B (206 Sqn)
Crashed into wood in fog near West Raynham on main Fakenham - Swaffham road. (near West Raynham Hall). Crew killed F/O H. A. Skeats, Sgt P. L. Brace, Sgt S. Bradley, Sgt J. H. Moss (WOp/AG)†.

23/11/40
Blenheim IVf LA-S (235 Sqn)
Hit bombing target and pilot (P/O Davison) wounded. Sgt Haslett wounded. One remaining bomb exploded on landing and set a/c on fire. Pilot helped to drag Haslett to safety.

23/11/40
Blenheim IVf T1999 (235 Sqn)
Also hit making attack. Sgt Lawrence (pilot) wounded and Sgt Ross (obs) also wounded. Crash-landed on return.

02/12/40
Blenheim IVf LA-Y (235 Sqn)
Crashed at Holbeach range in bad weather after sweep. Crew saved.

16/12/40
Blenheim IVf Z5754 LA-B (235 Sqn)
Crashed in sea off Titchwell after convoy escort of minesweepers. Crew killed inc. P/O Coggins (pilot), P/O N. A. Sadler (obs)†.

20/12/40
Hudson N7333 VX-E (206 Sqn)
Crashed on take-off on *EMRO* patrol 0405 hrs. Crew killed. P/O R. Ward† (pilot), P/O K. J. Dobbie, P/O R. Ward, Sgts G. R. Ellerington & N. G. Riddell.

01/01/41
Hudson T9287 (206 Sqn)
Crashed into barn after low flying near Langham. 8 Crew killed. F/O H. Featherstone (pilot), AC1 G. A. Meridew†, P/O J. B. Allen, P/O Mansell, P/O Bakiralky, Sgt Plowright, LAC Miller, AC Gilder.

04/02/41
Hudson T9331 VX-S (206 Sqn)
Failed to return from patrol. P/Os A. R. Blackett & H. W. Noble, Sgts J. T. Kennett and A. Soppitt.

11/02/41
Whitley T4217 (51 Sqn)
Abandoned near airfield on return from ops.

12/02/41
Hudson T9289 (206 Sqn)
Failed to return.

12/02/41
Hudson T9346 (206 Sqn)
Abandoned in fog off Caithness.

12/02/41
Hudson T9350 (206 Sqn)
Abandoned in fog off Caithness.

14/02/41
Blenheim IVf Z5970 LA-T (235 Sqn)
Crashed on cross-country 1 mile north of Croxton, near Fakenham at 2130 hrs. P/O Chamberlain and Sgt Burns injured. P/O E. R. Phillips (pilot) killed†.

14/02/41
Blenheim IVf LA-L (235 Sqn)
Crashed near Thetford on cross-country. Crew killed - Sgts Mason, Stanger, Pond.

14/02/41
Blenheim IVf V5431 (235 Sqn)
Hit ground on overshoot.

02/03/41
Hampden X3147 (61 Sqn)
Aircraft crashed at Syderstone on return from ops due to lack of fuel. 4 crew killed inc. Sgt R. W. T. Clarke†, Sgt H. G. Loates (WOp/AG)†.

08/03/41
Blenheim IVf V5896 (235 Sqn)
Crashed in forced landing.

08/03/41
Hudson T9357 (206 Sqn)
Damaged beyond repair, Docking.

13/3/41
Whitley T4140 (102 Sqn)
Overshot runway at 0100 hrs on return from ops to Berlin owing to engine trouble. Aircraft crashed at Blackburn Wood near Docking & burst into flames. P/O Malim (pilot) and F/O Cubitt killed.

23/03/41
Blenheim IVf L9404 LA-A (235 Sqn)
Shot down in sea on *Pirate* patrol after attacking enemy ships - flakship and E-Boat. Crew - Sgts C. R. Evans, E. H. Harvey, G. S. M. McLeod.

23/03/41
Blenheim IVf Z6085 LA-D (235 Sqn)
Shot down in sea on patrol after attacking enemy ships - flakship and E-Boat. Crew - P/O A. W.
B. Newman, Sgts H. Willis & V. S. Key.

23/03/41
Wellington T2719 (300 Sqn)
Swung on take-off & hit boundary fence at Langham.

23/03/41
Wellington R1273 (300 Sqn)
Swung on take-off & hit boundary fence at Langham.

01/04/41
Blenheim IV V5764 (235 Sqn)
Stalled and spun into ground near Hunstanton. P/O P. H. Blake† (pilot).

01/04/41
Blenheim Z6022 LA-B (235 Sqn)
Crashed in sea near Snettisham. Crew saved? Square search organised and wreckage sighted on
beach there - a/c had landed with u/c down and turned turtle - personnel warned about beach mines.

04/04/41
Blenheim IV PJ-P (59 Sqn)
Forced-landed Swanton Morley with engine trouble.

10/04/41
Wellington IC R1049 DF-B (221 Sqn)
Shot down by intruder and crashed in flames after take-off from airfield (or Langham). Crashed at
Burnham Westgate. Crew killed - P/O P. C. Brown (pilot), Sgt F. H. Butterworth (AG), Sgt E. R.
Owens (AG).

21/04/41
Hudson T9304 VX-C (206 Sqn)
Crashed at Castle-on-Dinas, Cornwall. All four crew killed - P/O R. L. Tanner (pilot), Sgt G. V.
Reeves (obs), Sgt C. T. Handley (WOp/AG), F/Sgt F. Allen (WOp/AG).

23/04/41
Wellington 'K' (144 Sqn)
Forced-landed. No casualties.

05/05/41
Blenheim IVF Z5742 LA-A (235 Sqn)
Crashed in North Sea off Borkum on anti-shipping patrol. Crew - Sgt B. L. T. Crawforth (pilot),
Sgt C. D. Robertson (obs) both killed. Missing - Sgt W. K. Blackford (WOp/AG).

06/05/41
Blenheim IV PJ-A (59 Sqn)
Failed to return from *EMRO* patrol. S/Ldr G. T. Palmer DFC, Sgt A. D. Whitson, F/Sgt C. E. A.
Dunlop DFM missing.

09/05/41
Hampden AD901 (144 Sqn)
Forced-landed in field at Syderstone with engine failure at 0500 hrs.

15/05/41
Blenheim LA-Q (235 Sqn)
Crashed on landing after *Pirate* patrol.

16/05/41
Hudson T9324 VX-N (206 Sqn)
Aircraft failed to return from *Pirate* patrol - came down in Thames estuary.
Crew killed - P/Os R. J. Tearle & L. Cooper, Sgt A. G. Knight.

25/05/41
Wellington N3010 (311 Sqn)
Swung on take-off & hit trees at Langham at 1130 hrs.

28/05/41
Blenheim IVf Z5968 LA-V (235 Sqn)
This a/c and V5453 (below) crashed in North Sea NW of island of Terschelling after attack by
enemy fighter during anti-shipping *Pirate* patrol. Both crews killed - P/O John O. Fenton (pilot),
Sgt R. H. Johnson (obs), Sgt O. J. Dee (WOp/AG).
A third a/c LA-D got back safely.

28/05/41
Blenheim IVf V5453 LA-O (235 Sqn)
F/Sgt H. T. Naughtin, Sgt S. Gordon, Sgt R. Oldroyd.

07/06/41
Blenheim V5722 (500 Sqn)
Crash-landed 1008 hrs near airfield with u/c up.

08/06/41
Blenheim IV V5689 (500 Sqn)
Flew into ground in mist at Holme at 1635 and caught fire. 3 killed. Pilot F/O F. W. Hall-Jones†.

16/06/41
Halifax L9506 (35 Sqn)
Crash-landed near airfield after being attacked by Me109 on raid on Hanover.

20/06/41
Anson N9732 MK-V (500 Sqn)
Collided with Hurricane L3391 and crashed 3m SW of Aylsham.

30/06/41
Wellington R1231 (3 Gp Tr. Flt)
Engine failure on take-off. Swung & hit fence at Langham.

01/07/41
Hudson AE609 (206 Sqn)
Failed to return.

02/07/41
Blenheim IVf Z6171 WR-K (248 Sqn)
Crashed in North Sea off Texel after being shot down by fighter (pilot Unteroffizier Metzler - II./
JG52). Crew missing - P/O R. J. Powell, F/Sgt W. G. Sharratt, Sgt H. J. Robinson.

215

04/07/41
Blenheim T2078 (248 Sqn)
Crashed on overshoot at West Raynham.

07/07/41
Blenheim IV Z6041 MK-O (500 Sqn)
Shot down by intruder when landing at Docking. Crashed near Burnham Market. All crew killed.
F/O A. Leeson† (pilot), F/O R. W. V. Smith, Sgt C. V. Pearce, Sgt A. N. F. Glide.

09/07/41
Whitley Z6625 (78 Sqn)
Hit tree and haystack near airfield on return from ops 0405 hrs.

13/07/41
Blenheim PZ-W (53 Sqn)
Overshot landing after *Nomad* patrol with 4 other a/c. Badly damaged but crew unhurt.

15/07/41
Blenheim 'A' (1403 Flt)
Failed to return from patrol. Sgts Culley, Anderson, Elliott.

15/07/41
Whitley 'E' (102 Sqn)
Crashed on landing on return from raid.

15/07/41 Stirling 'Y' (7 Sqn)
Crashed on landing after raid on Hanover.

25/07/41
Blenheim V5393 (500 Sqn)
Crashed near Burnham Market.

31/07/41
Blenheim Z6048 (500 Sqn)
Hit tree on approach at Langham.

07/08/41
Blenheim IV L4899 MK-E (500 Sqn)
Crashed on anti-shipping patrol to Dutch coast. Crew missing - F/Sgt R. L. Burton, P/O L. Ward, Sgt W. S. Robinson.

10/08/41
Hudson V AM672 (53 Sqn)
Crashed on anti-shipping patrol in North Sea off island of Terschelling - shot down by flakship. Crew killed - P/O A. F. Buck (pilot), Sgt L. H. Wood (obs), F/Lt I. P. Magrath (pilot). Missing - F/Sgt T. E. Stepney.

13/08/41
Halifax
Crash-landed at Docking.

15/08/41
Blenheim IV Z6063 (500 Sqn)
Crashed in North Sea on anti-shipping patrol. Crew missing F/O C. M. Elgar, Sgt D. A. Butterfield, Sgt J. Halls.

20/08/41
Henley L3320 (1 AACU)
Forced-landed at Langham with engine failure.

24/08/41
Blenheim IV Z6039 (500 Sqn)
Shot down by flak off Hook of Holland. Crew killed - P/O Gordon C. M. Fletcher (pilot), Sgt J. E. Mylrea (obs), Sgt Hartley Walton (WOp/AG).

30/08/41
Whitley Z6951 (102 Sqn)
Lost speed in circuit at Docking at 0500 hrs. Crashed nr Friar's Thorne Farm.

30-31/08/41
Blenheim IV Z6164 MK-V (500 Sqn)
Crashed in North Sea. Crew F/O Ian H. N. Terry (pilot), Sgt Harry D. Poole (obs), Sgt Alan C. Scrivens (WOp/AG). All posted missing

30/31/08/41
Blenheim IV V5525 MK-B (500 Sqn)
Shot down on general recce near Schiphol. Sgts David A. Crosbie (pilot), D. C. Hyslop (pilot), Alan H. Peek (obs). All posted missing.

31/08/41
Hudson RR-H (407 Sqn)
Forced-landed at Docking from North Coates.

03/09/41
Hampden 'P' (50 Sqn)
Crash-landed after raid on Kiel.

03/09/41
Hampden 'C' (83 Sqn)
Crash-landed after bombing aerodrome west of Berlin.

03/09/41
Hampden 'K' (49 Sqn)
Crash-landed after bombing railway station at Berlin.

05/09/41
Spitfire P8166 (19 Sqn)
Lost control at Langham and crashed in poor visibility during ferry flight from Coltishall to Matlaske. Pilot F/Lt Arthur F. Vokes killed†.[2]

---

[2] Detail about this crash in *The Inivisible Thread: A Spitfire's Tale* by Dilip Sarkar (Ramrod 1992) p29.

17/09/41
Beaufighter T3351 (248 Sqn)
Tail unit and port wing detached at 1500 ft near airfield.

20/09/41
Wellington II W5382 (12 Sqn)
Crash-landed at Docking after jettisoning bombs in Emden area.

23/09/41
Blenheim IV V5684 (500 Sqn)
Anti-shipping patrol. Crashed in North Sea. Crew missing - F/O R. E. M. Hughes-Chamberlain, P/O S. G. Nicoll, Sgt J. B. Crees.

10/10/41
Blenheim IV MK-F (500 Sqn)
Aircraft missing on *Nomad* patrol in Hook of Holland area. Missing Sgt R. H. Coomber, F/Sgt R. C. Roberts. F/O E. A. Webb (PoW).

16/10/41
Blenheim IV MK-H (500 Sqn)
Lost after error of gyro compass. Made landfall in Wexford area (Eire).

25/10/41
Blenheim IV V5538 MK-X (500 Sqn)
Crashed in North Sea on anti-shipping (*Nomad*) patrol. Crew missing - P/O L. W. Brown, Sgt P. A. V. Lyons, Sgt J. K. Mitchell.

31/10/41
Blenheim IV V5537 MK-M (500 Sqn)
Crashed on anti-shipping patrol to Frisian Islands. Crew missing - S/Ldr F. C. Phipps, Sgt A. A. Miles, Sgt T. P. Mowan.

02/11/41
Blenheim IV Z6163 MK-Y (500 Sqn)
Crashed on take-off, heading for strike mission.
(*Norfolk Crash Diary* states for that date Blenheim Z7449 of 500 Sqn: bombs fell off & exploded as a/c took off at 2215 hrs).

04/11/41
Blenheim IV Z5959 MK-X (500 Sqn)
Crashed in North Sea off island of Terschelling on anti-shipping sortie to Frisian Islands. Crew missing - F/O W. J. Sipprell, Sgt H. R. Davies, Sgt A. T. Hall. ASR by Beaus of 248 Sqn failed to find any trace.

01/12/41
Hudson AM718 MK-A (500 Sqn)
Crashed near Docking-Choseley road on night test flight, and caught fire. All 6 crew killed.
P/O A.F.N. Ladefoged (pilot)†, AC1 Richard Chadwick†, AC1 Hilton A. Lonergan RAAF†, Sgt. F. L. Morgan (WOp/AG)†.

11/12/41
Hurricane V7625 (56 OTU)
Spun into ground near airfield.

12/12/41
Hampden AD979 (49 Sqn)
Crashed after raid. F/Sgt Stuart C. Black RNZAF†.

15/01/42
Hampden AE441 'P' (144 Sqn)
Crash-landed near Langham after bombing raid to Hamburg 0045 hrs.

16/01/42
Hudson V9097 MK-N (500 Sqn)
Crashed in field at Lowlands Farm, Bacton, in snow storm. Crew of 4 killed & memorial erected at crash site. Crew P/O J. Macgillivray (pilot), Sgt J. S. Brownsell (WOp/AG), Sgt R. B. Wark (WOp/AG), Sgt W. A. Sanger (AG)†.

22/01/42
Beaufighter (248 Sqn)
Failed to return from patrol. Crew P/O Walker, F/Lt Blennerhasset.

30/01/42
Hudson MK-P (500 Sqn)
Went down in sea on *Nomad* in direction of Sylt.

30/01/42
Hudson MK-W (500 Sqn)
Forced-landed at Winterton after going through snow storm after anti-shipping strike.

08/02/42
Hudson AM845 MK-P (500 Sqn)
Dived into ground and exploded at Docking on return from shipping strike. Crew killed - P/O W. Hollingsworth (pilot)†, Sgts Pound, Morgan, Hazell.

08/02/42
Hudson AM677 (500 Sqn)
Crash-landed at Docking.

08/02/42
Beaufighter WR-F (248 Sqn)
Failed to return from patrol to recce enemy shipping. Sgt van de Walle and Sgt Brown.

13/02/42
Hudson V8993 OS-J (279 Sqn)
Missing after ASR. Sgts Garrard & Redhead.
279's first loss?

14/02/42
Beaufighter WR-Z (248 Sqn)
Missing after 'recco' patrol to Dutch coast. Sgts Theater & Ryall.

16/02/42
Hampden AD801 (144 Sqn)
Forced-landed at airfield at 1850 hrs after engine failure.

17/02/42
Hudson AE647 MK-D (500 Sqn)
Crashed on Brancaster beach on *Nomad* shortly after take-off.
Crew killed - F/Sgt A. B. Giles (pilot)†, P/O Stote.

17/02/42
Hudson AM663 (500 Sqn)
Crashed on beach at Brancaster after take-off.

21/02/42
Hudson MK-K (500 Sqn)
Failed to return from patrol - Sgt Pitkin and P/O Crozier.

26/02/42
Hudson PZ-E (53 Sqn)
Crash-landed at Docking on return from search for enemy convoy.

27/02/42
Wellington DF-Z (221 Sqn)
Failed to return from patrol. P/Os Joad & Walden and 4 others missing.

06/04/42
Hudson AM684 RR-D (407 Sqn)
Failed to return from *Reefer* patrol - one of 4 a/c. 407's first loss?
P/Os Foley, Lowry. WOp McCann and Sgt Leckie.

13/04/42
Hudson V8996 (279 Sqn)
Crashed in forced landing 3m W of Docking.

18/04/42
Hudson RR-P (407 Sqn)
Failed to return from strike patrol. Sgt Kennedy, W/O Girradote.

28/04/42
Hudson AM571 RR-D (407 Sqn)
Failed to return from *Nomad* patrol. P/O Majeau, F/Sgt Richard, Sgts Wheadon and Hancock.

08/05/42
Hudson AM540 (53 Sqn)
Damaged by Bf109 and crash-landed at Langham.

08/05/42
Hudson V8981 NO-M (320 Sqn)
Failed to return from patrol. Crew missing: Sgt Jansen, Sgt Vos, LAC Koehl and Cpl van Klaveren
- 320's first loss at Bircham?

09/05/42
Hudson AM783 (500 Sqn)
Crashed on take-off.

14/05/42
Blenheim Z7355 'A' (1401 Flt)
Crash-landed Flitcham Hill after take-off at 1700 hrs. Crew injured - F/Sgt Garthwaite, P/O Luddington, Sgt Dale.

15/05/42 to 16/05/42
Hudson III AE525 NO-H (320 Sqn)
(From Docking) Crashed in North Sea north off island of Terschelling - shot down by night fighter and exploded in mid-air (Hauptmann Helmut Lent II./NJG2).
Crew missing - Lt J. M. Mulder, J. H. Stork, A. L. Sens, E. De Weerd.

Four Hudsons (407 Sqn) failed to return from shipping strike off Dutch coast (P/O W. A. Haliburton & crew, WO J. W. Daubner & crew, F/Sgt N. C. Doehn & crew, F/Sgt G. F. Algar & crew: Hudsons, serials AM679, AM525, plus two other a/c).[3]

Hudson AM864 (407 Sqn)
Attack on enemy convoy off Dutch coast. On return crashed at Digby - all crew killed. P/O James W. Creeden DFM, RCAF (pilot)†, F/Sgt James A. Easton RCAF (WOp/AG)†, F/O Ralph K. Howson RCAF†, F/Sgt Douglas E. Parks RCAF (WOp/AG)†, F/Sgt J. H. Powell (obs) (latter buried at New Hunstanton).

Hudson AM906 (407 Sqn)
Damaged during the attack on convoy but returned to crash on landing at Docking. Crew included P/O F. Kay DFC (pilot) - injured. Navigator P/O Angus L. Kippen RCAF killed†.

27/05/42
Blenheim 'B' (1401 Flt)
Failed to return from *Rhombus*. Crew P/O Marshall, Sgt Thimblebee, Sgt Groves.

29/05/42
Hudson III AM939 NO-E (320 Sqn)
Failed to return after attack on convoy off Dutch coast. Ditched in North Sea off island of Terschelling (hit by flak). Crew - S/Ldr H. Schaper, Sgt A.C. Den Boer, Sgt A.J.I. Lensing, M. Loos. Crew picked up by flakship and became PoWs.

29/05/42
Hudson III V9122 NO-N (320 Sqn)
Failed to return after attack on convoy off Dutch coast. Crashed in North Sea off island of Terschelling (collided with barrage balloon cable). Crew missing - Maj. P. Buijnink (pilot), Sgt A. L. M. van den Broek (2nd pilot), H. L. Emmens (AG), M. J. Versluis (WOp).

29/05/42
Hudson V AM650 RR-D (407 Sqn)
Failed to return after attack on enemy convoy off Dutch coast. Crew - Missing F/O C. F. Race, F/O R. M. D. Robinson. Killed W/O W. P. McCarthy (WOp/AG), F/Sgt Clarke.

---

[3] Other 407 Sqn losses on 15/16 May include the following aircrew: Killed F/Sgt N.C. Doehn, P/O S.R. Balden. Missing P/O G.F. Cook, P/O A.R.R. Farley, P/O W.A. Haliburton, P/O L.N. Skinner, W/O J.W. Daubner, F/Sgt G.F. Algar, F/Sgt W.M. Crane, F/Sgt M. Knight, F/Sgt D. McDonald, F/Sgt G.F. MacNutt, F/Sgt A.J.W. Pottle, F/Sgt L.O. Scott, F/Sgt G. A. Tooth.

04/06/42
Hudson V9102 (1401 Flt)
Crashed on landing.

13/06/42
Hudson AM711 (407 Sqn)
Crashed in sea off Thorney Island.

20/06/42
Hudson FH346 RR-A (407 Sqn)
Missing from anti-shipping strike. Crew P/O Little, Sgt Aikenhead.

25/06/42
Tiger Moth DE166 (1 AACU)
Stalled and spun into ground near airfield.

26/06/42
Hudson T9435 NO-R (320 Sqn)
Failed to return from Op. *Millennium II* (1000-bomber raid on Bremen). Crew S/Ldr Graff, F/Lt
Mattysen.

26/06/42
Beaufighter 'M' (235 Sqn)
Hit water during sea search. Only pilot rescued.

30/06/42
Halifax W1062 (78 Sqn)
Crash-landed at Docking on return from ops at Bremen.

09/07/42
Beaufighter 'U' (236 Sqn)
Failed to return after recce to Dutch coast. Crew P/O Harding and Sgt Robertson.

09/07/42
Beaufighter 'V' (236 Sqn)
Failed to return after recce to Dutch coast. Crew P/O Smith and F/Sgt Taylor.

26/07/42
Mosquito DK289 (1401 Flt)
Missing - no details.

30/07/42
Hudson AM860 RR-K (407 Sqn)
Crash-landed near Ringstead after anti-shipping strike (out of fuel). Crew injured.

09/08/42
Swordfish 'B' (811 Sqn) FAA
Failed to return after 'gardening' op. Lts Bentley & Mayo.

09/08/42
Swordfish 'C' (811 Sqn) FAA
Failed to return after 'gardening' op. Sub-Lt Wilson.

18/08/42
Stirling R9151 (15 Sqn)
Belly-landed at Docking after flak damage in raid on Osnabruck.

06/09/42
Hudson AM701 RR-V (407 Sqn)
Failed to return after attack on targets over enemy coast and Frisian Islands. P/Os Wilks and Foskett.

07/09/42
Hudson EW923 (320 Sqn)
Crashed Thorney Island.

08/09/42
Mosquito TE-P (521 Sqn)
Failed to return from *Pampa* patrol. F/Sgt Farrell and Sgt Vince.

04/10/42
Hudson FH379 TE-W (521 Sqn)
Collision after take-off for *Rhombus* patrol, in thick fog with southerly mast of MF/DF Station, lost wing and crashed. Crew killed - F/O R. C. Porter (pilot)†. Others - Sgts Hatherly, Hawkins, and Harris (WOp), W/O Knights.

13/10/42
Wellington X3963 (420 Sqn)
Engine failed at take-off and stalled, Docking at 0100 hrs.

14/10/42
Wellington 'D' (420 Sqn)
Crashed near Docking after raid on Kiel.

27/10/42
Hudson N7302 (320 Sqn)
Missing.

01/11/42
Hudson FH466 (521 Sqn)
Destroyed after catching fire taking off on *Rhombus*. Crew OK and took Blenheim instead.

04/11/42
Hudson AE594 (279 Sqn)
Crashed.

09/11/42
Hudson EW912 NO-K (320 Sqn)
Failed to return (from Thorney Island) from shipping strike off Ijmuiden. Crew F/Lt van Loon and F/Lt de Boer.

11/11/42
Spitfire R6817 (521 Sqn)
Crashed in attempted landing at Coltishall after engine failure.

12/11/42
Tiger Moth W7954 (1 AACU)
Crashed on take-off at Langham.

19/11/42
Blenheim Z7365 (521 Sqn)
Crashed on take-off .

22/11/42
Hudson VI EW903 NO-E (320 Sqn)
Crashed in North Sea off Dutch coast after *Nomad* (shot down by night fighter - Lt Lothar Linke IV./NJG1.) Crew missing - Sgt C. L. G. Van Heugten (pilot), Sgt L. A. Hoogteiling, J. de Ligt, J. A. Den Ouden.

27/11/42
Hudson T9407 (279 Sqn)
Crashed on take-off.

23/12/42
Hudson AM695 RR-K (407 Sqn)
Now based at Docking. Failed to return from *Rooster* - crew F/Lt Ellam and F/O Woodward.

20/01/43
Hudson RR-X (407 Sqn)
Failed to return after anti-shipping strike. F/O Anderson and F/Sgt Mattison.

27/01/43
Hudson VI EW919 NO-C (320 Sqn)
Crashed in North Sea on anti-shipping op - target convoy near Borkum.
Crew missing - H. J. V. D. Berg, Cpl J. H. Cloesmeijer, Sgts T. J. De Gast, and C. L. Kost.

03/02/43
Hudson NO-G (320 Sqn)
Mid-air collision and damaged but got back to Docking.

04/02/43
Hudson OS-E (279 Sqn)
Failed to return from ASR. F/Sgt Marchand, WO Slugorski, F/Sgts Evans and Preece, Sgt Gendron.

04/02/43
Hampden AD906 (415 Sqn)
Overshot and ground looped at Docking 1730 hrs.

17/02/43
Martinet HN949 (1482 Flt)
Lost speed in turn, stalled and crashed.

18/02/43
Hampden AE435 'U' (415 Sqn)
Based Thorney Island? Crashed and burst into flames at take-off for convoy strike off Ijmuiden from Docking. Crew killed - Sgt Adams, WO2 Z. M. Niblock (WOp/AG)†, WO2 P. B. Campbell (pilot)†, WO2 R. E. Vokey (WOp/AG)† & F/O K. R. Maffre (obs)†.

18/02/43
Hampden 'O' (415 Sqn)
Failed to return from above op. Crew F/O Brenner, F/Sgt Rowe, Sgt Vautier, Sgt Glass.
Crew were rescued and later returned to the squadron.

21/02/43
Hampden (415 Sqn)
Crew saved after ditching & rescued by Walrus and landed Martlesham Heath.

25/02/43
Mosquito DZ475 (521 Sqn)
Missing. Presumed enemy action.

28/02/43
Hudson T9443 (279 Sqn)
Crashed on take-off from airfield.

05/03/43
Mosquito DZ362 TE-T (521 Sqn)
Crashed into sea after enemy action. P/O Hatton, F/Sgt Bartolotti. Hatton rescued.

12/03/43
Hudson AM558 (407 Sqn)
Swung on take-off and crashed at Docking.

16/03/43
Mosquito DZ477 (139 Sqn)
Crash-landed at Docking on return from ops.

17/03/43
Whitley BD425 PZ-O (53 Sqn)
Sgt Milligan overshot landing in cross wind at 1516 hrs. U/c collapsed and fuselage broke in two.

26/03/43
Whitley EB331 PZ-U (53 Sqn)
Failed to return from sea navigational exercise. (Pilot Sgt Kirby). Next day rescue launch picked up body of one crew member in sea - Sgt Matthews. Loss presumed due to enemy action. (Only fatal crash of sqn while at Bircham).

11/04/43
Gladiator N2307 (1401 Flt)
Tipped up while running up. Not repaired.

15/04/43
Hampden AD767 (415 Sqn)
Tyre burst on take-off from Docking at 1545 hrs, swung and u/c collapsed.

15/04/43
Whitley PZ-N (53 Sqn)
F/Lt Sutton overshot landing on return from navigational exercise causing u/c to collapse and break. Category 'B'.[4]

---

[4] Opinion expressed in ORB that Bircham runway too short for Whitleys (02/03/43) and night flying had to be done at Docking - letter from J.M.C. 'Jock' Manson 25/08/92.

17/04/43 or 18/04/43
Anson AX628 YF-B (280 Sqn)
Forced-landed 4 miles S of Wells (Little Walsingham) after ASR. Crew uninjured.

21/04/43
Wellington X9751 (304 Sqn)
Crashed on landing at Docking.

01/05/43
Halifax W7929 (78 Sqn)
Crashed at Docking after receiving flak damage over Essen.

13/05/43
Wellington N2989 (304 Sqn)
Crashed on landing at Docking.

15/05/43
Hudson (279 Sqn)
Damaged on ASR. F/Sgt Rusby killed.

12/06/43
Wellington MS486 'R' (196 Sqn)
Crashed and caught fire at Docking. 2 out of 5 crew killed. F/O R. P. Lea† - rest injured and taken to RAF Hospital, Ely.

18/07/43
Hampden P1291 'P' (1401 Flt)
Reported to have ditched after *Rhombus*. 279 Sqn Hudson on ASR and 4 crew saved.

23/07/43
Hampden L4193 (1401 Flt)
Forced landing after suspected engine failure.

03/08/43
Whitley Z9206 (1484 Flt)
Overshot, swung and u/c collapsed at 1215 hrs at Langham.

13/08/43
Warwick BV276 (Warwick TU)
Caught fire on ground at Docking.

17/08/43
Hudson EW904 (279 Sqn)
Swung on take-off and cartwheeled at airfield.

24/08/43
Hudson T9399 OS-R (279 Sqn)
Failed to return after being attacked by 2 Me110s during ASR. F/Sgt Neil and F/O Whapham.

04/09/43
Hudson V9044 (279 Sqn)
Ditched on ASR.

12/09/43
Gladiator TE-C (521 Sqn)
Forced-landed on *Thum* sortie on field at Mintlyns (*sic*) Farm near King's Lynn.

15/09/43
Hampden AE192 (415 Sqn)
U/c collapsed on landing at Docking.

10/10/43
Hampden L4204 TE-L (521 Sqn)
Crashed on take-off for *Rhombus* patrol at Docking. Poor visibility. Hit gun post.

08/11/43
Gladiator N2309 (521 Sqn)
Crashed in forced landing, Magdalen Road, King's Lynn.

13/11/43
Hudson AE531 (279 Sqn)
Failed to return from nav. exercise.

24/12/43
Hudson T9408 (279 Sqn)
Crashed in forced landing, Docking.

20/01/44
Albacore (415 Sqn)
Failed to return from anti-shipping sortie. Crew missing inc. S/Ldr E. W. Cowan (CO 'A' Flt).

30-31/01/44
Lancaster (626 Sqn)
Crash-landed at Docking after attack on Berlin. damaged. WOp killed.

07/02/44
Wellington (415 Sqn)
Crew missing on anti-shipping sortie.
F/Lt J. F. Acer (pilot), WO2 J. L. Dissing (2nd pilot), WO2 C. J. McCarvill (nav), WO1 E. J. Dorval, WO1 C. E. Simpson, WO2 N. C. E. West, WO2 J. E. Russell. (LAC J. W. Husselbee believed to be on board too).

08/02/44
Wellington (415 Sqn)
Crew missing on anti-shipping sortie.
S/Ldr M. W. Gibson (CO 'B' Flt), WO2 A. R. Armitage (nav), P/O E. Hanson, WO2 J. L. A. Champoux, F/Sgt R. Urban, F/Sgt R. MacGillivray, Lt O. A. Lamb (USA).

26/03/44
Hudson AM554 OS-E (279 Sqn)
Crashed on take-off, heading for sea search for 100 Gp a/c. A/c destroyed by fire but crew uninjured.

28/03/44
Gladiator N5621 (521 Sqn)
Swung off runway and hit obstruction at Gt Massingham.

09/04/44
Albacore (415 Sqn)
Crashed during training exercise at Thorney Island. All crew killed - F/O P. D. Mackie (pilot), F/O E. McFarland (nav), F/Lt G. Loft, AC2 A. L. Thomas.

06/05/44
Hudson AE585 OS-V (279 Sqn)
Recalled to base with engine trouble on ASR - engine cut and a/c crash-landed at Harpley but crew uninjured.

07/05/44
Wellington NH-G (415 Sqn)
Crashed at Langham after engine trouble on armed recce of enemy convoy route, Hook of Holland area. Severe damage but crew uninjured.

21/05/44
Beaufighter NE (or NB?)824 (404 Sqn)
Pilot raised tail on take-off, prop hit bump on grass runway and u/c collapsed.

23/05/44
Beaufort X8936 (Langham Station Flt)
Swung on take-off and u/c collapsed, Langham.

05/06/44
Beaufighter LZ435 (489 Sqn)
Stalled on approach at Langham.

12-13/06/44
Wellington (415 Sqn)
Missing after attack on 17 E-Boats. Shot down with engines on fire in Ostend area. Crew P/O G. C. Krahn (pilot), WO D. Laurie, WO J. R. Dryden (nav), WO G. E. Robertson (WOp/AG), WO J. M. Lacombe (WOp/AG), WO G. A. Henson (WOp/AG), WO F. L. Ladd (WOp/AG).

12/07/44
Wellington 7R-K (524 Sqn)
Failed to return after cross-over patrol.

13/07/44
Wellington NH-G (415 Sqn)
Failed to return after armed recce of enemy convoy route off Frisian Islands.

16/07/44
Ventura FP566 (521 Sqn)
Engine cut at 1616 hrs near Stanhoe Church on approach. Belly-landed and damaged by fire.

09/08/44
Beaufighter NT958 (455 Sqn)
Engine failure after single engined overshoot, and belly-landed in field at Langham.

19/08/44
Hudson AE513 OS-P (279 Sqn)
Spun into sea on ASR.

23/08/44
Hudson V9161 (279 Sqn)
Overshot on landing.

24/08/44
Beaufighter NE326 (455 Sqn)
Port engine failed on approach to Langham. Swung and crashed into building.

01/09/44
Wellington MF234 (524 Sqn)
Engine cut after take-off and flew into sea off Hunstanton. F/Lt H. J. Callin†.

09/09/44
Beaufighter NT892 (455 Sqn)
Engine failure over Dutch coast and returned to base. Landed heavily at Langham and u/c collapsed.

12/09/44
Beaufighter NT963 (455 Sqn)
Hit mast attacking convoy off Den Helder and belly-landed at Langham.

14/09/44
Gladiator N5594 (521 Sqn)
Hit mast on take-off in fog and crashed at Docking.

28/09/44
Beaufighter 'Z' (254 Sqn)
Failed to return from Exercise *Gilbey*.

02/10/44
Wellington 7R-X (524 Sqn)
Failed to return to base after armed recce. Last operational loss from BN?

16/10/44
Wellington MF299 (524 Sqn)
Undershot landing in fog at Langham.

27/10/44
Hudson TE-M (521 Sqn)
Docking-based. Failed to return from Special Met. flight.

29/11/44
Mosquito PZ461 (7 Ferry Pilots Pool)
Overshot and hit wind-sock pole at airfield.

15/01/45
Lancaster LM720 (61 Sqn)
Collided with radio mast at Langham returning from raid on Merseburg.

06/02/45
Wellington NB823 (612 Sqn)
Overshot landing in bad weather at Langham.

08/02/45
Lancaster PD348 (227 Sqn)
Engine failure after take-off and belly-landed near airfield.

20/02/45
Beaufighter LZ182 (144 Sqn)
Landed out of wind in wrong direction and overshot runway at airfield.

08/03/45
Beaufighter NE438 (254 Sqn)
Damaged by flak and crash-landed at Langham.

07/03/45
Beaufighter X (CCPP)
Crashed near Sculthorpe on training flight.

14/03/45 (also see above?) Beaufighter RD431 (CCPP)
Belly-landed in field near Sculthorpe.

18/03/45
Wellington NC623 (612 Sqn)
Bowser caught fire and a/c bombs exploded at Langham.

18/03/45
Wellington PF820 (612 Sqn)
Damaged beyond repair when NC623 blew up.

26/03/45
Wellington NB824 (524 Sqn)
Engine cut on take-off and crashed at Cockthorpe.

26/03/45
Wellington ND133 (612 Sqn)
Belly-landed in bad weather at Langham. Short of fuel on return from patrol.

09/04/45
Beaufighter NE212 (489 Sqn)
U/c collapsed in heavy landing.

23/04/45
Swordfish NF322 (Station Flt at BN)
U/c collapsed in heavy landing.

05/05/45
Wellington NC513 (407 Sqn)
Overshot landing at Langham.

06/05/45
Swordfish NF329 (Station Flt B/N)
Undershot landing, hit ditch and overturned.

May 1945: 2 fatal accidents:
S/Ldr R. L. J. Fitch DFC (No. 2 APC), and WO Underwood and F/Sgt. Adams (695 Sqn).

11/05/45
Wellington LP404 (24 OTU)
Engine cut and hit house on overshoot, Langham.

20/05/45
Martinet NR610 (695 Sqn)
Dived into ground half mile SE of Downham Mkt.

21/05/45
Mosquito RF858 (1 Prep Pool)
Overshot and dropped out of control at Docking.

08/07/45
Mosquito PZ178 (BSDU)
Broke up in mid-air and crashed at Docking.

05/10/45
Hurricane LF371
Hit mast at night and crashed at Langham.

09/10/45
Hurricane PZ806 (521 Sqn)
Hit HT pole at night on met. flight and crashed near Langham.

20/10/45
Hurricane PG470 (521 Sqn)
Collided with HT cables at Middleton.

26/04/46
Beaufighter RD501 (254 Sqn)
Accident while taxying - brake cable sheared at Langham.

12/08/48
Anson LT995/RF-A (1510 Flt)
U/c collapsed after taxying fast on landing at Sculthorpe.

16/08/48
Oxford HM678 (1510 Flt)
U/c retracted in error, damaged beyond repair.

24/10/49
Vampire VV684 (226 OCU)
Flew into ground near airfield during aerobatics.

APPENDIX V

OPEN DAY AT BIRCHAM NEWTON ARRANGED AFTER VE-DAY 1945 (Extracts from official guide)

Follow this Guide - and make the most of your visit to RAF Station Bircham Newton.

FIRST see the WAAFs' and airmen's quarters in the barrack-blocks on either side of the parade ground.

THEN visit the exhibition of RAF equipment, aero engines, airborne lifeboats and safety equipment, armoury, photographic section etc. in No. 1 Hangar.

LOOK OVER the operational aircraft lined up on the airfield by No.1 Hangar - Halifax, Fortress, Mosquito, Vengeance dive-bomber etc. The ground crew will be there to explain.

INSPECT the workshops and the equipment stores. Visit the Officers', Sergeants', and Airmen's Messes, and the NAAFI Institute. See the Information Room and the Cinema.

LISTEN IN to the air-to-ground VHF between Control and the aircraft overhead - it will be broadcast through the loudspeaker system during the afternoon.

AND DON'T MISS the Colour Lowering Parade on the Parade Ground, that will end the exhibition at 6 p.m.

GUIDES WITH WHITE ARMBANDS are posted at conspicuous points about the Station. If there is anything you want to know - ASK A GUIDE.

The Commander-in-Chief, Coastal Command, Air Officer Administrative, Coastal Command, and Air Officer Commanding 16 Group will arrive by air during the afternoon and inspect a guard of honour by the Watch Tower. Their arrival will be announced over the loudspeaker system.

THE LANGHAM BAND will be playing in No. 2 Hangar. Any information concerning recruiting can be obtained here, and any donations to the RAF Benevolent Fund will be gratefully received by the collectors.

MEDICAL ATTENTION can be obtained at SICK QUARTERS, the building with the Red Cross opposite the car park. Lost children may be found again here, too.

ANY BUILDINGS on view will be marked 'OPEN'. Please look for this notice.

PLEASE -
> don't wander on to the airfield - aircraft may want to land
> don't smoke near the exhibition aircraft or near equipment
> don't bring cameras on to the camp - this is not allowed

AND REMEMBER that we are not responsible for anything lost on the Station or from cars, or for cars and bicycles left in the car park.

APPENDIX VI

GRAVES AND MEMORIALS

Churchyard of St Mary, Great Bircham

The church and churchyard of St Mary, Great Bircham, are part of the Royal Estate at Sandringham. The churchyard contains 78 burials which include 1 sailor, 1 soldier and 37 airmen of the United Kingdom; 17 airmen of the Royal Canadian Air Force; 4 airmen of the Royal Australian Air Force; 6 airmen of the Royal New Zealand Air Force; 1 airman of the South African Air Force and 11 German airmen. The War Graves Plot, in the south-eastern corner of the churchyard, was used for the burial of airmen from RAF Bircham Newton, and includes a few German dead from coastal crashes. The Cross of Sacrifice, the first to be erected after the 1939-45 War, was unveiled by His Majesty King George VI on 14 July 1946. In the south-west corner of the plot stands a Canadian maple tree, one of several sent to war cemeteries as a gift from Canada.

BALLANTYNE, Pilot Officer Herbert G. (Pilot, RAF) No. 206 Sqn, 14 August 1940, aged 22. Hudson N7401, crashed in Docking circuit. See also Stephenson. (Other crew member Sergeant Eddie Fitzgerald (WOp/AG), aged 21, buried in The Rosary Cemetery, Norwich.)

BIDDLECOMBE, Sergeant Robert W. A. (WOp, RAF VR) No. 106 Sqn, 28 January 1942. Hampden X3058 lost in operation to Münster. One of four Hampdens lost from Coningsby.

Military funeral from Bircham Newton to St Mary's Churchyard, Great Bircham, c. February 1942. (Don Nelson)

War Graves plot, St Mary's Churchyard, Great Bircham. (author)

BLACK, Flight Sergeant Stuart C. (Pilot, RNZAF) No. 49 Sqn, 12 December 1941, aged 27.

BLAKE, Pilot Officer Peter H. (Pilot, RAF VR) No. 235 Sqn, 1 April 1941, aged 19. Blenheim IV V5764 stalled/spun into ground near Hunstanton.

BLEASE, Flying Officer John T. (Pilot, RNZAF) No. 97 Sqn, 14 July 1942, aged 24. Lancaster I R5558 based at Woodhall Spa crashed in sea off Wells.

BRISTON, Leading Seaman Eric V. (RN) HMS *Verdun*, 22 March 1946, aged 27.

BROWN, Flight Sergeant Raeside H. (WOp/AG, RAF VR), 28 February 1942, aged 22.

BUXTON, Sergeant Lawrence (WOp/AG, RAF VR) No. 514 Sqn, 22 May 1944, aged 22. Lancaster DS633 from Waterbeach crashed in North Sea.

CALLIN, Flight Lieutenant Harold J. (WOp/AG, RCAF) No. 524 Sqn, 1 September 1944, aged 23. Wellington XIII MF234 crashed off Hunstanton on anti-shipping sortie supporting attack Beaufighters.

CAMPBELL, Warrant Officer (WO2) -Pilot Paul B. (Pilot, RCAF) No. 415 Sqn, 18 February 1943. Hampden AE435 crashed at Docking (close to the railway station) on take-off for convoy strike.

CHADWICK, Aircraftman 1st Class Richard (RAF VR) No. 500 Sqn, 1 December 1941, aged 32. Hudson V AM718 crashed 1550 hrs near Docking/Choseley Road (G2257). Total six killed.

CLARKE, Sergeant Richard W. T. (RAF VR) No. 61 Sqn, 2 March 1941, aged 20. Hampden X3147 crashed at Syderstone 0430 hrs returning from ops. Four killed.

COTTERILL, Flight Sergeant Colin W. (RAF VR) No. 500 Sqn, 14 January 1942, aged 30. Hudson V.

CREEDEN, Pilot Officer James W., DFM (Pilot, RCAF) No. 407 Sqn, 16 May 1942, aged 20. Hudson crashed at Digby - heavy losses returning from anti-shipping sorties.

DALLAS, Sergeant Arthur F. (Obs, RNZAF) No. 105 Sqn, 28 October 1940, aged 22. Blenheim IV T2229 crashed at Cranmer Hall, Sculthorpe.

DAVIES, Flying Officer Llewellyn A. (RAAF) No. 97 Sqn, 14 July 1942, aged 33. Lancaster I R5558 based at Woodhall Spa crashed in sea off Wells.

DAVIS, Aircraftman 1st Class Percival A. (RAF VR), 6 February 1945, aged 42.

EASTON, Flight Sergeant James A. (WOp/AG, RCAF) No. 407 Sqn, 16 May 1942, aged 26. Hudson crashed at Digby - heavy losses returning from anti-shipping sorties.

FARWELL, Aircraftman 2nd Class Frank (Drogue Operator, RAF VR), 8 November 1941, aged 22. Henley L3265 crashed on heath at Holt. Two killed. Pilot, J. Czapinski (Polish), buried at New Hunstanton Cemetery.

FEATHERSTONE, Flying Officer Henry E. M. (Pilot, RAF) No. 206 Sqn, 1 January 1941, aged 27. Hudson T9287 low flying, hit barn near Langham. Eight killed.

GILES, Flight Sergeant Anthony B. (Pilot, RAF VR) No. 500 Sqn, 17 February 1942, aged 21. Hudson AE647 crashed on Brancaster beach.

HADLEY, Pilot Officer Ronald A. (Pilot, RAF VR) No. 58 Sqn, 9 October 1940, aged 20. Whitley V T4137 GE-K crashed on airfield on return from ops with engine trouble.

HALL-JONES, Flying Officer Frederick W. (Pilot, RNZAF) No. 500 Sqn, 8 June 1941, aged 21. Blenheim IV V5689 flew into ground at Holme and caught fire. Three killed.

HAMILL, Sergeant-Pilot James H. (Pilot, RNZAF), 20 April 1941, aged 24.

HOLLINGSWORTH, Pilot Officer William (Pilot, RAF) No. 500 Sqn, 8 February 1942, aged 30. Hudson AM845 dived into ground and exploded at Docking. Four killed.

HOWSON, Flying Officer Ralph K. (RCAF) No. 407 Sqn, 16 May 1942, aged 26. Hudson crashed at Digby - heavy losses returning from anti-shipping sorties.

KIPPEN, Pilot Officer Angus L. (Air Obs, RCAF) No. 407 Sqn, 16 May 1942, aged 25. Kippen was navigator in Hudson which crashed at Docking on return from anti-shipping sortie. Pilot, Pilot Officer F. Kay DFC injured. Wooden plaque on grave showing photo plus a brass plate with poem written by his sister (Mrs Armstrong) eight days prior to his loss of life.

LADEFOGED, Pilot Officer Anthony F. N. (Pilot, RAF VR) No. 500 Sqn, 1 December 1941, aged 20. Hudson AM718 crashed 1550 hrs near Docking/Choseley Road (G2257). Total six killed.

LEA, Flying Officer Ronald P. (Navigator, RAF VR) No. 196 Sqn, 12 June 1943, aged 28. Wellington X MS486 crashed and caught fire at Docking.

LEESON, Flying Officer Archibald (Pilot, RAF) No. 500 Sqn, 7 July 1941, aged 29. Blenheim IV Z6041 shot down by intruder in Burnham Market area, Norfolk.

LEFTLY, Flight Sergeant Nelson (Air Obs., RCAF) No. 405 Sqn, 8 April 1942, aged 28. (his brother Emerson M. Leftly also died on service).

LOATES, Sergeant Henry G. (WOp/AG, RAF) No. 61 Sqn, 2 March 1941, aged 25. Hampden X3147 crashed Syderstone at 0430 hrs due to lack of fuel.

LONERGAN, Aircraftman 1st Class Hilton A. (RAAF), 1 December 1941, aged 21. No. 500 Sqn Hudson AM718 crashed near Docking/Choseley Road (G2257) at 1550 hrs. Total six killed.

McPHEE, Flight Sergeant Allan J. (AG, RCAF) No. 97 Sqn, 14 July 1942, aged 23. Lancaster I R5558 based at Woodhall Spa crashed in sea off Wells.

MAFFRE, Flying Officer Kenneth R. (Air Obs., RCAF) No. 415 Sqn, 18 February 1943, aged 24. Hampden AE435 crashed at Docking on take-off for convoy strike.

MANSER, Flight Sergeant Raymond E. (WOp/AG, RCAF) No. 180 Sqn, 26 May 1943, aged 21. Mitchell FL696 crashed in sea off Wells.

MERIDEW, Aircraftman 1st Class George A. (RAF) No. 206 Sqn, 1 January 1941, aged 23. One of eight killed when low flying Hudson T9287 hit barn near Langham.

MORGAN, Sergeant Franklin L. (WOp/AG, RAF VR) No. 500 Sqn, 1 December 1941, aged 22. Hudson AM718 crashed near Docking/Choseley Road (G2257) at 1550 hrs. Total six killed.

MOSS, Sergeant John H. (WOp/AG, RAF VR) No. 206 Sqn, 19 November 1940, aged 20. Hudson N7300 crashed into wood at West Raynham Hall.

MURPHY, Pilot Officer Alfred H. (RAF) No. 235 Sqn, 26 May 1940. Blenheim IV P6956 spun in at Docking. Pilot baled out.

NIBLOCK, Warrant Officer (WO2) Zina M. (WOp/AG, RCAF) No. 415 Sqn, 18 February 1943, aged 20. Hampden AE435 crashed at Docking on take-off for convoy strike.

PARKS, Flight Sergeant Douglas E. (WOp/AG, RCAF) No. 407 Sqn, 16 May 1942. Hudson crashed at Digby - heavy losses returning from anti-shipping sorties.

PATRICK, Flight Sergeant Alexander G. (Air Obs., RCAF) No. 106 Sqn, 28 January 1942, aged 22. Hampden X3058 lost in operation to Münster. One of four Hampdens lost from Coningsby.

PATTERSON, Flying Officer William S. (Navigator, RCAF) No. 407 Sqn, 13 June 1942, aged 22.

PHILLIPS, Pilot Officer Ernest R. (Pilot, RAF VR) No. 235 Sqn, 14 February 1941, aged 28. Blenheim IV Z5970 flew into ground one mile north of Croxton, Norfolk. Three killed.

PILE, Gnr. Frederick R. (108 Battery 29 Lt AA Regt RA), 6 April 1940.

PORTER, Flying Officer Robert C. (Pilot, RAF VR) No. 521 Sqn, 4 October 1942, aged 30. Hudson FH379 crashed on take-off, hit mast and lost wing.

PRIESTLEY, Pilot Officer John S. (Pilot, RNZAF) No. 235 Sqn, 30 August 1940, aged 27. Blenheim IV L9262 spun into ground near Bagthorpe at 1115 hrs.

PRINCE, Leading Aircraftman Gilbert J. (RCAF) No. 407 Sqn, 24 May 1942, aged 22.

PROSSER, Pilot Officer Ian (Pilot, RAF) No. 105 Sqn, 28 October 1940, aged 22. Blenheim IV T2229 crashed at Cranmer Hall, Sculthorpe.

REEVE, Aircraftwoman 1st Class Audrey H. (WAAF) No. 279 Sqn, 12 March 1944, aged 32.

RHODES, Flying Officer Jack (Pilot, RAF VR) No. 153 Sqn, 1 March 1945, aged 25. Lancaster NG184 based at Scampton crashed in North Sea.

ROWLANDS, Flying Officer John D. B. (RAAF) No. 500 Sqn, 30 January 1942, aged 23.

RUDD, Flight Sergeant James C., DFM (RAAF) No. 78 Sqn, 1 May 1943, aged 20. Halifax II W7929 from Linton-on-Ouse crashed at Docking.

RUSTOM, Pilot Officer Robin (Pilot, RAF) No. 206 Sqn, 5 August 1940, aged 20. Hudson P5133 stalled and crashed at Syderstone.

SADLER, Pilot Officer Norman A. (Obs., RAF VR) No. 235 Sqn, 16 December 1940, aged 26. Blenheim IV Z5754 crashed in sea off Brancaster.

SANGER, Sergeant Wilfred A. (AG, RAF VR) No. 500 Sqn, 16 January 1942, aged 21. 'Bacton' Hudson, see under Memorials (below) for details of crash and four crew killed.

SCHMID, Sergeant Eric O. F. (Nav./Obs., RAF VR) No. 235 Sqn, 8 May 1940, aged 27. Blenheim IV P4844 crashed in circuit.

STEPHENSON, Pilot Officer John O. L. (Pilot, RAF) No. 206 Sqn, 14 August 1940, aged 25. Hudson N7401 crashed in Docking circuit. See also Ballantyne.

THOMAS, Sergeant Arthur R. (WOp/AG, RCAF) No. 407 Sqn, 13 June 1942, aged 21.

TOWNEND, Leading Aircraftman Ernest (AG, RAF) No. 206 Sqn, 3 May 1940, aged 28. Gunner in Hudson N7319 shot down one Bf109 and killed by second Bf109 attack. Aircraft returned safely with pilot (Pilot Officer R. T. Kean) slightly wounded. Kean killed on 5 August 1940 and buried in New Hunstanton Cemetery.

VOKES, Flight Lieutenant Arthur F. (Pilot, RAF VR) No. 19 Sqn, 5 September 1941, aged 23. Spitfire P8166 on ferry flight from Coltishall to Matlaske crashed in poor visibility at Langham.

VOKEY, Warrant Officer (WO2) Reginald E. (WOp/AG, RCAF) No. 415 Sqn, 18 February 1943, aged 21. Hampden AE435 crashed at Docking on take-off for convoy strike.

WALLACE, Sergeant Kenneth L. (Flt Eng., RAF VR) No. 196 Sqn, 17 October 1943, aged 19. Stirling III EH960 crashed in Wash on air test.

WARD, Pilot Officer Richard (Pilot, RAF) No. 206 Sqn, 20 December 1940, aged 22. Hudson I N7333 crashed near Bircham. (His brother Allan also died on active service).

WRIGHT, Second Lieutenant James M. (Pilot, South African AF), 16 January 1944, aged 20.

LUFTWAFFE GRAVES
6 December 1939:
Crash of Heinkel He115 on the beach at Sheringham, in mysterious circumstances. Only one member of the crew found, **Leutnant Emil Rödel** who was buried at Great Bircham with full military honours, the bearers being RAF men.

26 May 1941:
Crash as the result of a sortie to the East Coast - 1/Kustenfliegergruppe 506 - Junkers Ju88A-4 (0738). Crashed into the sea off the Norfolk coast in unknown circumstances. Oberlt. J. Lohr, Oberlt. F. Pohl and Obergefr. W. Nimwegen missing. Body of **Uffz. H. Biesterfeld** washed ashore and buried at Great Bircham, on 29 June.

22/23 August 22/23 1941:
Heinkel He111 of 8/KG40. Shot down by Wing Commander J. Cunningham DSO, DFC and Bar and Pilot Officer C. F. Rawnsley DFC, DFM and Bar, in a Beaufighter of No. 604 Sqn. Crashed into the sea north-west of Wells 10.05 p.m. Gefr. G. Dohmen, Gefr. H. Hadrich and Obergefr. K. Dandel missing. Body of **Gefr. R. Faath** washed ashore 31 August and buried at Great Bircham. Aircraft F8+BS sank in sea. (Source: *The Blitz - Then & Now* Vol. 3 (After the Battle) pp35, 68)

German graves in War Graves plot. (author)

Also: Unknown RAF man has normal headstone on which it mentions Pilot-Officer RAF 6.3.42.

Pre-war graves near gate leading to War Graves Plot:
Riddell, Robert Norman, Sergeant-Pilot (RAF) - killed 9.5.1939 aged 23

Sampson, Charles, Corporal (RAF), killed 9.5.1939 aged 39.

Berry, G., Aircraftman 1st Class (RAF) 26.6.1938.

[Note: for full details of the Great Bircham Graves see Appendix I (sources): private publication by Brian Hillman and John Beynon.]

MEMORIALS
Lowlands Farm, Bacton, nr North Walsham.

Memorial to crew of Hudson V9097 of No. 500 Sqn which crashed in field at Lowlands Farm, Bacton in bad weather conditions on 16 January 1942. Crew of four all killed - memorial stone erected by relatives, looked after by Royal Air Forces Association members. Each year, on nearest Sunday to 16 January, poppy wreath laid and small Service held there.

Crew
Pilot Officer J. Macgillivray (pilot), aged 25
Sergeant J. S. Brownsell (WOp/AG), aged 21
Sergeant R. B. Wark (WOp/AG), aged 26
Sergeant W. A. Sanger (AG), aged 21 - only member of the crew buried in Great Bircham. (See photo on p131)

Die peacefully young hero yet unnamed
Neath fading bomber's moon on grass dew wet
We who remain may live to feel ashamed
But even so we never can forget

From *Returned Airman* by Pauline Lendon[1]

---

[1] Quote from *More Poems of the Second World War, The Oasis Collection*, J. M. Dent & Sons Ltd: London/Everyman's Library p192.

INDEX

Note: Page numbers in *italic* refer to illustrations

241